LAW SCHOOL AT FIFTY

Read It Now, Thank Me Later

Denny Fraser

COWCATCHER Publications

HILTON HEAD ISLAND, SC

Denny Fraser/COWCATCHER Publications
2 Village North, #17
Hilton Head Island, SC 29926
www.do-the-write-thing.com

Published in the United States.
Law School At Fifty Denny Fraser. -- 1st ed.
ISBN 978-0-9960533-9-6

DEDICATION

This book is dedicated with love to my girls, Debbie, Lizzi and Page, who made a far greater contribution to my law school adventure than I did. I owe much gratitude to the many people who encouraged me during my law school quest, of which there are far too many to mention by name. To all those folks, I say thanks for everything.

To my smart friends who were good and patient enough to encourage and guide me through the writing of this book, I owe you a great debt of gratitude. To Jennifer Montero, Charlie McOuat, Dave Oakes, and my publisher, Jodie Randisi, who encouraged my dreams of becoming a published author, thank you all. And to Debbie, who read and re-read the manuscript, fixed all the errors and took out the bad words, there aren't enough words to thank you.

Most of us have a dream or two buried in the basement, packed away in a storage unit, or hidden in the attic. More likely, we've thrown the dream out the window, or under a bus. Not many of us choose to unpack the dream and go for it when it involves sacrifice. My family and I went after our dream, and in doing so, some things went terribly wrong. Some things went delightfully right. Everything left a mark.

—DENNY FRASER

CONTENTS

CHAPTER ONE

The Interview

The call went to voice mail before I could catch it. Someone from the South Carolina School of Law called to tell me that my request for an interview had been granted. Interviewing with the Dean of Admissions (DOA) turned out to be one of the biggest moments of my forty-eight year old life. I'm told interviews are mostly a courtesy with little value. What could I possibly lose? I decided to go for it. For all I knew, an interview might be the closest I'd ever get to a real law school.

The interview could change the course of my entire life, no big deal. All I had to do was show up and be myself. Well, maybe not myself—the old guy with a mediocre GPA who isn't a good liar. I couldn't go as that guy. Who in their right mind would want that ME in their law school? I figured all I had to do was to polish the old me into a new and improved me.

Being older gave me a leg up. I already looked like a lawyer and had all the right costumes hanging in my closet. The kids coming straight out of college looked and sounded like they were twelve, maybe twelve and a half. All I had to do was practice sounding lawyerly. I was tempted to rehearse using a British accent because British people sound so smart. In the end, I decided to keep it low-key, not so dramatic.

The DOA had assigned an interviewer and a date. Fifteen minutes was all that was allowed for the all-important interview. My research suggested I should request the last time slot of the day, believing it to be the one interview that would be remembered. Also, if we clicked, we could go overtime. Ever the strategy-maker. If the law pursuit falls through, I suppose I could become a political campaign strategist.

The interview was scheduled for three o'clock. Plenty of time to get to Columbia and find a parking place, which was the wild card. I allowed an extra hour and a half on top of my plan to be seated in the lobby an hour early. My plan covered all contingencies—flat tire, car rental if necessary, attacked by rednecks at a rest stop, lunch and parking. What could go wrong?

Bad question.

The trip went okay, but Columbia was in some kind of monsoon. The news said something about the ten-year cycle of the reversing of the Humboldt Current on the Pacific coast of South America coupled with El Niño and global warming, or some such scientific crap. The bottom line—it was horizontal rain and the streets were flooded, however, the relentless traffic continued unabated. I think there were even more cars on the road competing for the last parking space in that godforsaken town. Sorry, Columbians, your town can appear cheerless when your dream is on the line. I found a sketchy, halfway-legal parking space about a half-mile from the law school.

For the occasion, I chose a navy blue pinstriped Hart Shaffner & Marx suit, accented by a crisp white spread collar shirt with French cuffs and a Ben Silver midnight blue tie with white polka dots. I was a stunning lawyerly sight to behold. Armed only with a small umbrella, I had to schlep a half-mile in a godawful cataclysmic, apocalyptic event that was causing animals to pair up. Feet, shoes, legs, all soaked. Squish. Squish. Leaning into a forty-knot gale, I forged onward.

Thank God I had an hour to air dry before the all-important interview. Fortunately, I brought a slim nylon laptop case I could put the umbrella and rain jacket into so it wouldn't look like I was a twelve-year-old coming for a sleepover. I squeegeed myself into the lobby/cavern, which became the impromptu storm shelter for about a hundred students, professors, and assorted homeless types. If there is no shopping cart for reference, I never know for sure if someone is just a cool-looking dude or homeless until I get within the olfactory clue zone, then I know.

It was standing room only, no seating at all, so I stood there looking like a wet jackass, thinking that maybe, because of my attire and demeanor, people would take me for a visiting professor from the Czech Republic, or somewhere like that. I killed my hour-long grace period trying to will myself dry; however, since it was early Carolina spring, it was a touch warm outside and the A/C was running around sixty degrees. The wet, fine Italian merino wool next to my skin was cold, really cold, and kind of sticking to my skin, sort of creepy-like.

My pants were beginning to look a little like tights. Really wet tights. And wool, which I had never thought much about, was not a plant product like cotton. Wool, even fine Italian wool, was made of animal hair. Sheep, to be exact, and when sopping wet, it does begin to take on the slightest odor of a farm animal. Yep, smelled like a sheep, a big wet one. Because of the internal temperature of the room, there was no drying taking place. At this point, I was trying to control my shivering and fight off hypothermia, with little success, unfortunately.

Ten minutes ahead of my appointed time, I decided to make one last trip to the men's room, for the obvious reason. The downstairs lobby men's room was just down the hall toward the Dean of Admission's office. It wasn't particularly clean, but it was functional. Little did I know, my contingency plan was about to take a hit.

Like all guys who are not bullfighters, I lowered my zipper to take care of business and the darn thing dislocated itself at the lower end of its run. Yep, it fell apart right there in my hand. Don't know if anyone has ever had any success getting a derailed zipper back in place once it has removed itself from its little toothy track, but I can tell you from experience it is IMPOSSIBLE. I tried.

With frozen, shivering hands, I struggled to re-engage the closure system to my man parts. No luck. I prayed to God. Aloud. One guy bellied up to a wall urinal, sneaked a glance in my direction only to recognize the fatal folly of interfering with a madman praying aloud into his crotch.

No luck. Now my heart rate was playing the drum solo to a rock song that inhabited my panicked mind. Out of time and nearly late, I had to think like a ninja bear fighter marine. I had to improvise and overcome. I figured I could use my portfolio case to camouflage the scene of the accident. I'd just have to be very careful. I've not done much reading on the subject of interviewing, but I feel pretty confident that, even in these modern, diverse, anything-goes times we live in, going to an interview with one's genitals exposed is inappropriate, at least on a first interview.

With little time left on my clock, I quickstepped to the elevator with my jacket buttoned and leather bound writing pad covering my man part area. The dehumidified sixty-degree air combined with my body temp had actually started to dry my sheep suit. The slacks, which were tailored with a perfect break at the mid heel, now hovered a good three inches above my shoes in Capri fashion, and the sleeves of the jacket exposed a similar three inches of white shirt cuff. The long hall that led me to my appointed destination included several open doors, revealing professors tucked inside their stereotypical and messy professorial nests.

Not my guy. His office was located at the end of the hall and on a corner, affording him about twice the space when compared to the other hovels I'd passed. His nest was immaculate, decorated with bookshelves housing mementoes, books and art objects expertly staged for proper display. His desk was a large mahogany one, fit for any successful corporate senior partner, which he was. He was dressed for the part: expensive suit, French cuffs, Windsor knotted tie. Hell, he looked like I did before I turned into shrunken wet sheep-dip.

And, the guy was genuinely nice. He had read my stuff and showed a personal interest in me. Shocking, actually. Took me by surprise, I can tell you that.

Realizing I had a wardrobe issue going on, he broke the ice by saying, "Guess you got caught in the storm?" That gave me the perfect opportunity to describe my misfortune with a little humor. He graciously confessed he had arrived just ahead of the bottom dropping out. I kept the secret of the wide-open fly because I didn't have a good explanation. I kept the leather bound pad squarely planted in my lap.

He was a great guy and it was a great interview. We got on wonderfully. He ended by saying he felt he could really support my candidacy to the admissions committee. I felt great. Well, I felt great until he offered me his business card from across his wide desk. When I reached out to take the card, the pad fell off my lap. I tried to stop it but it flew right off.

Now, I don't know if anyone knows much about men's slacks, but when seated, if the fly is down, it gapes wide open. Yep, wide open, exposing whatever's in there for all to see. The interview concluded with this classy gentleman seeing me to the door and politely waiting until I was well down the hall to burst out laughing.

Leaving the elevator, I had ceased to give a crap and walked right through the crowded lobby, fly wide open, tiny suit getting tinier, right out into the pouring rain. I didn't even use the umbrella this time. Screw it. I went to the first convenience store on the way out of town, bought gas and a giant beer that was placed in a little brown bag that convenience stores keep for the single beer buyers, and I sat in my car wearing my tiny soaked suit, pondering why in hell I was doing this. I had a great life. I made a good living. I had some degree of respect, at least in my small circle. I did not need this. That's when the City of Columbia cop pulled up beside me.

What an appropriate ending to the lousiest day ever. I could go to jail. But no, for some reason God was done with me. The cop looked my way, waved and went into the store. I guess middle-aged white guys are treated differently from the average black guy drinking a Colt 45 from a brown bag. Or maybe he didn't see it. At least, I was given a wake-up call.

I could now go home and arrange to resume the great life that I had lost appreciation for. Thank God, this obsession was over. I'd soon get my rejection and I could forget this stupid adventure and go back to work with the hope that only a few people knew that I had tried such an impossible thing for someone my age, and maybe those few would forget in time.

Two weeks later, my acceptance letter arrived in the mail. The big envelope. I held it with the full range of emotions— joy, fear, and trepidation, all of 'em. I thought for a moment about the last words of the DOA.

Be careful what you ask for. Sometimes you get it.

CHAPTER TWO

The Breakaway

I turned out of my driveway and onto the street for the last time as a non-law-student. It was South Carolina in mid August—hot, humid, and threatening to storm. The rearview mirror framed my family of girls, Debbie, my wife, and Page and Lizzi, my daughters, all waving goodbye to dad and getting smaller and smaller as I drove off toward a new future.

It was 165 miles and 150 minutes to Columbia, South Carolina, at the time, the location of the state's only law school. I was forty-eight, at least for eight more weeks, and about to enter the freshman class of law school at the University of South Carolina School of Law (SOL). If I could cut it, the odds of which were vastly against, I'd have to make the grind to Columbia several hundred times.

Picture this. I'm off to my first day of school, family waving at me. I'm almost half a century old and nervous. No wait. Let me be honest. I was actually scared. No way I belonged in law school. No way I was smart enough. No way I'd fit in. No way I could do the work. No way I could keep up. No way we could afford it. No way the family could cope with my absence or a good marriage survive it. There was just no way this could work. Nevertheless, I was on the way to what I figured would be a quick turnaround.

Two and a half hours on the interstate was not good for someone suffering near terminal self-doubt. The thunderstorm stopped threatening and became reality. The five o'clock sky turned black as night and rain pelted down in near whiteout torrents. Traffic, usually running about eighty, slowed to a crawl. Every overpass provided sanctuary for cars not brave enough to push on through the blinding storm. If I were one to read the signs, I'd say Mother Nature was trying to tell me something. *Turn back. Go home. You're safe there.* I kept going. I'm a dad and we do things like that, which is why the male life expectancy is somewhat less than our female counterparts.

Three and a half hours of white knuckle driving brought into view the dark skyline of Columbia. The city was nestled under the cover of a big black storm—an evil sight. Not deterred, my destination was the downtown Holiday Inn, which would be my new home for the next three years, maybe. Why the Holiday Inn? Well, it squats conveniently and indelicately right next door to the law school, has underground parking and gives business rates for long stays. It was a no-brainer, and I truly qualified on the "no brain" part of the deal. The business guests were put on the top floor—the ninth—in "business suites," meaning rooms with desks and a computer connection. My room looked directly at SOL, a four-story brick cube built during Columbia's signature design era featuring brick and concrete cubes.

The storm continued unabated as night descended upon the already dark city. I was morbidly drawn to the window. I looked at the law school building, which was partially illuminated by the streetlights below, kind of like someone holding a flashlight under their chin to be scary. The occasional flash of lightening gave it the sinister look of the castle on the hill in every black and white horror movie ever made.

For the sake of my sanity, I needed to stop looking out at the concrete sarcophagus, but for some reason I kept drifting back to the rain-drenched window for another look. I could swear I heard organ music each time thunder blasted over this evil scene. Worried, I sat on my business suite sofa and prepared to read my cases for the next day—Property Law, Constitution (or Con) Law, Civil Procedure, Contract Law and Torts. SOL was kind enough to give us newbs assignments before school even starts, a sort of "Welcome aboard!"

Although staring out the window and scaring the crap out of myself was pretty fun, I had cases to read and nervous energy to burn. I needed to get down to the business of law schooling. Debbie bought me an Orvis leather and canvas briefcase for my first day of school. I had hoped for a Spiderman lunchbox, but the expensive soft case would have to do. I opened it and started what would become the first of several thousand hours of case reading.

I grabbed the Con Law book. It was the biggest, and I figured I knew a little about the Constitution. First case in the book was named Marbury v. Madison, and I read it start to finish with pen and paper ready to brief my first real law school case. Perhaps I was too focused on the lightening show going on outside, or maybe I was just really stupid, but after reading every single word, I didn't understand anything about the case. It was written in English. I understood most of the words (except for Writ of Mandamus, still don't know what that is). But I simply didn't get it, like at all. So I read it again, going slowly with a finger under each line so not to miss a word, and still, I got nothing. Zilch. I figured I would jump into Torts, which I thought might be a refreshing break after learning I knew nothing about the Constitution. For those who may not know, Torts refers to the law of civil wrongs. People suing people over stuff—as in personal injury cases—that kind of stuff.

The first case made sense, at first. Guy drives down the road, has a seizure, and ends up driving his car through the window of a bike shop and crunches the bike shop person. This kind of thing is easy. I mean, come on, who doesn't know how this turns out? Well, apparently, the person who didn't know was me because on the last page was a big surprise. The court held that the driver wasn't at fault. Not even a little bit. Because he had taken his medication for his seizure problem, he didn't owe the crunched bike shop person anything, not even an apology.

How, how, *how* could that be? Had I entered the world of reverse logic? What had I gotten into? I was doing better looking out the window.

After that exercise, I was pretty sure I was ten hours away from being exposed as an aging imbecile who was admitted into the school to help the curve and boost the self-esteem of the real law students. Thinking a good night's sleep was essential for surviving the ordeal of humiliation that would begin in just a few short hours, I decided to bed down. I needed some rest, and maybe the butterflies flopping around in my stomach needed to get some shut-eye, too. As it turns out, butterflies don't need sleep; they keep churning.

Trains. Surprise! Columbia's got 'em, and they rumble through town all night long. They stop at every road, cattle crossing, or rat dropping and blow the horn, blowing not once but several times at each intersection. I live on an island, Hilton Head Island, to be somewhat exact, and we don't have trains. In fact, we don't have much of anything that makes noise. Maybe a leaf-blower now and then, but nothing like a train. The earth-shattering sound of five blasts from a locomotive every ten minutes from midnight until dawn helped me and the butterflies stay wide awake.

Downtown Columbia also has traffic that never stops. Cars hissed loudly on the wet pavement below, kind of like Satan might hiss so someone in a business suite on the top floor of the Holiday Inn would know he was out there...waiting.

The sun mercifully found me lying funeral parlor style looking fixed and dilated at the popcorn ceiling. Finally, the night was over and I could get up, go next door to the law school, quit while I could still go home, and resume my career. I could tell everyone it was just a joke, and that I was paying off a dumb bet. Let all the naysayers have their laugh. Hell, they were right all along. I couldn't do this stupid thing. Damn, I was nearly fifty.

CHAPTER THREE

The Affair

This whole half-baked idea of following a dream to a new career began three long years prior to my actual arrival. One just doesn't just walk away from a job and family one day and into a three-year commitment to law school the next. No, that is not how it happens. Not at all. It's a process, an incredibly long process that becomes an investment one cannot simply drop.

And for the record, my preparation process couldn't be kept a secret around town. Before long, lots of people knew about my scheming. Some had to be told, some figured it out, but eventually, my people knew I was contemplating a life change that was far beyond my grasp. I became like the kid in the schoolyard who called out the school bully. Everyone was now watching to see how this dumb idea would turn out. I had to stick with it. Die right there in that schoolyard, or by some miracle, come out alive and a lawyer.

The word "great" conjures up several meanings. It could mean something of high quality, like a great concert, or a great present, or a great teacher, or a great rollercoaster ride, or a great kiss on a first date, that's greatness. Or, it could refer to the quantity aspect of the word, such as a great journey of many miles, or a great adventure, or a great mass of crap in my life, or the great toe (that's the big one). Going to law school at forty-eight was most of those all balled up into one. Not that my going to law school was greatness with a capital "G" like Gandhi, but it was great as in something supremely difficult, something supremely large, something that required a great degree of excellence.

I've studied enough successful people to know that there are many similar steps in any great undertaking. There are commonalities in all giant steps—planning, commitment, dedication, goal setting, tenacity, hard work, setbacks, failure, drive and focus, to name a few.

And let's not overlook luck. Most ego-driven big shots opt to leave out the "L" word from the inspirational story that comes later down the road. If you look closely, you'll see "L" is involved in most great achievements.

My guess is that my story of returning to law school at an all grown-up age could be overlaid on top of most success stories and there would be more pattern matches than not. Most great things start small, deep inside one person. The beginning of something great is not a group accomplishment.

Usually, a concept comes first. At the molecular level, I am certain the cells that made up my idea began to divide and multiply silently. They had not yet debuted at the cotillion of wacky ideas that is held monthly in my imagination. Instead, they were hatched deep within some level of my consciousness.

The Notion, as we shall call it, began to grow and fester. Out of the blue, from time to time, The Notion showed up unannounced, but not unwelcomed in my perfunctory daily routine. She would drop by and entertain me for an afternoon when I was supposed to be doing something not so fun.

Not that I would know, but I think this is how men (and in all fairness, women, too) begin having extra-relational affairs. A life desperate for something new and different welcomes the little flirt.

In my case, The Notion developed a skill and intuition to visit when my daily grind was at its most sucking. More, and more, this dalliance grew into an anticipated and regular thing. Then, sadistically, the little tramp began to stop by unannounced, just to see if I had taken the bait. And the vixen was right—I was "fish on." I'm now missing her when she's not around. I call her up to take me away from my world.

Okay, I confess. I enjoyed the intricacies of imagining a life together with The Notion. That's pretty much how it went, at least before Debbie found us out. Debbie's my wife, partner, girlfriend, best friend, business partner, co-parent of kids—all that.

Debbie knows me so well. She always catches me when I stray into another affair with a Notion. The telltale signs are all too familiar. The preoccupation, the daydreaming, the lost in space look on my face—she knows. You see, I'm the guy who makes a passionate hobby of conjuring, nurturing, and grooming business ideas, most of which never see the light of day. They get aborted when it becomes clear they cannot sustain viable life outside my internal cocoon.

One of my favorite authors, Elspeth Huxley, described her father, Robin, a British ex-pat who tried coffee growing in colonial Africa, as a man who could make any business concept seem successful on a plan on the kitchen table late at night. I'm that guy. Although, I have had some success, more successes than failures, there have been failures.

Debbie surprised me when she exposed The Notion affair to me. She didn't force me to break up and come back to earth where my family lived and I belonged. My girls needed a dad seriously focused on all aspects of family life. I'm talking financial, emotional, punitive, the whole enchilada. Much to my surprise, my wife somewhat embraced The Notion. Honestly, I did not see that coming.

Debbie is the one who tethers me to reality, which is why this refreshing but frightening endorsement felt a little off. I started to feel akin to the circus elephant chained by one ankle to a stake, which the beast could easily uproot so he or she could take a little walkabout terrorizing the town's folk until someone shoots him or her with a tranquilizer gun, or worse.

Debbie has held me back from barroom brawls and talked me off more ledges than I care to count. I take comfort in knowing that she will almost always gently coax me back to safety. But nooooo, not this time. This time it seemed she was metaphorically suggesting that I go talk smack with the drunken savage who took my seat at the bar, rationalizing that though he was bigger, younger, meaner and drunker, I was wiry and would likely prevail if I used some of those ass-kicking skills I'm always bragging about.

So the planning phase began. The Notion floozy was now our adopted child and we were going to raise her right.

CHAPTER FOUR

The Burden

Although Debbie and I enjoyed working at our construction-related business, the two of us were approaching burnout. We were ready for a change, and to be honest, most any kind of a change would have been entertained.

We were perfectly willing to wear blinders with rose-colored glasses underneath our "readers" to help us do a proper job of due diligence in choosing a safe and smart career path. In other words, we were both having an affair with the floozy law school Notion. We were business people, so we didn't run toward this idea in slow motion across some imaginary field of golden wheat, under a cobalt sky, flecked with gently drifting dandelion crystals, like two lovers in a Viagra commercial. No, not at all. We were running flat out. To hell with slow motion!

My plan of attack began on multiple fronts. I arranged to meet separately with several respected friends known to have pretty good business sense. My focus group included a banker, an attorney, a retired business executive, a marketing guru, and a preacher. Though they all swore on a death oath to guard my particulars confidentially, I am certain they headed straight for the comedy club, not in the least bit concerned about using my name and story as a routine. I suspect this because I began to field the occasional odd, thinly veiled question.

"Hey, what's this I hear about you going to law school? Are you crazy?"

So word had leaked, only a little bit like that fissure on the side of the Titanic, but that was to be expected in a small town. The focus group gang was drafted because they were not only smart and successful, but because they were also hard-nosed conservatives who would never gamble with one's future. Skeptical, cautious, laboriously inquisitive, they each, save the preacher, gave me guarded encouragement. The preacher smiled, prayed, and told me to trust in the Lord, and that He, that is the Lord, would not give me more than I could handle and would carry me and the family through all trials and challenges that lie ahead.

Not a bad thing.

My confidence was on the climb, if not from the stingy encouragement, then from the fact that these good people believed in me. They actually saw a quality in me that maybe I had overlooked. If the whole affair had ended at this point, I felt kind of good about myself. Also not a bad thing.

Okay, I'll admit it. I also talked to a therapist hoping to address the many issues of emotional trauma associated with such an odyssey. Think what you will about lawyers in general and me in particular, but I have been, and am, a good dad and husband. Those are the only words I want on my tombstone and obituary. Don't say what clubs I belonged to, or what boards I served on, or what civic group I helped, or what dragons I slayed, or any other crap. Just chisel out DENNY FRASER, A GOOD AND LOVING FATHER AND HUSBAND. That's it.

I know more than a smidge about the shared burden a family carries in a home with a work-away-from-home dad. My dad, Denson Fraser, was a good man. He married at twenty-one in 1933, in the heart of the Great Depression. As a dowry of sorts, he inherited his ailing widowed mother and seven of his ten younger brothers and sisters. In a few years after helping to win WWII, he would inherit my maternal grandfather, a mean Irish Patterson who devoted his remaining days to the care and nurturing of his chronic alcoholism.

After the last of the seven brothers and sisters left Dad's nest, we began to take in assorted cousins to help with other assorted difficult family situations. I was a kid then and enjoyed the sibling-like younger ones. Then we took in my mother's elderly, crippled aunt who had helped raise my mother while her Irish Patterson father perfected his drinking skills. Yes, my parents were those people. They helped everyone.

After the Big War, it became abundantly clear to my dad that he needed more money than a man could earn in my little hometown of Aiken, South Carolina, so he hit the road to follow the post-war American construction boom.

He worked through the industrial build up of the Ohio River Valley, then the TVA, then the chemical-textile build-up around the I-85 corridor in South Carolina, then the nuclear plants popping up all throughout the southeast, and lastly, the jewel of a gravy job, the construction of the US Naval Base at Guantanamo Bay, Cuba. He really loved that one, and like several thousand others, he was on the last plane out of Havana, just ahead of Castro's revolutionary insurgency against the ruling Batista family. Jeeps with 50's on the back, screaming down the tarmac, bullets a-flying, chasing the final plane headed for the safety of Miami, USA.

I vowed that I would NEVER work and live away from my family. Perhaps like the father I so brutally criticized, I rationalized that my jaunt to law school would be, in the end, better for my family than having me at home for those three short years. Yep, I was doing it for them. It was in their best interest. It was a silent vow I made only to myself, no one else.

Debbie worked the numbers. She crunched, massaged, caressed and dissected them. She studied our business books, met with our accountant and created a budget with every line item imaginable. Not a single Q-tip, legal pad, Post-it Note, or any minor necessity was overlooked. And, at the end of her painstaking process, the numbers worked. Cash on hand, plus future income, together with the cost of law school, and we would be just fine.

Red Flag.

CHAPTER FIVE

The DOA

The Law School itself held some answers that could not be gleaned anywhere else on earth. I had to go there and talk to a person. I had to find out if an older (sort of) white guy could be of interest to such a fine institution.

I made my initial appointment with the DOA, not to be confused with the now legendary interview appointment wherein I showed up in a shrunken suite smelling like a wet farm animal. I wanted to talk with the guy who held the gate key for hundreds of youngsters who, along with their parents, grandparents, and in some cases, great grandparents, held onto the dream that someday, somebody would someday be a lawyer. ABA accredited law schools receive ten or more applications for each admission, so the DOA possesses unbelievable power.

This capacity to make or break someone's dreams is a little hard for me to understand. I know doctors and lawyers, though respected professionals, make only a representative fraction of what their professional peers made years back. Nonetheless, the lives of pre-professional people are relegated to the DOA, as irreverently as that sounds. Not since SS officers of the Third Reich stood staunchly greeting the line of arriving souls at Auschwitz, pointing some to the right to a life of misery and toil, and pointing some to the left to condemnation, has one person held such power over others. I would never trivialize the horrors of the Holocaust by comparing that situation to not getting into a professional school. However, many young aspirants place so much emphasis on acceptance into a particular field that they come to believe that these DOA initiated rejection letters permanently alter, even end their lives.

In all schools across the nation, and for that matter the world, there is a DOA guarding the gate, or to abuse a more modern analogy, a bouncer holding the velvet rope at the most popular club in town. Eighty percent of applicants, despite praying for acceptance into law school, are given the small thin envelope of rejection, most of whom go on to have great lives. Probably way better and way happier than if they had grabbed the tar baby of the law.

Most of the rejects were at the top of their classes, incredibly bright and laden with excellent potential and talent. While their world may have felt as if it collapsed during the moment of rejection, the truth is, rejection probably catapulted them into an unexpected new beginning.

In fact, the current job climate for new attorneys is so lousy that many of the bottom ninety percent in class ranking are offering to take jobs for no pay. That's right, zero dollars. Attorneys are willing to show their stuff and maybe earn an entry-level job. Also, somewhere around ninety percent of these hopefuls carry big student loans, which by the way, are non dischargeable in bankruptcy and will follow them to the grave.

My appointment with the DOA was set and Debbie and I made the first of many trips to Columbia. My shot at livin' the dream was established. Yeah. However, I found USC's School of Law much like a disappointing inner city school campus, meaning no open parking spaces, no parking spaces for visitors, no room at the inn, so to speak. We parked at the nearby Kinkos and wondered which impound lot would have our car upon our return.

The Cube, as I like to call it, has a bank of glass doors preceding its massive cavern of a lobby that passes straight through the building to an opposite wall of glass through which the Holiday Inn, my future home, could be seen in all its glory. The vast cavern has several scattered pieces of assorted, stuffed seating, arranged in little clusters around cubical formica coffee tables, perhaps to give the illusion of cozy gathering spaces for lively and engaging exchanges between the students and professors.

Several actual law students, or law student posers, lounged on these obese chairs, staring into their laps at huge books, completely oblivious to the world and its petty events. Opened newspapers littered the floor around some of the seating arrangements, showing a paradoxical contempt for the media institution that held such critical importance to the inhabitants such a short while back.

Against the vast left wall of the cavern was a pedestal topped by the dark bronze bust of the late Senator Strom Thurmond, who was the longest serving United States senator and an alum of this fine institution. I would learn later that his namesake son, Strom Jr., was attending the School of Law. Ol' Strom had married late in life, around sixty or so, to the beautiful and young Miss South Carolina. Nancy Moore happened to be from my hometown of Aiken and two years ahead of me in high school. She and Ol' Strom produced a wonderful family of kids, yet as the world would soon learn, Ol' Strom had produced another secret mixed race child with a black family servant many years prior. So there was Ol' Strom's bust, preserved in bronze-face for all of history.

A hallway directed the masses from the cavern to the left, and above its maw was a small sign: ADMISSIONS. We took a left. The DOA's office was barricaded behind a counter three feet inside the door stretching from wall to wall. Without having ever visited Russia, I wouldn't really know what "Soviet era" architecture and construction looks like first hand, but here I go. I'm thinking any DMV bureaucrat from Stalingrad, transported via magic into this room, would weep with joy at such a sight and raise a glass of potato vodka to the spittin' image of his home.

A wonderful older lady, whose name I am embarrassed to say escapes me now, greeted us. All the years I attended that institution, she faithfully called me Mr. Hazel. Bob Hazel was a classmate of mine ten years my senior and the delightful lady in the DOA office could not keep us separated in her mind. I guess all us older students look alike.

After a brief wait, I was allowed behind the barricade and directed to a private office against the back wall. I met an elegant, fortyish-year-old man named John Benfield, aka the DOA. He appeared kind and pleasant. No pitchfork, horns, or tail that could be seen.

So far I had met two humans associated with the law school who were actually nice people. Benfield gave up his time freely and I would soon learn that time was not a commodity he could waste. Benfield had the mandate, as do a couple of hundred of his wizard-like counterparts in law schools across the country, of securing exactly the number of rear ends as there are seats in the first year law classrooms. In the case of USC, that would be 240. Seems easy enough, right? Just pick the top 240 out of two thousand or so, and you are done for the year.

But it doesn't work that way.

Of those top 240, a good number of them have applied to several law schools, and to hedge their bet, they pretend that each school is their number one choice. When someone snags a big envelope from Duke, Harvard, or Yale, the big envelope from little ol' USC doesn't even get opened. Somehow the Benfields of this world have to know how many acceptances to hand out in order to have 240 rear ends.

Therefore, while wasting this good man's time, the businessman in me had to ask what happened if the whole crowd showed up, say three or so hundred. He informed me in the nicest way possible that dealing with that problem was far easier than not having 240 rear ends on opening day.

The budget (all institutions live or die by the budget) was based on 240, and this DOA had damn well better have 240 rear ends on Day One. He shared how his magical system of prayer and expertise had consistently produced the exact number within a one percent margin of error. Holy Crap!

Refocusing on my reason for stealing his time, he advised me that in light of my less than stellar academic past, I needed to focus on crushing the Law School Admissions Test, the dreaded LSAT. Unlike the SAT, the LSAT was an actual admissions test. Do good and you get in; do poorly and you don't get in. It's that simple.

As an example, an acquaintance of ours graduated from a prestigious research school in North Carolina, sporting a perfect 4.0 GPA. He took the LSAT without preparation or concern because he was a genius for God's sake. He blew the test. LSAT retakes don't help much because the old score hangs around the neck of the applicant like the proverbial albatross. This much I knew.

I thanked Benfield for his time after taking notes regarding his potion of magical selectivity.

1. Good LSAT.
2. Good personal statement on my application.
3. Good interview.
4. Good grades on a few yet to be taken undergrad courses.

And most importantly and in big letters, GOOD LUCK!

Debbie and I had no problem finding the car. It was right where I left it, waiting for me to start my new life, eager to help me find my way back to The Cube, after I got accepted, of course.

CHAPTER SIX

The Undergrad

In the years since law school, a fairly steady stream of people have sought me out to talk about the experience of returning to professional school all grown up. Two common denominators were (and are still) a part of every conversation.

First, and perhaps most striking, is the fact that all of them confessed to harboring within their hearts and souls some unfulfilled dream. Perhaps put on hold by family, money, love, or maybe by war, or maybe, like my good dad, all of the above. Whatever the reason, the lot of them still grieved the postponement of a dream that resulted in its fatality.

Second in the list of commonality amongst the seekers was the belief that they could not survive the rigors of academic life at the advanced age of forty or fifty, or so. This self-doubt I fully understood. I was infected with it also. No way could I run with the smarties that make the cut and get into law school.

Prepare yourself. I am going to break the suspense by sharing one of the two secrets involved with going back to and succeeding in school as a seasoned person. Here it is. Secret number one is...I spent thousands of dollars to learn this, so pay attention. Perhaps slide your finger along under each word so as not to miss a single nuance. I'll even put it in italics and bold so it jumps out at you. Are you ready?

If you have average intelligence and are accustomed to working nine hours a day at a job with two breaks and lunch, then you will do just fine in law school.

But don't be getting all "I'm in. Piece of cake!" on me because secret number two is the most important and success will not come without following secret number two, which will be revealed soon enough. Hang on.

You might ask, why should secret number one make me feel more confident? Here's why.

Traditional students come straight from undergrad, and if you recall, you'll remember that undergrad consisted of three hours of class per day, usually four, maybe five days per week. Studying was completed just prior to an assessment or test. The real world, where you sit at a job from eight in the morning until five-thirty in the afternoon, with two days off at Thanksgiving, three off at Christmas, one each for Labor Day, the Fourth of July and Memorial Day, has already prepared you for the work of law school, or med school, or any professional school.

Every traditional (and by traditional, I mean younger) student who makes it into a professional school will enter a temporary state of shock. They're used to having a social life, going drinking with their buds, and playing catch-up with assignments. Law school is much more of a system shocker to the kid coming straight from undergrad than it is for the career person.

Don't get me wrong, undergrads aren't just smart, they are the smartest of the smart, and if you old guys try to run with them they will eat your lunch. However, if you grown-ups forget about having a life, put your butts in a chair, and study law eight to ten hours per day, you will definitely survive law school and do well. Anything less than that, you had better be a freaking genius.

I had no one to tell me secret number one, so I had to find out the old fashioned way. The only way to find out was to jump into the college classroom. USC has an extension campus in my hometown, so I signed up for a few courses. As a non-degree candidate, there was no need for me to fill out an application. Pick a course, put your money down, and at the end of the term, you get a grade.

This did two things for me. One, it gave me the answer to my brain doubts, and two, it gave me a chance to tweak my old GPA because law school admissions want to see every college level course ever taken. So, off to school I went.

Pubic Communication, Business Management, and Business Law. Public Communication was my gravy course. Fifteen years of training in the Toastmasters International program plus five years teaching public communication in one of our local high schools made this an easy "A." Good for the GPA but not an answer to my academic insecurity.

Business Management and Business Law were the real courses, and both were only offered at night at the other extension campus forty miles from home. These classes were a little more of a workout than Public Communication. Business Management (401) started inauspiciously enough at eight o'clock at the Beaufort Campus of University of South Carolina.

The professor was a nice enough guy, ten years my junior. Dr. Somebody, I forget. They are all Dr. Somebody. Not MD like a real doctor, but PhD, and buddy, you better call them DOCTOR like they call themselves or there'll be hell to pay. I don't get the DOCTOR thing with these guys. Sure, they took four semesters on top of a masters degree, and sure, they wrote a paper. Okay, I get it. But most real doctors I know don't call themselves DOCTOR SO-AND-SO. Well, except for the optometrists and chiropractors. They usually want to be called Doctor.

Dr. Business Management Guy handed out a syllabus and told us that he taught the Socratic Method, which he clearly did not. In case you may not know, the Socratic Method asks questions of students rather than lecturing them. If nothing else, this method causes the student to prepare more diligently for each class. Looking like a fool in college is not much fun. Yes, Dr. Business Management did ask the occasional question, but he'd obviously never seen a good ol' law school Socratic grilling. At any rate, he did a pretty good job of lecturing. Remember, this is undergrad, where students memorize terms, dates, and lists.

The class makeup was diverse. It included regular students, business folks, military personnel from Parris Island, our local Marine Corp Recruit Depot, and me.

I eyeballed the room for the smart ones; the ones who may make it to something like law school, or USC's Darla Moore School of Business, one of the best business schools in the nation. I studied their faces. I was able to ID the vacant ones and the ones with potential.

Being older is like being invisible; no one gives a crap about you, therefore you don't count. This enables the older student to be completely ignored and somewhat like being dressed in Real Tree Camo. You go completely unseen.

Too bad for the curve, I was the wolf eyeing my prey. I was a businessman and a phenomenal public speaker armed with a Platinum card just looking for an excuse to kick some undergrad ass. Bring it on, Dr. Business Management Guy.

Dr. BMG was pretty good. He had the seventy-dollar textbook pretty much down pat and was insistent on the naming of business management axioms rather than the underlying reasoning. But this was the college method handed down for the millennium. Teach lists, bullet points and definitions, but for the sake of Jesus, Mary, and Joseph, don't educate.

He was a really good guy, working and praying for tenure so he could really kick back and not give a crap. But for now, he had me on the prowl, not only looking for an "A," but also looking to pit myself against the best in the room. I had them figured out after a class or two. There was an older guy who worked in town as a banker, and two younger girls who were in careers, smart and hard workers. My kind of peeps.

The class turned out to be lecture after lecture with the occasional question thrown in, so one could say the process somehow mimicked the Socratic method. Halfway through, he assigned a team project and asked us to form teams. I played enough dodgeball in my life to know that the older guy wasn't going to be picked by anyone, so I volunteered to be a team leader and immediately picked my chosen ones, the smart ones. They didn't seem to covet the idea of being on my team until they realized I was in it to win it, meaning a sure "A" for all.

The assignment involved following some business model and creating a fake business plan. I picked the hardest working girl and assigned her the research, which made her happy because she was scared witless just thinking about making a presentation. I gave the older banker guy the job of compiling data. He acquiesced to me just because I was older, just like in grade school. Plus, he knew I owned my own business and I knew he was hoping to make it to branch manager sooner rather than later. That made me the alpha dog.

I turned my office staff loose to develop a Power Point presentation to make our case, which allowed us to avoid using the school's horribly scratched Soviet-era overhead projector. My team met after class and used email to devise a battle plan. On the night of our team presentation, we rolled in four deep, confidence firmly established. We had everything we needed, except someone should have had the theme song from Rocky playing out loud instead of in my head.

I slapped down my laptop, brought up the screen, and I delivered. By delivered, I mean, if you want to win the coveted Best Speaker ribbon at Toastmasters, you need to either make 'em laugh, or make 'em cry, and if you want to deliver and dominate, you make 'em do both, and that's what I did.

I looked at Dr. BMG. I'm pretty sure that through his laughter I saw a tear streak down his velvet complexion. Then I looked at surfer dude in the front row, along with his team of valley girls who were scheduled to follow us. He was somewhat visibly pissed. The utopian non-achieving society he yearned to shed was challenged.

All of a sudden, I realized I could beat the crap out of these modern day co-eds on their own playing field. BOO and YA!

Business Law was a bit of a different story. A local lawyer who also served as an adjunct professor taught this night class of about twenty students. We learned about business law in a biology classroom in the old Beaufort USC campus. No desks, only lab type tables, the kind that seats two students to the side. Dr. Business Law was young, about ten years behind me. The guy was a pretty cool dude, a second career lawyer after being a successful local banker for a few years.

I'm convinced second career lawyers bring something unique to the table. As counselors, they certainly have a broader and more diverse experience to draw upon right out of the starting block. From my perspective, the kid who finished twelve years of grade school, four years of undergrad, and three years of law school, has little more than academic experience to pull from—that's what I think anyway.

Let's face it. Counseling is mostly what lawyers do. People come to them and seek guidance. Maybe I'm biased, but I've learned that legal counseling is more than telling someone the law. They expect a more rounded steering that may include business, ethical and personal slants, along with statutory and common law interpretation.

The assortment of business law students included a few slightly older CE (continuing ed) guys, a dozen or so traditional students, and me. And yes, I was the oldest and still invisible, except this time around I had an ally, a black girl named Tonya. It seemed she was invisible too, so we kind of hung out, unseen by the rest.

Tonya was maybe twenty, tall, beautiful, and infatuated with The Notion that a college degree would at least give her a shot that the average African American from Beaufort County didn't have. I certainly would do nothing to dissuade her of that belief even though I knew the market and held serious reservations about her prospects. I've seen too many talented, degree-holding young folks, white, and especially black, being relegated to teaching, waiting tables, or flipping burgers. Tonya took full advantage of her status as a person of color being condescendingly ignored.

At least once in every class she would ask a question that would completely derail Dr. BL. "Question. Mind you this is entirely hypothetical, but say a girl was to kill her boyfriend but had a pretty good reason. Would she serve any serious time?"

The first time she threw one of these stereotypical grenades, I caught on immediately. She was screwing with the professor. He handled the hot potato fairly lawyer-like, but this was to become a regular game of dodgeball for him because she came to class locked and loaded, a round in the chamber, so to speak.

My personal favorite was "Professor, if somebody, not sayin' who, it's nobody you know though, was to catch their man having relations with that person's best friend, would a jury convict this person that you don't know—for murder if, let's say, these two adulterers didn't ever show up again, and I mean ever again?"

These questions were the highlight of my evening. I got to class early, as did Tonya, who would often let me in on her GOTE (grenade of the evening). She knew how the system worked. She knew she was being tolerated instead of educated, and she found a way to have some fun. She was hilarious!

One night, we both got there early and the ancient science building was locked and dark. The school was closed save for this one class, so there was no government employee with master keys hanging around at seven-thirty to open the building. Being a dad and a contractor, I fished out a pocketknife and picked the lock. This gave me instant cred with my invisible partner in crime.

We had a great gig going. Tonya came with at least one fake ghetto story and I came in insanely prepared to destroy the curve. I pretty much knew there were no future lawyers in the room but me and the real lawyer teaching the class.

Despite the shenanigans, Business Law was a good class. The textbook was a casebook much like the real law books, no actual text, just condensed written appellate court opinions, and cases showing examples of common law. Business law involved the law of contracts; offers and acceptance, considerations, quasi-contracts, promissory estoppel, quantum meruit, and the like, with several cases thrown in to exemplify.

Professor vowed to teach in the real Socratic method to simulate a real law school class setting, which I liked because my hope was to be sitting in a real law class in about twelve months. For those who may not be aware, adjunct professors were different from institutional professors. Adjuncts come out of a real career to teach something they love for little or no pay, and this guy had a real passion for teaching. He was funny and seemed to enjoy the whole thing. He even got good at catching Tonya's grenades and tossing them back. He was on to both of us after a few classes.

Prof's standard practice was to start the class by putting a student on the spot with a question about a case; what were the facts of the case, what was the holding, what was the rule of law, etc. He would then give his take on the case to help with the understanding because the law is pretty darn confusing, even to lawyers.

Now in real law school, the Socratic Method is just questioning, no explanation. If the answer is wrong, the professor moves on to the next victim without a hint of right or wrong. Many classes left students confused because they heard two or three conflicting answers with no clarification from the professor. It's a very weird system. Function by dysfunction.

In Business Law we were given a mandated midterm exam. In real law school there was no such midterm mandate. In real law school there was one exam at the end of the term. We had to digest a whole semester of legal cases packed into one three-hour exam. How'd you like them apples?

Business Law turned out to be quite valuable and relevant to my intended landing zone. I did quite well and came away with a letter of recommendation.

The No-Brainer

As I said earlier, public speaking is a no-brainer for me. Public Communication, thank God, was offered during the daytime in my hometown, Hilton Head, which is also where I developed my public speaking skills. This class was a piece of cake. Although not a natural part of my anatomy, I was comfortable speaking in public. Twenty years ago I did not have the confidence to stand and deliver in front of human beings.

Prior to enrolling in this class, I sought help, not necessarily for nerves, although the fear of a meltdown on stage did manage to keep me in the background. When I say in the background, I mean that if asked to speak to a group of my own species, I would fake a stroke, and maybe I wasn't faking. I dodged this embarrassment with great skill; however, as my career progressed, I kept finding myself having to fake more and more strokes. I needed some relief from hitting the floor and twitching. I simply lacked confidence due to my lack of skills.

I had heard about Toastmasters being good for career development, but I was skeptical. A club playing parlor games could help a dodger like me? I doubted. Still, I was desperate and a little curious. I did some research on the clubs in the area, which led me to the Friday morning FastTrackers Toastmasters Club. I now credit the educational process offered by Toastmasters as being the key to my career change to law.

I showed up on the threshold of the meeting like a refugee from Cuba washed up on the shores of South Beach. The room was crackling with activity. About thirty people, all of whom appeared to be employed. Everyone was super prepared for what would be their standard one-hour (not one minute more, not one minute less) meeting. At exactly eight o'clock, the president, a known Toastmasters Nazi, took control and called the meeting to order behind what I know now is a lectern, not a podium. He got things moving at a healthy clip. No nonsense, no parlor games. He was serious as a heart attack.

I, of course, was the center of attention, because, like most members, I came in from the cold to improve my skills, or in my case, find some skills since I had none to speak of. I soon learned that the one thing these Toastmasters folks loved more than standing, applauding and blabbing was to mold a blob like me into a confident speaker.

Back to the Public Communication class—the main difference between this college course and Toastmasters is that Public Communication is required for all degrees in the university system, which means students are not there by choice. They are forced to be there, which affects the level of energy and enthusiasm within the class. One glance around the classroom revealed boredom, nervous anticipation, and disinterest. All were young except for me, of course. No older continuing ed folks.

The good professor, her name escapes me, made an effort. It was easy to tell she had already been through several years of teaching students who absolutely, completely, totally, and wholeheartedly could not care less about her course. However, since it was an established prerequisite, a few students intended to do the minimum to maybe get a B.

University professors teach by books, test by books, and live by books. Public Communication came with a textbook as well as a written test that covered the material in the book. Other than that anomaly, her class somewhat mimicked a Toastmasters program, or let's say a Toastmasters Light program. She assigned a progression of speeches starting with a personal introduction speech, followed by a speech using props, then humor, then readings, and so on.

No boasting here, I killed it.

Yet, a few events took place in that class that deeply saddened me. The class had two black students. Understand that I cling to the term "black" to describe race. I know it is much more modern to use the term African American, but I was an impressionable young person in the sixties who witnessed people of color fight for and demand to be called "black" instead of colored, Negro or other less complimentary terminology. I listened to the cadence of "Black Power," "Black Pride," and "Black is Beautiful," and feel I owe the respect to those good people who demanded to be called black. I intend to honor that simple request.

Anyway, one of the black students was a young lady and the other was a young man. They were not the sassy, confident Tonya-from-Business-Law types. They were visibly intimidated by the young, white, sorority and frat wannabes. They were not embraced by the group any more than I was, except in this case, we did not have the opportunity to bond. The young man only made it through a few classes. He went off the radar, never to appear again. The young lady stayed. I applauded her for staying.

For her first speech assignment, she was to give a personal introduction. She elected to talk about her personal passion for the plight of those stricken with HIV. She worked from a stack of file cards, which is considered a big mistake under the best of circumstances. Her notecard stack was rather large.

Apparently, her notecards had gotten mixed up in her bookbag, shuffled like a deck of playing cards. She didn't realize the mess she had going on until she started her speech. Painfully and quietly, she labored to make sense of the thought or two she had jotted down on her previously arranged note cards. She was mortified but stayed planted alone in the center ring.

She finished, even tried to force a sheepish smile at the end, although her main job in life at that moment was not to let us see her cry. In front of the preppy brats, this kid kept on trying. I was so proud of her.

To my amazement, Professor praised her presentation without critique. She offered no tough love or helpful suggestions for next time. She simply said, "You did a GREAT JOB!"

If my super power had been mind reading, I might have been able to discern something quite the opposite. *Have a seat. Move along. Let the kids with futures do their thing.*

By this time in my life, I'd seen enough discouraging incidents to break my heart. Young black students were being put on a conveyor belt through the system. Look, I'm not the guy to fix the system, but these kids deserve better, that's all I'm saying.

I stopped the young girl after class and offered some suggestions right there in the hallway. I was probably saying all the wrong things while she fought back tears. Despite being the older white guy (which sometimes sucks), I tried to give her the three "C's": Compliment what was done well, offer constructive criticism as encouragement and suggest specific doable challenges for next time.

I'm not sure if what I said helped, but I couldn't let her slip away feeling lousy. In the end, she settled down and did somewhat better. May I please take some credit?

There were a number of underperformers in that class worthy of mention, such as the front row surfer dude who everyone knew by his nickname, something like Tiger. He was popular. He came in late, showing his contempt by carrying some food product, chewing like a llama, shirt completely unbuttoned, and shorts soaking wet from surfing. Hey, we do live by an ocean.

His first speech was about his silver surfer action toy. He actually brought a little plastic toy of a superhero on a surfboard. Worst speech ever but everyone laughed, including Professor. Then there was the girl who made a smoothie as a part of her How To Use Props speech. Oh, dear Lord, at least it tasted good.

One final thought. If anyone is formulating a plan for a new career or self-improvement, please consider enrolling in a good public speaking educational program. Toastmasters International is one of the best and clubs can be found in most communities. If you think you're a good public speaker, and especially if you think you're a very good public speaker, I'd have to say you probably aren't. I was in Toastmasters with people who made their living speaking in public. The motivational speakers I met stayed sharp by continually exercising their public speaking skills. Much like professional golfers who never stop working with instructors, these guys knew they could improve.

The importance of this piece of advice cannot be overstated. Hence, I call this secret number two.

Those who communicate well, both in written word and as speakers, will succeed in life. The best communicators always rise to the top.

I crushed Public Communication. I got the highest grade in the class, which allowed me to move on to graduate school. No more undergrad. It was time to prep for the LSAT.

CHAPTER EIGHT

The Bear

A bear, hungry and mean, prowls outside the only entry door to law schools in America. His breath is as foul and rancid as Satan's crotch, with three tons of claws and teeth and the venomous drool of a Komodo Dragon. With no way to sneak past to the door, The Bear must be fought to get in.

The Bear goes by LSAT, short for Law School Admission Test. Plain and simple, fight The Bear or go home, and sometimes it's fight The Bear *and* go home. Many a lifelong dream of a law career ends with The Bear.

I am told American law schools' reliance on The Bear as a gatekeeper began in the year of my birth, 1948, or somewhere thereabouts. It doesn't matter. The Bear lives to this day and that is all that matters. To describe this test as difficult would be fair, but the difficulty comes from two ancillary factors, the first of which is time.

It is a huge test with only a small amount of time allotted to complete it, three hours to be exact. The second factor is stress. The LSAT is the quintessential admission qualifier that trumps everything else in the applicant's file— grades, experience, character, everything. Do poorly on this test and you don't get in. It doesn't matter how many other things you've aced. The pressure is massive, almost palpable. For many young people, this is the single most important test of their entire life, except for the bar exam, of course.

Here's a paradox. The three-part LSAT is actually an easy test, one that most any test taker could ace, that is, if they were only given enough time. Each section of the test has approximately twenty-nine questions and a thirty-minute time limit. Chew on that for a while!

Let me offer a more detailed explanation. Two parts are reading comprehension, just like you've had all your livelong life, except on steroids. You read a story, then answer questions. The story doesn't go away. It's right there in front of you, so when you read a question, you can go back to the story and find the correct answer. What could be easier? The third part is a logic quiz. Easy breezy.

But wait, there's more. The reading comprehension tests are broken into two parts, short passages, maybe one paragraph of 150 words, and long passages, maybe 600 words, or two book pages. Remember, each section has about twenty-nine questions and each passage has four or five questions. So, on the short passage section, for instance, there might be five passages to read and digest with four or five questions to answer.

You have thirty minutes and if you spend, let's say, three minutes scouring each short passage, that adds up to fifteen of your thirty minutes. Then you have to answer twenty-nine questions in the balance of the fifteen remaining minutes. Are you beginning to get the picture? Holy crap, that's thirty seconds per question! No worries though, it's only the most important test of your entire life, that's all.

The sadists who write these tests know the system. They are the house in Vegas and the odds are on their side. The questions are multiple choice, A through D. Here's the catch: two of the multiple choice answers are clearly wrong and somewhat easy to spot. The other two choices are both right. Yep, right, but one is more correct than the other. See what I mean about Satan being involved here?

Kick that up a notch because we're moving on to the long passages. These passages consist of four or five hundred words and have slightly more complex storylines. In other words, there are more names, dates, and squirrelly facts to consider. And there are a few more questions per passage, let's say up to seven. You get three or four passages, which will take maybe five minutes to read. That's a full twenty of your thirty minutes! And that's before you attempt to answer the twenty-nine questions in the remaining TEN Mother F-ing minutes! Pardon my emotion, but writing this chapter has taken me back to hell for a brief moment.

I had to stop just now and take a couple of deep breaths, visit my happy place, and chant…*I passed. I never have to do it again!*—but with "NEVER" inserted forty or fifty times. To those of you who might be thinking about taking The Bear, good f-ing luck!

Logic. It's a comforting word, right? Like common sense, we all have it. Heck, I've got plenty of logic. You probably do, too. Forget that BS. Clearly, The Bear's logic was thought out by the Prince of Darkness. Here's an example of a logic passage:

Mary lives in a red house and must live alone.

Tim lives in a green house and can never live next to Fred or Tom.

Tom can never live next to Fred.

James can only live next to Mary and must live in a green house.

Bob cannot live next to a blue, red, or green house.

Carol has a cat that cannot be next to Tom and has never sprayed a red house.

Question:

Where does Nancy live with her cat?

    a.   In a green house with Mary

    b.   With James in a blue condo.

    c.   With Bob

    d.   With Carol

My answer may be the same as yours: Who the hell is Nancy?

Next question:

Who can never live next to Bob?

    a.   Fred

    b.   James

    c.   Nobody

    d.   Jane

Who the hell is Jane, and where did she come from?

Use your minutes wisely, friend. The Bear is not your pal. My appointment to do battle with The Bear was three months off, so I had time to prepare. However, my enemy was time, not because I had so little of it. No, it was quite the opposite. I had too much time.

Let me confess. I am a member of a subset of humanity that suffers with chronic debilitating procrastination. Oh yeah, I know, everyone says that, but at my level, procrastination almost becomes a mental illness. Give me three months and I'll take that to mean I have eighty-nine lazy days to occupy. And I am not only good at avoiding the idea of working, but I am also very good at forcing the thought along without any shred of guilt every time it comes a-knocking, which, by the way, happens several times a day.

The way procrastination works is simple, yet I have to admit its complexity. The mental reminder comes up on my brain screen, causing a momentary reaction of anxiety about the looming crisis, or whatever, and almost instantaneously, I convince myself that first, I have time, and second, I will *seriously* get on it tomorrow.

And guess what? The butterflies (or seagulls) that started the commotion deep in my gut and caused my heart rate to elevate suddenly calmed down. A morphine-like calm washed over me from gut to brain. It's hard to explain, but it's something like waking up from a sound sleep only to discover you are late for work and you have a huge project to turn in. But then you suddenly realize it's Saturday. It is a singular human emotion that dogs and other animals can't access. It's that moment of waking up from a bad dream and realizing that your bed has never felt more comfortable.

For perhaps the first time in my procrastination-addicted life, I went cold turkey and laid out a plan to use each of the ninety days to prepare for The Bear. But seriously, how does one go about getting smarter and faster? The easy and obvious answer was to take a course. Of course, a course, it's what everyone does these days.

Remarkably, I turned in a lackluster performance as an unprepared walk-on for the SAT back in the sixties, but since then, there has been a fundamental change other than grade inflation. You know, B is the new C, A is the new B, and 4.5 GPA is the new 4.0 GPA, 1250 SAT is the new 950 SAT, and so on.

The HUGE game changer in test taking is the advent and universal acceptance of the multi-billion dollar industry of prep courses. That's right, there is a prep course for every type of test—SAT, LSAT, GMAT, MEDCAT, CPA, Bar Exam, USCG Captains test, General Contractors test, and probably even Large Animal Taxidermy test.

I paid a thousand bucks twice for each of my daughters to prep for the SAT, and both managed to score lower on the second time around. It was something about the AC was set too high, or the fluorescent light was flickering, or some such something. The test sellers, of course, offered free do-overs if a higher score was not achieved, but I decided to tell them to go romance themselves.

So, to prep for The Bear, I decided to start with a study guide. What a great idea! Barnes & Noble has an entire section devoted to this endeavor, housing no less than twenty study guides, most having at least a thousand pages. I lucked out after three hours of perusing these volumes while consuming three cups of Starbucks coffee. What a mean idea to put a caffeine bar in a bookstore. I found a study guide written by a guy who had a career as a test writer for the LSAT people. I bought it for a little less than I paid for the four cups of Starbucks.

LSAT Study Guide Guy put it right out there, sort of. The test writers are tricky so-n-so's. They've developed skills while developing test questions so unique that they are difficult to be assessed by the study guide industry.

It is possible to spend much time studying a not so perfectly crafted question, the result of which is to screw one's self up completely. LSAT Study Guide Guy touted test taking technique and strategy over trying to make an educated adult smarter. For example, on the passages sections, both long and short, he had several alternative approaches to the old standard of just read the story then try to answer the questions.

I liked his approach. He provided a sample test or two and strongly advised going to the LSAT people and buying actual exams given in past years. Now I had a plan. Other course takers may have maintained a false sense of empowerment, thinking they were totally prepared by the end of the one-week course. Not me.

After studying my study guide, I decided how I would use each of my remaining eighty days. The first few weeks would be devoted to taking individual sections of the actual exams I now possessed. There were ten books with three complete tests per book and three sections to the test. In all, I was looking at test taking approximately 250 sections.

Each time a test section was completed, I compared my answers to the correct answers provided in the back of the book. This way I could see what the test writer was looking for while keeping in mind there are two very nearly correct answers in each multiple choice grouping.

I began to see a pattern. I also learned how to quickly identify the two wrong answers, giving me the opportunity to make an educated guess. My chances were up to 50/50.

Phase one of the study process was to spend two hours a day working on former LSAT tests. My first focus was on the logic madness, so I sat with logic tests in my lap each night. This routine accidentally increased my potency.

Surprise, surprise, I began to not only like the logic quizzes, but I got pretty good at them. I could spot where Nancy lived in an instant. I started to like the illogical stuff so much that I had to break to use the time allotment for other passages. Similarly, I got pretty good at these passages. So, I guess this stuff is just like sex. If you practice enough, you get pretty good at it, or at least that's what I'm told.

Anyway, I started living with The Bear. I got better at the sections and was ready for phase two of the study process, which was to start taking full tests under the clock and calculating a score.

I needed to do extremely well on The Bear to overcome my lackluster undergrad performance. My early scores were in the 140s, not good enough. I began to creep slowly into the 160 range, which was the automatic acceptance level for my chosen school. All schools have what is called a presumptive admission threshold—USC's being a 3.4 GPA with a 161 LSAT. Meet or beat that level and they mail out the big envelope. All applicants falling below that bar get dumped into what is called the discretionary category.

Even with a 160+ LSAT, I'd be in the discretionary category due to my soft GPA. In the discretionary gang, other things come into play as well as the numbers alone, things such as experience, achievements, ethnicity and age. Perhaps my year was the year they were adding to the pool of older students. If so, I'm taking it. I might even land on top of the pile. No phony pride here.

Once I began taking timed tests, I had to move off the couch into a cocoon. I needed a space with no distractions, so I surveyed my options. The most logical cocoon in our home was our bedroom closet. It was big, huge actually. It contained two sub-closets of its own. I couldn't hang myself on a hook, so I went up in the attic and dug out my sister Lynn's old desk, an oak drop leaf secretary, meaning the desk part dropped down to make a writing platform, and when closed, it looked like a small dresser.

My father found the desk in a junk shop and refinished it for Lynn, who used it all through school. The hardwood exterior was stripped, sanded, and hand rubbed with multiple coats of Tung Oil, my father's favorite wood finish. He said it dried hard, like a rock, and the more coats, the more it shined. He embellished it with antique drawer pulls he scavenged from some other relic, polishing them to a high luster.

When opened, the older desk revealed pigeon slots for letters along the backside. Maybe the desk had seen service in a small inn where guests signed in and fetched mail from time to time. Between the mail slots were two small drawers, maybe eight inches wide and two inches tall. This is where my sister, Lynn, kept her most secret things. Under the drop down leaf were two full-width drawers for storage. When my dad delivered it to our home for our kids to use, Lynn's school papers and crayon drawings were still in the drawers.

Sadly, Lynn died three years before I found a good secondary use for her desk. She died after a long, lonely fight with illness. She was abandoned by her husband, a good guy and a lawyer, as a matter of fact. He just couldn't take the emotional meltdowns that travels with dying.

I liked using something she had used daily. Lynn was an excellent student, not at all like me. The desk still smelled of varnish, old wood, and crayons. Unfortunately, it was where my sister hatched young dreams of a great life that didn't quite materialize.

So it was just the closet, an antique desk, my study guides, and me. I spent hours upon hours in my cocoon suitably pressurized, taking tests. It served me well and would later become the hideout for my next huge hurdle, bar prep.

CHAPTER NINE

The Bear Fight

It came time to meet The Bear. I could hear him breathing. My appointed test center was in Charleston, South Carolina, on the campus of the College of Charleston, an old institution known for educating the South's elite, while only a few blocks away horrified Africans who had been kidnapped from their homes and shipped across the ocean were inspected and purchased like a mule or ox. The campus is home to many antique buildings, wedged shoulder-to-shoulder and tightly clustered on a peninsula between the confluence of the Ashley and Cooper rivers.

For those who may not know, the city of Charleston sticks out like a fat finger in Charleston Harbor. Her buildings are bunched together like yaks in Mongolia, as if to form a unified defense to unwelcomed hurricanes and invaders. Charleston witnessed the British yield to America's battle to free its white folks and later see its own countrymen battle to free its black folks. Over the decades, Charleston has seen a lot, but on this particular test day, she got to witness a nearly old guy desiring to change his life fight The Bear.

The assigned classroom for my group of test-takers was in a modern brick building. Our room was filled with rows of schoolhouse desks, all facing a dry erase board. Apparently, the era of chalkboards ended whilst I was away.

Even though the acoustical tile ceiling had a few tiles missing, it was able to support fluorescent lights, one of which was humming. And for old times' sake, there was a big round analog clock hanging over the board and a proctor.

The proctor, a female to be exact, was hired to watch over us during The Bear fight. She gave instructions and warnings. It was her job to yell out when to start and when to stop. She was to keep anyone from cheating and call 911 if someone succumbed to the pressure and died before The Bear even entered the room.

I was crazy prepared.

Debbie and I came up the night before and stayed in a killer hotel downtown in the overpriced tourist mecca. I had assembled a pack of essentials for The Bear fight that included #2 pencils, two real Cokes, three power bars, and a newly purchased sports watch for timing.

LSAT rules state that no watches with audible alarms were allowed, but I couldn't take the time to look at the big wall clock to figure how much time was gone and how much was left. I had to have a stopwatch. I needed to know my place at a glance and know whether I had time to ponder or needed to hit the gas.

I had gone to Walmart the day before and made the clerk open every cheap sports watch they had and make them beep until I found one that was mostly silent. I'm not allowed back in that particular Walmart. There's a photo of my mug with a big red X drawn through the middle of it.

I entered the arena with thirty or forty young people, some smartasses, some sick with fear, some there to take a shot without hope, like the drunk guy shooting from half court at a basketball game trying to win a car.

I was freaky calm but not making eye contact with anyone. I was there to kill The Bear, and it wasn't going to be pretty or merciful. I had no intention of making friends or joining a fraternity.

Security was tight. I was required to show my ID along with the ticket from the testing folks. I also had to submit a fingerprint. Not kidding. They took my fingerprint. I found a seat in the front row because I didn't want to see the back of a kid. In fact, I didn't want to see anyone. I just wanted to draw first blood before The Bear knew what hit him.

Proctor gave a few more admonitions, passed out the actual test booklets, offered a few warnings, said something about thirty minutes, and then said, "Open your booklets and begin." And that's when The Bear slammed into the center of the room, pawing the floor and slinging his horrendous head side to side with venomous saliva flopping around his head like a wet beach towel. Game on!

It was the fastest hour and a half of my life. Three sections done. Proctor said we had a ten-minute break to go puke or something. Twenty minutes into the fight, two students got up, crumpled their tests, threw them in the trashcan by the door and left. That's right, they left the room. Proctor had said if anyone quits the test before the end, it didn't count. Four more would leave before the mauling ended.

The ten-minute break allowed me to consume two of my power bars, along with my whole Coke fully loaded with sugar and caffeine. One of the sections was impossible and rattled me a little. I tried to control my nerves while still avoiding eye contact. I knew The Bear would offer me different degrees of difficulty and that the grading is supposed to allow for this, but getting kicked on one unnerved me.

Maybe I shouldn't be here?

Also, the LSAT people sneak in two sections that don't count at all. These sections are there just for kicks. They are given to the test-takers so the test-makers can determine whether the questions are too easy or too hard. No one knows which ones are which. Bastards.

Back in the pit, the mauling continued, and in what seemed like a blink, it was over. I gathered my stuff, handed in my test, and walked out, stunned and shell-shocked. I was in a speechless trance, walking like I was the sole survivor of some devastating tragedy. I was unable to hear, unable to speak. Not in the least did I care whether or not I went to law school. I leaned toward not going to law school. I walked zombie-like straight out the door, immediately startled by the searing sunlight. If Debbie had not been there, I would have surely walked right into traffic.

Yep, Debbie was there, as she always is. She caught me and turned me down the sidewalk toward wherever we were going. It was a beautiful sight. If I could have made a word or two, I'd have told her so. It felt good to be led like a lobotomy patient. She could have led me anywhere. I would have gone to the Battery, where 150 years back, the young Citadel cadets fired the first cannons aimed at Fort Sumter. She could have left me staring seaward until someone from the nut house threw a net on me. Thank God she kept me moving along and a safe distance away from those godawful horse-drawn carriages filled with tourists who don't mind soaking up history from some kid in a confederate uniform. Does no one see the abject absurdity of that?

While we walked down King Street with normal people who had not fought The Bear, I wondered why in hell I was doing all this. The Bear fight began to wear off and revelation of all revelations, as it turns out, fighting The Bear leaves you hungry and in need of alcohol, preferably the drinking kind. Debbie and I spent the rest of the afternoon and night behaving like two freshmen after the last day of exams.

I tried to not dwell on the trauma and aftermath of the fight. I took comfort in knowing that I probably made the worst grade in history and could soon forget this stupid adventure.

Then, one Saturday morning, the envelope came. Having a secret urge to throw it away, I put it on the kitchen counter to rest for a couple of hours. Instead of hurting my fragile ego (again), I decided there was much yard work to do.

Debbie saw the envelope and insisted that I open it. She also made a promise to love me no matter what the contents revealed. Relenting, I negotiated the perforated edges of the one-piece computerized mailing and scanned the entrails.

Damn, I did good. Well, pretty good, above average, but not the great I had secretly desired. Not the 165. However, I had done enough damage to The Bear that I would never have to fight him again. I can't say I killed The Bear, but I never again had to get tangled up in his pressurized lair. However, what havoc I did manage to inflict in Charleston wasn't good enough to be given an automatic big envelope.

The process continued.

I still harbored stupid ideas, like savoring the good life I had and forgetting the law school idea altogether. And yet, I started planning. Devising strategies and planning, that's how I roll.

At this point, I needed a winning campaign, one consisting of a good application, strategic recommendations, a great personal statement, and a killer interview. If you started at the beginning and read Chapter One, you know how that turned out. Anyway, that was the plan.

There is a lot to do after LSATs and before a law school class can even become conceivable. The application process is the typical school application process—a personal and academic history and two hundred bucks. The law school allowed applications to come in piecemeal. God knows why, but they put each piece in a file until all the components are complete. The application was a five-page book. SLAM! BAM! Thank you ma'am! Out the door it goes.

Then again, recommendations take serious consideration, especially those destined to be strategic. Everyone asks their minister, senator, boss, parent's friends, etc. I mean, what kind of idiot sends in a bad letter of recommendation? I needed a better than average approach, so I selected people who could comment on a particular aspect of my life, speak to my character, or portray my past career in a positive light, not just five humans saying what an asset this little boy would be to such a fine institution.

For my recommendations, I selected one business associate who could speak of my business practices over the last twenty years, another associate who could comment on my service to the home building industry, and a business adversary who could speak of my character as a decent, honest, and aggressive competitor. Also, I chose my business law professor who could assess my ability to think and speak legal mumbo jumbo. And, yes, I asked my minister, only because I had taught Sunday school and served on every committee a church could dream up. One could say they owed me big time.

Of course, since no one submits a recommendation from an adversary, I planned to reference him in my personal statement so the review committee would be at least tempted to take a peek. I was confident they would take delight in the notion that I included the sealed recommendation of a business enemy.

It was a big risk, but I knew the guy to be honest and fair. Even though he hated my business guts, I think he respected my trustworthy character. Seeing as the legal profession was taking a public relations beating from every direction at the time, highlighting the character aspect I thought would be a great maneuver. Plus, I think this particular business guy wanted me out of the marketplace. It turned out it was a good gamble. I think that one gutsy move got all my recommendations read. Who knows? By now, you do know I am a lawyer, right? So something worked.

This might sound like a lot of over planning, but my undergrad numbers weren't great and the application process was mostly based on numbers. It's all about GPA, LSAT, and not much else. I needed to display my desirability over some smartass little brat, and there were thousands of smartass little brats trying to get into my school. My plan was to work every angle of the system.

I knew the DOA to be nice. I was hoping I could impose on His Kindness to help me lessen the weeding out process. Turns out he remembered me. He relented and gave me a half hour. I shared my application thoughts and sought his opinion. He told me he felt my personal statement concept seemed a little rigid, lawyer-like, and that maybe a little passion would be useful.

I can take a hint like a klepto can steal a ribeye from a Walmart Superstore. Forget the lawyer talk. These guys were all lawyers. May it be, they were sick of lawyers? Nevertheless, I used all my powers to pour my soul out in human language onto the computer screen. My intent was to touch their hard little hearts while teasing them with recommendations. Think about it. Who sends in a recommendation from someone who hates them? Who the hell wouldn't read that one?

I got with some of my old public speaking buddies and gave them a challenge. Interview the crap out of me. We set up mock interviews in a real office. The pros came up with questions and I came in dressed for the occasion—suit, tie, shoes, socks, and underwear. I arrived on time, made eye contact, and sailed through the hard questions as well as the easy questions.

Then came the merciless evaluations with the proverbial Toastmaster three C's: compliments, critiques, and challenges. Rinse and repeat. How many times?

Whatever it takes.

CHAPTER TEN

The Question

You know how we can "know" someone through phone or electronic communications for such a long period that we are able to create an image of them in our minds? Even though we've never met them in person, we have a visual. Then, you know how, when you finally meet in person, it's always a bit strange because your image of them doesn't match the real person? Makes you tilt your head like a dog to try to make sense of a weird situation.

I had envisioned the acceptance letter for so long that I had fooled myself into believing that I had seen it, that I knew what it looked like, that I knew what it said and knew how it felt to hold it and read it.

"Congratulations, we are pleased to inform you . . ." in black and white, right there in my hands. It seemed unreal, the visual all lined up. What I had imagined had become real, and yet, as I read it with my head slightly tilted for enhanced comprehension, my heart rate eased up in spite of my beta-blocker meds. In fact, it seemed as if my heart had actually eased up from my chest cavity into my lower throat region because the beat seemed to be emanating from right behind my thyroid gland.

A full range of emotions was beginning to stimulate my endocrine system into full crazy mode. I had achieved the thing I had lusted after, and it was to the exclusion of all else sane in the world. I got what I asked for, my bluff was being called. I had to do something. But what?

I didn't have an exact plan. I am an insane planner, so that would happen in short order, but at that moment, I had nothing. Standing in front of my mailbox on my street was like inviting a retiree to run me over as if I were a squirrel. I had nothing but the inclination to gaze at the letter inviting me into the University of South Carolina School of Law.

I had them fooled. I pulled it off.

Oh, for God's sake, it had to be a mistake. I was interviewed with my zipper down in a shrinking sheep suit. Could that be why they accepted me? Was I interviewed by a perv? Was it God playing a trick on me? Was I going to get a phone call saying...?

"Mr. Fraser, this is the DOA calling to say with my sincerest apology that an admissions package was sent to you by mistake. Yes, sir, we understand you have told your family and both of your friends, and sold your business at a loss, but we cannot accept someone of your caliber. On behalf of the University of South Carolina, I apologize and wish you the very best in all your endeavors in life, which unfortunately, will not be fulfilled here at the University of South Carolina. Perhaps we could forward your application package to the Jackson Creek Community School of Law in South Jackson Creek, Missouri, located on the nation's fifth largest bison farm. I am told they accept most anyone who wishes to practice law within the city limits of South Jackson Creek and specialize in the legal issues surrounding home heating with

bison dung, a most interesting growth field. Their motto:
"They plop it, we profit" is no joke. Or perhaps we could
forward the package on to the Barrow School of Law in
Barrow, Alaska, where the great Will Rogers died while
visiting the Arctic Circle. Perhaps you and your family would
like to relocate to the greater Barrow area. However, the
Barrow School of Law has yet to be formed. Nevertheless, I'm
almost certain they would grant you early admission based on
the recommendation of the interviewing professor here at the
great USC SOL. Oh, and please don't promote the rumor that
"SOL" stands for "you know what outta luck." We don't
appreciate that around here. Again, I apologize and remind
you that this call may have been recorded for quality
assurance and training purposes. Goodbye, Mr. Fraser, and
good luck."

That call did not take place.

After some more reflection, I felt it necessary to take pride
in knowing that I had achieved something that was, for me,
extremely difficult.

Debbie and I knew we had to take the plunge, which meant
risking everything, or we could decide to savor the
satisfaction of being accepted and go on with our great life.
Few more difficult decisions have been put before me. Major
life decisions are not easy for me because I'm not a gambler.
I'm a conservative, a sure thing kind of guy. I know only a
few lawyers who are doing as well as in their practices as I
did in my construction business. You know the types—they
have assistants and time for Starbucks in the afternoon.

I often wondered why I was consumed with the will to
accomplish this outrageous goal without a clear end-game
objective. Was it because I wanted to take a stab at what some
believe to be the successful lawyer's pot o'gold? I know

plenty of lawyers smarter than me, but I don't know many (or any) wealthy lawyers, so that wasn't it.

Could my obsession to reach the law school summit be compared to Dr. Beck Weathers' dream to climb Mt. Everest? Weathers' dream cost him his nose, some toes, and both hands but saved his marriage. This guy took a few seconds for a photo op at the top of the mountain, then descended the mountain to go assess the damage to body, mind, soul and family. Think about it.

I have been asked the "why" question many times. I should have a canned answer, but, in all honesty, I do not. No doubt, I wanted to change careers and get into something that didn't have so many personnel headaches. So sure, that is one reason. And yes, I really wanted to excel academically. I always knew there was a better student inside me somewhere. Maybe that was the driving force.

I have a friend who (along with the rest of the community) heard what I was going to do, and in all seriousness said, "The only reason I can think of that would explain why someone would do such a thing at your age was to satisfy some deep feeling of inadequacy."

Seemed like a lousy thing to say, but I'm certain he wasn't the only one to have such a theory. Maybe he was right. I, of course, would never admit that, but I'm pretty sure he won't be reading this book.

My bluff was called. Debbie and I thought long and hard about this day, and then after prayer, we very nervously decided to go for it. The Platinum card and I were off to law school.

Dear God, do you know how many things have to line up in order to sustain extended stays away from home? Arrangements, so many arrangements had to be made! I was notified of my acceptance in May, which meant I had three months (until August thirteenth) to rearrange normal life so I could start what would be an exceptional three-and-a-half year trek.

We gradually let people know about our decision, especially those who would be most affected by the process. Debbie, with the help of two key employees, was to manage our business in my absence. Surprisingly, they were both on board and even excited about the prospect. Perhaps they hated me being there. Doesn't matter, they both quit within my first two months away from home, leaving us devastated and scrambling. They said they had great opportunities placed in their laps and felt certain we'd understand. No comment. Later down the road, I realized it was painful but worth it. Beck Weathers knows what I'm talking about.

I've always wanted to give Dad something to really be proud of, so when he came for a visit with his new wife, I gave him the best gift a dad could ever want. I told my dad, my only living close family member since my mother and sister passed away, that I was going to become a lawyer.

It's kind of weird when your eighty-three-year-old father gets married. But then it occurred to me that the news of his semi-worthless son going off to do what every parent dreams of their kid doing—becoming a doctor, lawyer, or astronaut— kind of balanced our new situation perfectly. He took a moment to absorb the news for a second or two and then quizzed me.

"Law School? Really? Why?"

Dammit! Again with the question! Why all the whys?

Too many whys—I wish I had an answer written on a slip of paper or on the back of a business card hidden in my wallet so I could whip it out and read it like a press release every time the question arose. Maybe I should have accepted how completely absurd this sounded to sane people. Well, if they didn't get it, then that was their problem, 'cause I was doing it and that was that!

Forget the question, there was work to do, and it had to be done in a summer so brief that I cannot recall a single detail of summer activities. No Fraser vacations. The sole focus was getting our business affairs in order and organizing an assault on Columbia.

The business part was a piece of cake. We had ourselves fooled into believing we had a plan that couldn't fail. Money would continue to roll in and the worker bees would simply whistle whilst they worked—very much a utopian society. Why wouldn't it work? We had happy employees and plenty of work scheduled. We were like two deaf kids playing *Go Fish* on a train track. What could go wrong?

Mid-summer Debbie and I were invited to campus for a pre-orientation. We got there early so we could say hello to the DOA and the wonderful lady who called me Mr. Hazel. The orientation was little more than a presentation in the auditorium highlighting various Deans and the DOA himself. I listened to my school leaders extend a warm welcome to us, the Chosen Few. The Few would be arriving for the first days of school in a few weeks, and I felt deeply honored to be among them.

The distinguished speakers spoke about who we were as a group. They described some of the many paths that led to that very day, which featured a physician, an engineer, a US Air Force officer, a pharmacist, a contractor (maybe me), and recent grads galore, average age twenty-eight. It was stated that ours was one of the oldest classes to date. I'm guessing Mr. Hazel and I helped with that one. So many males, so many females, so many African Americans, so many Asians, and so on and on until he had convinced us that we were a part of a very unique and diverse freshman group. All joking aside, this was a very proud moment—me, squeezed in with my new best friends.

Ethics and Character were huge topics in the presentation, and here's why. Our Supreme Court was generally fed up with the beating the legal profession's image had taken in recent years. At the time, I think we ranked just above car salespeople and just below Catholic priests. The still unfolding horrors of the Catholic priest molestation and keen affection for altar boys was giving us an opportunity to move up in ranking, but for the time being, we landed right above car sharks.

Our Supreme Court, the arm of government that rules over the state bar, was damned unhappy. Word was out that they had told the bar examiners to weed out the dumbasses for good measure, figuring the dumb lawyers are the bad apples.

Speaking for the dumb lawyers of these United States, I don't agree with that assessment; however, my opinion does not carry with it the power to tell the bar examiners not to make the bar exam decidedly harder. How could it be that as soon as I get accepted by accident they make the damn bar exam harder? Crap! Oh well, one crisis at a time. I still had to pass a real law course. What a great day!

I kind of wished my dad could have been there. Other parents were there with their kids. It would have been so cool if my eighty-four year old dad could have taken his forty-eight year old son to college just like he did in 1967. That wasn't to be though, so Debbie and I just soaked up the pride, enough for him and all the rest of my kin.

I knew my wife was proud. She knew all the crap I had been through to get there, but did she know why we were there? It was a bit of a reality check though when one of the other parents asked, "Which one is your kid?"

"It's me. I'm the rising first year."

And, of course, they had to ask, "Why?"

Jesus! Again with the why! Damn it! I don't know. I just don't freaking know why. I really wish I had tee-shirt that could speak for me. "I DON'T KNOW WHY I'M HERE!"

Even with the occasional bubble-popping smack of reality, we just slurped up the prideful day. And hell yes, we went by the little room where they sell stuff and bought a USC School of Law tee-shirt with a little scale of justice over the right boob, much like the kind my friends used to use to measure out an ounce of product. What a great day! I was really going to law school!

Oh crap, I WAS REALLY GOING TO LAW SCHOOL!

CHAPTER ELEVEN

The Routine

My kids call me OCD, which is far from correct. I want things a certain way, and yes, I get a little hysterical when anything dishevels my little batch of life. So I organize and arrange things.

Yep, I am the Ruler of Redundancy, the Prince of Preparation, the Dean of Design, the Orator of Organization, the Legionnaire of Listing, the Raptor of Regiment, but I am definitely not OCD. As remarkable and enviable (and fun to ridicule) as these talents are, they come in damn handy when one is preparing to go live in a motel room for three years.

Back to reality and the earthly world of preparation. The Holiday Inn, located right next door to the law school, the one with guest parking, was to become my home away from home residence. Even though it was more expensive than renting an apartment, when you deducted for weekends, holidays and summers, it came out about the same.

One drawback was that I had to check out every Friday and get a new room on Monday. One more drawback, there was no kitchen. These challenges I could handle with ease. I wasn't sure about passing law classes, but I could organize the crap out of this new life. This was my playing field.

First order of business was to avoid overload. I needed to be prepared to make one trip to the car, one trip into the Holiday Inn, and one trip back to the car to come home. I needed custom equipment, and this, by God, was what I was made to invent.

Tanger Outlets had a luggage store. We went there on a mission from God. American Tourister made the most ideal piece of law school luggage imaginable—a standing trunk, like those little rolling carry-on pieces of luggage everyone pulls around in an airport, except this was big, and I do mean BIG.

At attention, the trunk stood three feet tall with a handle that came out of the top and wheels on the underside. And, as you'd expect, the front door, when zipped open, it swung like a door, revealing three shelves. The top shelf I decided was for the computer, the middle shelf for the printer, and the bottom shelf for books and paper supplies.

The Tourister became an engaging project. I found dense foam yoga pads and cut them to make the top shelf a soft igloo, allowing my laptop to fit perfectly without any wiggle room. I "MacGyver-ed" the second shelf for the printer in a similar fashion. The damn thing was taking on a NASA look.

I left the bottom shelf for books that were not in use. Books switched out on an every other day basis. I also stored my power strip and phone hookup in there. After leaving my power strip behind one Friday, never to be seen again, I painted a new one in safety glow orange so that when I left my room each Friday, I could scan for orange and know if I was cleared for departure. The thing was so cool!

With academic supply transport properly taken care of, I went on to food and clothing. I had to do a little thinking and experimenting with the food concept. My new home in the Holiday Inn was a motel room consisting of a bathroom, a couch, a desk, and a king-sized bed. I had to figure out how to eat there at least three nights a week, those nights being Monday, Tuesday, and Wednesday.

It was important that I ate out on Thursdays. I'd have gone crazy if I didn't have that amenity built into the regime. Of course, I couldn't answer the "why" thing, which some thought was a clue for crazy. Never mind that, I had to have some time outside of the cell, so Thursdays became my retreat. I went home on Fridays, so I considered Thursdays my one indulgence. Remember, no TV, just law books. Thursdays were a big deal.

Having dinner in the room took some real planning. I was (and still am) an adult male who is accustomed to eating a full meal every night. I'm not a bird on a diet of seeds. Meat and three, that's me. So I bought a food saver vacuum device and a small electric fondue pot with temperatures that ranged from warm to 350 degrees. The fondue pot was good for boiling water for coffee or warming the boiling bags from my FoodSaver® meals.

Over the weekends, Debbie and I would cook all kinds of packable and freezable yummy things. Chili, hamburger, chicken breast, salmon, steak—whatever we wanted for the weekend, plus a little extra. I simply had to freeze three main entrees rock solid for transport to the Holiday Inn.

Chicken breast grilled with lemon butter and garlic was a favorite. Something like canned green beans, lima beans, or fruit cocktail worked for a side, and I was good to go for three days. I bought a small soft cooler to transport the frozen entrees to the hotel, and then added Holiday Inn icemaker ice to sustain the meals until the blessed Thursday night in a restaurant rolled around. I also purchased a duffel bag to house the fondue pot, a few minor cooking utensils, and my one plate.

Not having to think about packing to go away or come back loomed as a necessity, and the hodgepodge of miscellaneous toiletries and health supplies stood out as a potential nuisance. I bought a soft cooler, the kind designed for a six-pack, and bought a duplicate of everything I typically use at home—toothpaste, toothbrush, deodorant, soap, shampoo, mouthwash, shaving stuff, meds like aspirin and cold pills, band aids, and other essentials.

Okay, maybe I am a little OCD, but only a little. I don't count bathroom tiles or anything weird, but I do like having my stuff where it's supposed to be. This way I don't have to think. Meanwhile, my essentials all live in the little cooler, just waiting for a chance to go away somewhere.

The cooler occupied one end of the big Orvis duffle, leaving the other end for the fours—four boxers, four shirts, four pairs of pants. An extra pair of shoes went in the end compartment and my one windbreaker and rain jacket went in the other end compartment. The routine I devised was some of my best strategizing.

Pack the fours. At the Holiday Inn, open the duffle and use one of the fours each day. Fold the dirty items and place them by the duffle. On Friday, place the dirty fours into the duffle. Back at home, enter the house through back laundry room door. Remove the fours for cleaning. Go upstairs to the home closet, put in a new set of fours, zip closed, and forget it until Monday morning at 5:00 a.m.

What could be easier? It was a simple, repetitive routine that an overtaxed mind could keep without thinking, which also left the most time possible for family, 5:00 p.m. Friday until 5:00 a.m. Monday. I made a simple vow that I would have no life other than law studies during the week. Class, study, and sleep. Nothing else. My weekends would be devoted to family.

I pretty much lived by this vow with very few exceptions. The sadists who teach law will occasionally assign a project that spills over into the weekend, but I found with the three-for-one method (meaning three hours of study outside of class for each hour of study in class), the bulk of the work gets done.

Doing school "right" and playing by the rules actually paid off, which was a first for me. I admit to having enough smarts to have been a major screw-off in my previous years of schooling, so yes, doing things the right way was a refreshingly new experience. Just think what might have happened if I didn't wait until the age of forty-eight to figure that one out.

Now, so the record is somewhat straight on the depth and breadth of my slackness, it was confined to school, an endeavor that, for some unfathomable reason, I always felt conscripted into, like an indentured servant, doing the minimum and praying for the servitude to end.

God, did I miss the boat, or what? I was presented a free education and thought I was cool by not packing everything I could into my little head. What a dumbass! I showed the school system. I didn't take what they were giving away. Look at me, teaching them a lesson!

We've all known the good student who turned into a lazy bum later on in life, so I guess I did it the better way. I'm still a little pissed that I didn't make better use of the educational opportunity placed in my lap. When I build a time machine, I'll go back and fix all that.

Work was a different story. Come early, stay late, never take a sick day, no vacations, and overachieve wherever possible. Sometimes I wondered who in hell was this new guy, and what he did he do with the slack-ass Denny?

How I spent (or wasted) my time preparing to transport myself to and from law school was significant for one big reason. The task of attempting to keep up with the crowd of young geniuses was daunting enough, and I could not embark on the undertaking with inconveniences and annoyances nipping at my heels. The thought of reinventing the packing wheel each week, dining at restaurants every day, and living like a disorganized slob would make an already painful endeavor unbearable. I know me. Hell, I should know me at forty-eight.

I know all too well how obstacles divert my attention and get me off target. Every investment in efficiency, no matter how small and seemingly insignificant, removed one small pain in the neck from my life. The idea of selecting toiletries so they would all stand upright in my little cooler so that when needed, they could be seen and accessed without having to dig around like a bear going through a trashcan. That can actually made my life slightly easier. The idea of folding dirty clothes and placing them by the duffle until the last clean item came out so they could then be placed in with one motion, and the assurance that they were all accounted for without having to search the room looking for clothes to pack on Friday, was genius.

Fridays were pleasantly predictable. I rose early, studied, packed, checked out, loaded my car with one trip, went to class, and then launched myself toward home exactly one minute after my last class.

Debbie and I found that little extra effort was necessary if we just cooked a little extra on the weekends. If we cooked chicken breasts on the grill, I'd grill four extra. It literally takes the same effort to cook eight breasts as four. If the menu happened to be hamburgers, then I'd cook four extra hamburgers. If we made chili, then we'd make a bunch more. If we had spaghetti, we'd make a bunch more. We'd vacuum-pack and freeze, so when it was time to go back to war, all I had to do was go to the freezer, grab three different packages and three cans of sides, and I was good for the week. The little things made my nearly impossible academic life possible, but just barely. It was enough to keep me in the game without saying "to hell with it" and throwing in the towel. And yes, I had to talk myself off that ledge more than once.

Some plans were little and other plans were big. Some tweaks and improvements came through the usual evolutionary process, as expected, but by the first week of August we were ready.

SOL, the law school, mailed my schedule along with advance reading requirement for orientation and course case assignments. This was not like getting an undergraduate degree where you get to have preferences. SOL classes are assigned. First years are not offered a choice of course or professors, but there was method to this insulting madness. SOL arranged the class schedule so daily classes were separated by at least one off period, for study or whatever. For me, it was study. Time to proceed to Columbia for book buying and orientation. Time for the real thing.

CHAPTER TWELVE

The Mountain

Columbia sits atop a lump of sandy soil that once was part of the ancient seabed when the oceans thought covering this part of the world was a better idea than leaving it dry. After the ocean receded, it left behind barren soil to bake in the sun for a million or so years. Only tenacious plant structures found its composition habitable. This included the scrub oak, a dwarf and angry little tree with claw-like branches invented to grab anything that comes near, animal or human. Scrub oaks like sandy soil and live a graceless existence sucking minimal nutrition from dry dirt. Pine trees could deal with this pale soil even though they didn't grow fast like they did in other places. But these Columbian pine trees, they could live by sheer determination, rooting themselves in the old beach sand.

Let me be clear, Columbia sits on a lump, or a knoll—a much more flattering term. Because of this, it can be seen from a distance when being approached by interstate. On a clear day, it begins to show itself about fifteen miles out. It's not engulfed by smog like Los Angeles, but a shroud of light fog clings to the city in a similar fashion.

The fog is made from, in part, car fumes, some industrial matter, and brooding humidity. Columbia is known for its heat and humidity, and rightly so. Hard surfaces, concrete, asphalt, and the ever-ready sandy soil giving whatever moisture it may possess to the unrelenting heat, contributed to the hazy vale.

It was August, and by the looks of it, Columbia appeared to be cooking. But it didn't matter because all human life contains itself in an artificial atmosphere. Columbians exist mostly in cars or buildings. No one remains in the haze for long. It's not even visible when you're in it.

It was midmorning when I arrived. The early rush was over. The parking place wars had ended—some poor stiffs lost while others had won. The bookstore was across the street from the law school. It was small but big enough to have what I needed, plus other school-related stuff such as license plates, window stickers, t-shirts, hats, visors, and so much more. List in hand, I found the section marked Law Books. Good name, very helpful.

Two twenty-something girls sensed my stupidity and offered to help me. Being completely helpless, I handed over my computer printout of my schedule like someone in a foreign country handing over all his money to a vendor because he was too stupid to acquaint himself with the currency. It turned out to be a good choice on my part. The girls cut right to the chase and had my thousand dollars worth of books yanked out in no time.

Then, for kindness or sport (not sure which), they offered a critique of my courses and professors. They said I lucked out. A few classes were not praised but not trashed. One course and professor, namely Contracts, came with a short and sweet admonition. *Don't go in unprepared.* Not a particularly scary thing to say, but it traveled with me for the next few days.

I gave a thousand dollars weighing less than an ounce and got eighty plus pounds of books. It's funny what we trade in life. I should have felt that I got the best end of the bargain by weight or volume, but the suspicion that I had been screwed went along with the admonition about the Contracts class.

Well, I had a lot to think about, so these nagging suspicions were in good company; in fact, they were in the back of the room, which was already filled with anxiety and doubt. At this point, nothing was going to scare me. Hell, I was already scared at the quantum overload level. I was way into the red.

I've already mentioned this, but it bears mentioning again. Even before school starts there is homework. It's a tradition, like arriving at 3:00 am on a bus for Day One of Marine training on Parris Island. Also traditional, first years have to attend an actual orientation of some substance the week before class. This was the real orientation, not like the one where we listened to speeches and got all comfy.

Real orientation was designed to laden rising freshmen with all the information needed to immediately dive into learning without any interruption, like, for example, where's the bathroom. In this program, first years were introduced to the library—its study closets (corrals) and passwords to research tools. It's important to know the layout of the building as well as the concept of the honor code, and so on.

And for this, there was homework. I had to buy and read three books so I could prepare for orientation class discussion sessions. I believe the idea was to simulate the class environment. I couldn't tell whether it was to diffuse the fear, or cause greater panic.

One of the books was *The Buffalo Creek Disaster*, which is about a West Virginia coal mine dam that broke, causing several downstream dams to break leading to massive flooding, destruction and death, hence the disaster part. As it turns out, the lead counsel for the Plaintiffs chose to retire in my hometown. He was an acquaintance of mine, so I used my adult powers, gave him a call, and got the lowdown on the case.

Of course, the orientation, led by sophomores and juniors, simulated a real law class, which meant these books and cases weren't even discussed. These guys didn't care. They probably wanted our first day of real classes to suck the most.

Having no regard for trees, we were loaded down with paper, lists, documents, pamphlets, schedules, and ads for campus clubs and such. I left orientation and went home to enjoy my last weekend as a civilian. Loaded down with hundreds of pounds of stuff, I wondered how all this stuff was going to fit inside my cramped little contractor's head.

By now, I felt like I'd already been through law school or its equivalent. I had prepared for the LSAT, took the LSAT, passed the LSAT, got accepted, and designed my new life as a first year law student. I had been oriented, not once but twice.

Nearly two years of my life had been given to this process and it was finally sinking in that I had not even started school yet. How big was this mountain? I felt the need to call Beck Weathers, who had just finished his trip up Everest and was likely healing from his multiple amputations. Surely he would have time to chat on the phone about doing something large for one's little self.

So, Beck, what'd ya think? I should have given him a call. *The mountain looks mighty high and you're only at base camp. Better be careful climbing that thing.* I'm sure that's what he'd say.

My last weekend as a non-law student was kind of weird. Debbie and I tried to act normal and tiptoed around the subject while making last minute preparations and hanging out with our girls because on Sunday our world was going to change. We were betting everything would work out and we would not lose everything we had built over the last twenty years.

Having kids is a wonderful thing. They are fun to make, ask any guy. Kids are fun to play with, ask any dad. Kids are fun to spoil, ask any grandparent. And believe it, or not, kids provide a service. The reality is children are by nature self-orientated. Kids are not interested or burdened by all the craziness whirling around in your head. They don't care what you drive or where you live. They want to do kid stuff and receive attention.

Mine were two of the best at achieving selfish fun, love and joy. They did their job of keeping me from dwelling on myself. The kids made sure we did the whole family thing throughout that last weekend. We built a fort in the family room and watched Saturday morning television—Angry Beavers, Ren and Stimpy, and Foghorn Leghorn.

CHAPTER THIRTEEN

The Kids

Page, my first born and first opportunity to raise and educate a human being, was twelve at the time of my departure. She was my best friend and constant companion for nearly all those twelve years. From the time she could climb out of a bed, she would find her way to my bedside. Inherently shy, she stood there, staring. She made no commotion. She just stood there willing me to wake.

At some point during the "willing," my subconscious would make me aware of a presence in my room and I would open my eyes. There she would be, smiling, ready for her playmate to get up and start the day. Often I wondered how long she had been standing there. Minutes? Hours? Who knows—this was before she could tell time.

We lease a small island for hunting and family recreation, and like most Saturdays, Page and I went out to the island and walked the fields looking for illusive Indian relics. It seemed appropriate. In two days I would be a relic going back to school.

Families just like us, with their own set of dreams and challenges, lived on this coastal island before us. In the process, they lived out their allotted time here on earth, leaving behind shards of pottery and bits of flint. My time with my kid out on that island, finding the history of other families long since gone, gave me a new perspective. I thought about what bits of my life would be left for someone to come across.

What would the things I left behind tell about me? I kind of hated to leave the ancient world but the new world I had craved for so long was waiting for me just a few hours away.

Lizzi. Lizzie. Liz. Given name Elizabeth Harris Fraser, she was sent to us by God late in life. She was born almost seven years after Page.

We wanted a second kid so badly but it wasn't meant to be, at least not without help. We went the medical fertility route. Had every test, did sperm counts, tried in vitro and artificial insemination. I made more trips down the OB hall at the hospital with a plastic cup of potential baby swimmers than I care to count.

I got to know the nurses in the hospital pretty well, so much so that some would smile and give a familiar knowing nod, a kind of an "atta boy" thumbs up as I carried my cup of potency to where the experts got my best boys ready for a journey upstream.

The procedure never took. We don't know why. It could have been that the little swimmers were easily distracted like me, or maybe they had my mother's sense of direction and just kept going in circles. It doesn't matter why things didn't happen. In the end, no egg got fertilized.

Ever exasperated with the easy fixes, we tried surgery to see if there was something plumbed wrong the way. Now, you do understand when I say "we" tried surgery, I mean a doctor performed the surgery and he did it on Debbie, right? My job was simply to produce and deliver robust swimmers, which I did a lot. A whole lot. Hey, someone had to do it. Debbie, on the other hand, was suffering through this process as only a hopeful mom could.

Finally, the doctors, realizing we had been drained of all of our money and likely couldn't afford to raise a child anyway, sat us down for "the talk." It just wasn't to be. *Go home, you are not to have another child unless you kidnap one from the mall.* This nearly killed Debbie. She was thirty-nine and had vowed that forty was the cut off anyway.

We were done. Wrung out, cried out, kicked out. The Charleston voodoo baby doctors were through with us. We carried our sadness home to report to our local OBGYN guy, a good doctor and lovely person named Dr. Love, believe it, or not. He had sent us on this scientific odyssey with great confidence that a baby would be made. It was his turn to have "the talk" with us. His was a little kinder than the Charleston fertility bunch where we were merely passing through the system, never to be seen again. Our doc was a local and had more human compassion, probably because he might see us in the kumquat isle at the grocery store one day.

Dr. Love gently reminded us that we had the gift of one great kid. "Maybe it just wasn't meant to be and things have a way of working out for the best," said the stress of all the medical tests and failures and our doctor. This was something our marriage and family simply did not need.

Dr. Love encouraged us to enjoy our good life and to give one hundred percent to the family we already had. He reminded us to be thankful for our blessings and invited us to relax. We took his words to heart and went back to normal life. No more doing you-know-what in a plastic cup for me, although I stood ready to make the sacrifice if needed. The girls in the OB ward would just have to smile at some other guy carrying his cup full of swimmers down the hall.

Yep, we were completely done fixating on the idea of a second child. Debbie got pregnant in one month, just before her fortieth birthday. Thanks, Dr. Love!

Our luck in this department led us to decide not to announce the long-awaited pregnancy until the new baby was in the second grade. Much deliberation and prayer convinced us that would be a stupid idea, so we decided to wait until we were absolutely certain this pregnancy was viable.

We had been down this road once before.

It started with cramps and spotting, which is a stupid doctor term for bleeding. The euphoria of expecting a baby suddenly gets replaced with the dark and suffocating realization that the little life is being sent out of the womb. I know many moms-to-be and couples have experienced this sadness, but we never knew the pain of the loss until our own child's little life was rejected.

And to boot, we had announced to the world, yelled from the rooftops that we were expecting a baby, so for weeks, maybe months after the miscarriage, people would ask about the pregnancy. Everywhere we went, the grocery store, at church, the dry cleaners, the wound kept being reopened.

So in this case, we waited silently for three months. We kept our mouths shut until Debbie was showing and sonogram images confirmed there was an unstoppable baby in the hopper. Things worked out for the best, without all the infertility crap. One of my really good swimmers met up with that one special egg, punched its way through, and make the little human we know as Elizabeth Harris Fraser, aka Lizzi, aka Liz, aka Ittybit.

I, too, was given life despite similar circumstances. My mother had three late term miscarriages. She was told by the medical wisdom of the 1930s that she would never carry a pregnancy to term. She waited until WWII was won and in 1946, she was blessed with another pregnancy. She gave birth to a little girl, only to be told in the haze of ghastly amounts of anesthesia that her daughter was born with an abnormality called spina bifida, which was incurable and not survivable.

It took that little angel two months to leave this world, and how the death of that sweet baby did not take my mother along, too, I'll never know. But one thing is for sure, had that tragedy not taken place, I would not have seen this earth. They tried again. Fifth time was a charm because here I am.

Debbie's pregnancy was carefully observed, first of all, because of our age, and secondly, as you may have guessed, because of my family's history with spinal column abnormalities. We were strongly advised to have a procedure wherein they take amniotic fluid from the sac and analyze it for all sorts of problems.

This was beyond frightening because the procedure causes spontaneous miscarriages in about one out of a thousand cases. When it comes to your kid, no point spread is acceptable, but our doctor all but insisted on it. He said the procedure could diagnose a host of birth defects, like spina bifida and Down syndrome. I argued that Down syndrome was certainly no reason to terminate a child's life. I used to be a big "women's right to choose" guy, but now I had grown to cherish this little life growing inside my wife. But we placed our trust in our physician, Dr. Love, who sent us back to Charleston, the same cold place where months before we were told we'd never have another kid.

The doctor pushed a foot-long needle straight through Debbie huge pregnancy dome while watching a monitor screen to help guide this awful-looking instrument around Lizzi, my kid, so he could capture some fluid. There are no words for the fear when your kid's life is on the line. The nightmare finally ended and everything and everyone was fine. No problems at all. We were relieved. Actually, we felt much better. Once again, thanks Dr. Love.

Can someone please tell me how two genetically almost identical humans, siblings from the same parents, be so completely different? Page was a little shy, eager to accommodate, eager to please, accepting of parental guidance. Lizzi, on the other hand, wasted no time letting all three of us know that she was in charge. We were put on this earth to see to Lizzi's every need, and this could be accomplished in one of two ways, the easy way, or the hard way. The choice was ours, but the end result was always the same. Home was Lizzi's domain.

Having kids separated by nearly seven years means that around the time one settles into full teenage mode, the younger one enters the perfect playmate age.

When Lizzi was young, our church started family camping. The timing was perfect. I taught Sunday school and was involved with the church youth, so we bought into the whole camping experience, big time. We bought enough camping equipment to live in the woods under any and all conditions. We took on camping like all things Fraser, balls to the wall, take no prisoners. For good measure, I bought a small fleet of kayaks, ocean, and river.

For Lizzi, the progression into the camping world started big and ended small. First, we went on large group trips with huge family tents and incredible equipment. Gradually, we gravitated to backpacking. Eventually, we grew into backpacking purists and noticed the wimpy families were gone. They would call themselves normal, but I'm sticking with wimpy.

Finally, it ended up being two dads with daughters. As father/daughter teams, we went everywhere. We dragged our girls and kayaks over rivers and oceans of North Carolina, South Carolina, Georgia, and Florida. And we backpacked every mountain trail in North Carolina, Georgia, Tennessee, and South Carolina. Of course, I bought every imaginable piece of high-tech equipment to face every contingency in the wild or on the water.

Lizzi, the girliest girl ever, became unbelievably proficient as an outdoors person. She could do it all, and since the teenage parental repulsion did not hit her as early as it did Page, I had a camping and backpacking buddy for a few extra years. I was a lucky dad. I had two daughters, both beautiful and athletic, who did the girlie stuff with Debbie and the guy stuff with me.

Beyond having fun with my kids, I have only one job in life, and that is to be the protector of my kids. I don't care how nice the boys are or how much, under different circumstances, I might like them, my job was to distrust and question all situations. In this regard, I'm not cool, not modern, not open minded, and never apologetic. God gave me two girls to look after, and I will do that so long as I live.

'Nuff said.

For my last civilian meal, Debbie fixed a special Fraser family dinner, the kind reserved mostly for birthdays, anniversaries, holidays, and most anytime we felt like making something special, like fried May River shrimp with coleslaw and hush puppies, made with love, of course. That's what special dinners are all about, right? Mine was a going away last supper but nothing like a last meal for a condemned man.

Debbie and I tried to act like nothing big (like going to law school) was going to happen the next day. And the kids did their usual sibling thing, not really understanding the impending enormity of what was about to happen. Sure, we had talked to them about the impending change in pretty calm and reassuring terms. It was to be an adventure.

However, kids are barometers. They detect the pressure in a relationship. They can sense it. They can see it in our body language, feel it in the mood of the household. They can absorb clues and warnings that go back to the survival instinct that we all had a million years before we exchanged freedom for the illusion of government protection.

Kids are keen. They know when things are not right in their sphere of security. I view parents as protectors, teachers, and providers who do not have the right to inflict parental anxiety and concerns upon their children.

To me, that's child abuse and neglect. It's not the worst kind of abuse, but it's a bad one, nonetheless. Children need love, protection, and guidance. They do not need to feel every emotion their parents have.

Most parents don't get this. They operate under the belief that true honesty in a family means puking out your every feeling for all, including the kids, to absorb—which is what kids do. They're like sponges, they absorb. They can read the wind. Parents should use caution when it comes to sharing their emotions. Debbie and I did our best at keeping ours buried deep within ourselves.

Therefore, on the last night, we kept it upbeat, everything cool and peachy. We actually had a pretty nice evening just hanging out. We stayed up late and watched Saturday Night Live. I commented on how back in the day, the show was funny.

Amazingly, I slept, really slept. I suppose at some point exhaustion sets in and a body shuts down. Deep inside I knew this would be my last rest for a while. I should ask Debbie's dad if he slept the night before Normandy. Come Monday, I would face what I considered to be the metaphorical German 88's.

Sunday brought with it packing and loading the car and acting normal, as if nothing was up. The countdown to three o'clock (zero hour) was in motion. And damn, didn't the hours slip by too quickly.

"Life is like an hourglass glued to a table." Suddenly that made sense.

CHAPTER FOURTEEN

The First Week

Somewhere between the train horn blasts every ten minutes and swishing cars on the wet pavement of Assembly Street, I must have enjoyed some moments of unconsciousness wherein regeneration takes place, but I couldn't say for sure. All I could remember was staring at the popcorn ceiling illuminated by the mercury glow from the artificial lights on the street below.

No need for caffeine. My heart rate seemed to be up around 120. I have a bad heart valve that flops all around, so it's not unusual for me to feel beats, but these beats were registering in my eardrums, so my heart rate had to be above 120. However, I didn't come this far to quit because of a heart attack. I—no, we were going to school.

I was scared. I don't know why. Hell, I was older than all the kids, except for Mr. Hazel, whom I had not met yet. There was a very small cadre of returning codgers that I actually called old. Yep, that's right, I discriminate against old people, so sue me. I shouldn't be afraid of the professors; I was their age and certainly more successful. I think it boiled down to the fact that I don't like standing out, and I really, really did stand out. Does anyone like looking stupid?

These professors were smart. The kids were smart. Sooner, not later, they would find out I was let in by mistake, that I was stupid as a stump. They'd realize the term "stumped" came from my ancestral lineage. They'd say, "He's stumped," because that's what folks said when one of us was unable to answer the most basic of questions. We'd sit there all dumbstruck, waiting for the questioner and life to mercifully move on until someone eventually said, "Yep, he's stumped." To the academically elite, with whom I was now associated, I would be known by my ancestors, the Stumped. My destiny was much like the unfairness that beset the Crapper family after one of their people invented the flush toilet.

Oh Lord, having that thought, I realized I needed to take a crap to avoid any unfortunate mishaps in front of my new classmates. The only thing I could imagine worse than the horrors I was about to endure in law school was to be "stumped" and "dumped" in front of my peers. Heavens, why (this damn question again), *why* didn't I just get in the old Volvo and go home where I was never stumped and surely never dumped except in the appropriate crapper. People shouldn't be persecuted because of their ancestors, even if they did good stuff, like invent a toilet.

I opened the glass back door to law school and was instantly greeted by sheer pandemonium. The lobby was one crazy long flight up. All 720 students in that lobby talked using persuasive levels all at the same time. I came in from the back street entrance—the back door was fine with me. I ascended the long flight of stairs with the twenty odd people who also didn't mind entering law school through the back door. There was a television studio with high ceilings in the basement, so the first flight up measured thirty feet or so.

There was something odd about the stair risers. They were a little taller than usual, not by much, just a little, maybe eight and a half inches instead of the usual seven and three-eighths. I'm a contractor. I know these things.

Half way up, dear God, I'm carrying my new bookbag, with all my new school supplies, raincoat, umbrella, books, a snack, and I tripped. Fell face first, cracked my knees and shins on the concrete steps. I landed on my chest, eyeball to eyeball with a stair tread. The misfortune knocked all the wind out of my lungs, allowing me only enough breath to let out a pathetic sound, kind of like the noise an old dog makes as he's lying down for what very well could be his last nap.

All the kids on the stairs went silent after letting out a collective "ooooh." Then, to cap off the humiliation, a young person tried to help me get up.

Of course, I couldn't tell them to leave me the hell alone because both my lungs were collapsed and I could not make a sound. I pushed the youngster away and composed myself.

All systems checked, I began breathing again and discovered that I had not, in fact, evacuated my bowels in my drawers. All was okay. I took extra high steps and made my way to the top of the weirdly sized stairs into the giant lobby. Once there, Ol' Strom Thurmond, or his brown face bust greeted me. I made my way, dry and unscathed, into the law school scene.

It was human chaos. People going in every direction, everyone talking, nobody listening. My first task was to get through this ant bed of humanity and find a classroom. Time to get this one-act Tennessee Williams play started.

The first day of school is predictably the same for all of us. New people, new surroundings, new sights, new sounds, new odors. In the third grade, it was the distinct odor of a new painted metal lunch box, sandwich wrap, a thermos and a ripe banana. Law school wasn't much different.

Schools have a unique odor. It's a combination of humans, office supplies, books, janitorial supplies, and poor ventilation. Professors go to schools to get to full retirement so they can collect a paycheck for the rest of their eternity, and the students are there to get a degree so they can go do something until they can collect a paycheck for doing nothing for the rest of their eternity. I don't mean to sound all dark and dismal on the subject, but for many, that is the whole story in a nutshell.

I set about finding my first classroom. I knew where it was because I had scoped out the geography earlier. I tried to get my bearings once I knew for sure I was on the firm, flat surface of the cavernous lobby at the top of the treacherous stairs. Still in the midst of human chaos, I started to negotiate a path through the throng when it suddenly became apparent that I was still using the gait of a walking horse I had used to make my way up the crazy tall steps. The last thing I wanted was another embarrassing scene, or having EMS summoned to come take me away.

People were already looking at me, so the stupid high stepping had to go. At this point, anonymity was my deepest desire, which is why the appearance of gliding seemed preferable to appearing to be stepping over invisible trip wires. Having no idea where my self-confidence went, I wished I didn't have to be me, the older person going back to school.

My father would have loved being in this environment. He was a born showman. Always in need of attention, he would have stirred up things as much as possible. By the time he passed the evil brown face bust of Old Strom, he would have known everyone in the room by their first name. And he probably would have copped a feel or two along the way by pretending to be blind.

My father got more mileage from macular degeneration than anyone could imagine. No doubt he had a serious vision problem, but when he needed both attention and sympathy from a really hot young lady, he'd go totally midnight, coal mine, blind. Once, in a restaurant, he held his menu upside down, intimating blindness. This was my dad's way of asking the waitress to read the menu to him.

The waitress was honored to turn his menu over and read while he held her hand for comfort. Looking at us like the elder abusers we surely were, she patiently read deliciously described items. Between categories, he told her stories of losing his sight on the last flight out of Cuba.

If he were here, in law school, he would fumble into class late, walk up to the professor, and feel his face, explaining that a person's face reveals a lot. He'd stumble around the room looking for a place to sit while accidentally groping the good-looking girls until the hottest one offered him a seat next to her so she could take notes for him. Okay, that's him, not me. I was just the guy trying to vanish into a crowd and make it to Property Law class without another incident.

Mercifully, I made it past Ol' Strom, who seemed to harden his scowl to let me know he was watching me. He knew I didn't belong. If he had a brown hand to go with the brown severed torso, he'd have pointed two brown fingers at his angry eyes then jammed an index finger toward me so I'd know he was watching me.

I followed the throng.

"Hi, Mr. Hazel." Shocked, and somehow knowing it to be directed at me, I recognized the voice of the lovely lady from admissions who would call me Mr. Hazel for the next three years.

"Welcome!" she sung out. "How is your first day going?"

"Fine, so far. It's Denny."

"What's that, Mr. Hazel?" she asked, looking puzzled.

"My name is Denny Fraser," I tried again, muffling the compulsion to scream, "I've met you ten times and my mother-freaking-name is Denny Fraser, not Mr. G.D. Hazel!" But I kept it within, only because of my overwhelming desire to blend in.

"That's fine, have a wonderful first day, Mr. Hazel," she blissfully chirped. I pushed on, caught in the flow of humans with backpacks moving like a great river of logs, downstream, leading me to the room where it would all begin.

CHAPTER FIFTEEN

The Truisms

Law school classrooms actually do resemble what is depicted on television—a horseshoe of tables facing a lectern, each row higher than the one below, constructed so all the listeners can see the talker, and more importantly, the talker can see the listeners as well as the non-listeners.

My classroom was arranged in classic law school horseshoe style but was a long skinny one instead of a short fat one. The lectern and blackboard were located at the skinny end, near the two main entrances. No modern dry-erase boards, not here anyway. Narrow formica tables, about sixteen inches wide, made up three sides of the horseshoe. Anchored behind the narrow tables was a row of swivel plastic chairs attached to fixed posts sunk into the concrete. Those babies weren't moving.

I picked the first front row seat on the right. Actually, it was the second seat because the first seat and its post had been sawed off for some reason. My theory was that sitting in the front of the class communicates to the professor that you are prepared. So, if you are a professor trolling for slackers, they can and will be found in the far back rows. Plus, I'm about half deaf, so being close to the speaker helps.

Maybe it's the dad in me, but I noticed two small pieces of masking tape stuck to the floor, forming a small X about six feet in front of the lectern. The X, I presumed, was a mark to stand on for filmed presentations. It was worn and dirty like it had been there a while. The dad in me wanted to get a razor scraper and pull it up, but then I changed my mind. I made it my goal to see how long it would be left there, defacing the school.

The room was abuzz. No professor in sight and everyone talking, except to me. And then a young lady, a pretty stout gal, sat down next to me and said, "Hi. Are you a student?"

"Yes, going back for a second career."

"Why?" She looked at me as if staring at me she would be able to ascertain the answer.

"Oh, just something I've always wanted to do."

"Oh." End of conversation.

Don't get me wrong. The kids were unbelievably nice to me. I mean, really nice, as in "yes, sir" and "no, sir" nice. There was never any attempt at any actual conversation, just gushy politeness. Never "how's it going?" or "how's it hanging?" Of course, that probably was best because I wasn't sure I should be "hanging."

Seeing and sensing the level of anxiety in the room was reassuring. I knew I was a faker soon to be exposed, but I expected everyone else to be cool, and to my great pleasure, nearly all of them looked scared crapless.

For those who may not know the inner workings of law schools, the traditional, full-time standard law schools divide up the freshmen class into sections. First years are given a non-negotiable schedule of classes and professors, and all classes are with your assigned section. Same people, every class, every day. Each of the three USC SOL freshmen sections had eighty students, which would account for the 240.

My eighty looked like the proverbial mixed bag, mostly young, some older, both genders equally represented. The girls were generally dressed nicer than the boys. It was August in the hottest city in America and I picked long pants—khakis and a polo.

It didn't take me long to get to know my section. In fact, I knew them fairly well, but only by observation, not on a personal level. For example, older students were like the untouchables from the Far East. They were not going to be on the guest list to any social functions.

By day one, personalities were beginning to display themselves. The terminally shy ones were admitted because they were super smart studyholics. The boisterous, loud, showy types were admitted because they learned to cover weakness with outlandish behavior. The ones who really didn't give a crap—not shy, not loud—they were the ones to watch because they feared nothing.

Then there was everyone else. I fell into that group, although I was also in the over forty, unclaimed freight group, of which there were six, maybe seven of us. Professors would surely evaluate our section the same way. The weak, the timid, the lazy, the fakers, the strong, the smart and the old. If we were African Wildebeests, the question would be, which ones would the lions go after first?

Finally, the wait was over and the door opened. In walked Property Professor, a real, living, breathing law school professor. He was about my age, plaid shirt, no tie, casual slacks, goofy shoes, not goofy like Disney goofy, but the kind of Dad goofy that says, "I don't care what they look like, they're comfortable!" goofy.

"Good morning, my name is Dr. Property Professor. Welcome to the law of property." He smiled genuinely and seemed to have an air of kindness. I found this fairly disarming. All of the stereotypes about law professors brought up the image of the devil incarnate, but this guy seemed genuine, a guy-next-door kind of person.

"We're going to learn a lot...about the law of property." I wondered if he knew he had just punned the heck out of his intro. "I expect you to work hard, but I also expect you to have fun." His tone remained steady and genuine. Throughout his introduction he maintained a devilish smile. It wasn't the satanic kind, more minor-league devilish kind, as if he was the sort who could play a practical joke on you.

Just then, at the door, there arose such a clatter that I turned to see what was the matter. Oh, I'm sorry, I've fallen into a nursery rhyme. What I meant to say was it sounded like somebody was taking an axe to the door trying to beat their way in. I figured it was Satan coming in to possess the body of this really nice guy pretending to be a professor, but it wasn't. The prof opened the door to reveal a young man in a wheelchair trying to find his way into the room fifteen minutes late.

"I'm sorry for being late," he offered, "but all the handicap spaces were taken." Prof motioned him to the empty spot next to me by patting his hand on the tabletop so he'd know his spot.

Of course, Prof spoke in an overly polite and condescending tone, which I'd soon learn is the way all people speak to a person with a severe handicap. Then it hit me. The vacant space next to me was for the handicapped. It was the sole parking place for wheelchairs in the classroom.

This guy wheeled himself into the spot and with some difficulty was able to extract a book from the nylon bookbag hanging off the back of his chair. He fished out a writing pad and attached a Velcro strap around his hand, pulling it tight with his teeth. He retrieved a pen from the bag and stuck onto the Velcro device. After he made a fist around the pen like he was ready to stab something, he was prepared to write, his style.

This young fellow's disability was way beyond the average wheelchair-bound person. His ability to use his hands and arms in the ordinary fashion was noticeably affected, but he dealt with it skillfully. It looked like he'd been down this road before. After negotiating the seemingly impossible task of getting a book opened to the proper page and getting a notepad open, he readied himself to take notes, the ghastly entrance a distant memory.

Prof went back to his pleasant introduction to the law of property, the law of land and dirt. I, on the other hand, was relieved that it wasn't Satan coming to get Prof. I'm not necessarily the best judge of people, but I'm not too bad either. This guy seemed decent, or at the very least, okay. Prof went on to talk about the general philosophy of law school, how to get by, how to get through, and so on. He talked on about his exams and the bar exam, which were two things seemingly far in the future. Hey, how about we get the first day in the record books?

He encouraged participation, and by participation, he meant questions. *Good luck with that one, buddy.* These young geniuses were, for the first time in their educational lives, no longer alone at the top of the class filled with average achievers. Most of these kids harbored a fear of looking stupid in a room packed with smart people, I could tell. There would be almost no participation and very few questions.

Although, I must say it wasn't long before we discovered who the talkers were in our group. It doesn't matter if we're talking Sunday school, group therapy, or law school class, every class has at least one talker, and sometimes it's a handful of people who cannot keep their mouths shut. They just adore the sounds that come out of their gaping maw. Lovers of their own voices can't help themselves. They emerge slowly and bubble their way to the surface so they can start making noise, whether their words make sense or not.

In our section, there were three talkers. Since we were herded from class to class with our same group of eighty, we got to hear these three talk, and talk, and talk. In the coming weeks, I could pick up on the barely perceptible moan every time one of them would raise a hand and begin to spew. Within a month or two, the moan was replaced with a noticeable and collective groan. After a while, there was just an "Oh crap, they're running their mouths again."

In the undergrad world, these blabbers were a godsend because they took up class time to allow for daydreaming, or doodling, or staring at the best-looking girl in the class, but not in law school. The majority of law class was devoted to the grilling of victims. Teaching time was precious and we were desperate to hear what these gods of law had to say about the subject, so when some dumbass suffering from some lifelong lack of attention was free associating under the misconception that anyone wanted to hear whatever was on his mind, it became painfully irritating, to say the least.

Finally, Prof concluded his philosophical outline of living through law school via a balance of hard work and personal time. Later, he gave us his take on the actual practice of law. This is when he introduced us to his favorite saying, "Decorate the mahogany!"

We heard this many times over the next few years. It means show me the money! Putting money on the table wasn't an ad for greed. It was a pithy reminder that we were amassing professional knowledge that would one day become a marketable product—one that could be sold to those in need.

Property Prof announced the time had come for a visitation to the first real written appellate opinion, better known as a case. Carefully scanning his roster of students, he selected a victim. All professors have a system of dealing with a room of scared students. Some have a chart identifying each seat. At some point during the first class, they inform everyone that the seat their butt is in is where they will sit for the rest of eternity. Others, being Doctor geniuses and all, take the first couple of weeks to memorize the names of all students, which I think is pretty cool.

Prof worked from a list, and after taking his watch off, placing it face up on the lectern (another professor-ism), he called out, "Mr. Hazel, Robert Hazel, are you here?"

Hell, I nearly answered!

"Right here, Professor."

And there he was, Mr. Hazel, across the horseshoe from me and up two rows. Mr. Hazel turned out to be a decent-looking guy, about ten years older than my present situation but with a full head of dark hair. He was a neatly dressed fellow who had recently retired from South Carolina Electric and Gas. Mr. Hazel had a pleasant southern accent. It's hard not to like (or pick on) a guy like that.

"Mr. Hazel, our first case is Blackacre v. Greenacre. What's going on there, who did what to whom, and what did the court hold in this case?" Prof asked.

Hazel did pretty well. I don't know if he was right or wrong, but he handled himself well. He was calm, pleasant, and kind. I got to know him pretty well over our years in law school. We've even had the opportunity to cross paths a few times while practicing law.

Law school has a few truisms, one being that many of us will see each other throughout our careers, so if you show your rear in law school, it follows you down the road. Another truism is that while someone is being grilled, you're safe for a few minutes. Property Prof was a kind and dedicated teacher. He always made the victim feel good about their reasoning behind the answer, even if it was dead wrong. He called on one more victim after Mr. Hazel, and just like that, my very first, real, honest-to-goodness law class was over. It was all over except for a little surprise.

At the end of the class Prof announced, "We're going to play a little game on Fridays. Two of you will be assigned to study a case, then prepare and deliver closing arguments in front of the class. You'll sit right here in the middle of the room so you can experience a real courtroom atmosphere. You can have a lot of fun with this assignment. I think you're going to enjoy it."

After dropping the bomb he called a game, he named the first two victims for center ring arguments, and that was when my first law school class officially came to an end.

I turned to the guy next to me who was struggling to shed the penholder and get his book and pad into the nylon bag. "Nice entrance," I offered, hoping he had a sense of humor about using his battering ram of a wheelchair to knock in the door of the classroom. Still trying to cram his stuff back in the bag, he gave me a "yep."

Deep voice, few words, sheepish smile like he knew what a scene he caused, but at the same time, saw the humor in it...I liked this guy. His name was Matt.

My first law class wasn't a horror story. No one died, yet most everyone looked scared witless. I was beginning to feel a little better about this possibility.

Older people share their fear with me of not being able to handle the academic side of returning to school. I certainly had that fear, too, but undergrad was the only environment these smarties had ever known. Even if I was let in by mistake, I had a shot and a work ethic that might get me through. Getting the first class in the rearview mirror was a definite plus. Of course, I had not been victimized yet, so my confidence wasn't off the scale. It was just slightly out of the negative range.

Law school, for all of its indecipherable reverse logic, did seem to have a few things figured out. First year students are assigned at least one free period between each class, which was great for me because the more cramming I could do right before showtime, the better. Going into a class full of child prodigies with my lesser brain freshly packed with knowledge was a good thing. I liked this.

Actually, the new thing at USC and other law schools across the USA was to promote the success of the handpicked students. When I graduated from regular college in 1972, law schools seemed to take great pride in how many they flunked out, kind of like how Navy Seals drive the weak ones out.

Nowadays, schools brag on a low attrition rate, most claiming fewer than five percent, which in my class of 240 would mean somewhere around 230 would receive JDs (Juris Doctor). Of the ten not getting JDs, only a few would get the boot for academic failure. Most of them elected to leave for personal reasons.

Law school, and for that matter, the practice of law, isn't for everyone. So the real deal is that the school has a vested interest in getting its little angels to the cap and gown. Setting up first years so their schedule offered the best chance for preparation pre-class was a great idea. Otherwise, it was old school intense—extremely tough workloads and hard exams.

Students studied all the time. They hunched over law books in every chair and corner of the building. All day and evening, people studied like nothing I'd ever seen before. It didn't affect me because my healthy dose of fear of failure drove me to put in twelve solid hours of class work and study daily.

USC is a classic law school in the sense that it had no part-time or no night program. I was there to get through as quickly as possible while still putting in my time as a dad and husband, which meant just like regular college, I attended three one-hour classes on Monday, Wednesday and Friday, and two hour and a half classes on Tuesday and Thursday. Three hours of classes each day followed by legal reading and writing for an hour, and of course, nine hours of independent study.

CHAPTER SIXTEEN

The Hand Raiser

My first free hour between classes didn't jell exactly as I had planned. First of all, where would I go? Many people dotted the building landscape studying, but the building was also filled with bull sessions and socializing, and I'm easily attracted to bull, so I ran to my room figuring there would be fewer distractions at the Holiday Inn.

I packed my head with Con Law, a name I felt was a better fit for criminal law. In reality, Con Law was the law of our good old American Constitution. This was the assignment I read where I didn't know what the hell it was about— Marbury v. Madison. Something about a federal magistrate who didn't get a job, and something called a writ of mandamus. The case was heard by the US Supreme Court after the Revolutionary War, or after Jesus ascended into heaven, or some such ancient event. I read it a few more times. Still didn't get it.

I got to class early, of course, because I'm a dad and that's what we do. Again, I picked the first front row seat adhering to my theory of show no fear. I sat next to the missing seat again, and soon enough Matt came banging through the open door frame, hitting everything as he fought his way into the open space next to me. He was on time this time.

Again, I witnessed the fight to get supplies from his bookbag and strap a pen in his hand. I would see this a few hundred times over the next three years, but for now, the world of a severely handicapped person was brand new to me. It was painful to watch, and like most guys, I had no idea what to do or say, so I opted to pretend not to notice. That's what we do. Guys pretend to ignore something as outrageous as a person struggling with a massively difficult situation. We sit there doing nothing, frozen with guy stupidity.

Help, don't help, offer to help, don't offer to help, take a chance of offending. I was clueless, so I did nothing except offer the olive branch of humor. "I think you missed a spot on the door this morning, going to take another whack at it tomorrow?"

"Give me a couple of weeks and I'll have this building accessible," he offered.

"So why were you so late?" I asked.

"No parking," he came back.

"I thought there were lots of handicap parking spots right outside the front door?"

"There are fourteen to be exact, all full," he said.

"Damn, are there that many handicapped students?" I said, a little dumbfounded on my part.

"No, just me and one other," he tossed out.

"So who's filling them?" This was rather difficult for me to process.

Matt clarified, "Mostly students with someone else's hanging tag. A mother, father, grandparent. They're using someone's tag to get a better space."

I'm such a hayseed. "Isn't that against the law? Isn't there a fine for that? Aren't there campus security cops crawling all over the place? What's with that? Did you report this?"

"No, I'm not going to be that guy. I ride around until I find something. My problem is that I have to have the space with the big blue striped area to let down my wheelchair side lift. If I can't find something, I just park in the loading zone and take my chances. I figure the campus security knows all those cars are probably parked illegally, but they can tell that my van is for real. Anyway, I'm pretty used to dealing with no handicap accessibility. For instance, they don't have an auto-opener on the library door, which means I can't get into the friggin' library."

Damn, my first lesson and peek into his world. How far behind was our world when it comes to accommodating people with physical limitations?

The class was filling up with the Gifted and Chosen Few. It was time for class number two, and on the appointed moment, the professor appeared from wherever professors come from. Who knows, maybe they pop up through a trap door behind the lectern like a rock star.

I had heard about this guy. He was previously with the Department of Justice (DOJ) and had argued many cases before the US Supreme Court. He was USC's new superstar. They had wooed him and pitched him like the football team recruits a star quarterback. And they flaunted him with great pride. He was shockingly young, dammit. Way younger than me. Maybe mid forties, max.

He had a genuine easy smile and a real air of nerdiness. His demeanor expressed that he was a scholar with few outside interests and new to this professor thing. He attempted to interact with the students. Like most, he removed his watch, placed it face up on the lectern, and proceeded to introduce himself. Then he provided the short, general overview of Con Law.

He smiled a lot. This was ruining my preconceived notion of these monster professors. Had I simply watched too much television and become completely unaware of the real world? Was I wrong about the whole thing?

We all know the Constitution, right? It's what we invoke when something doesn't seem fair. It is the great playing field leveler. It keeps religion out of government, keeps people from being fired from jobs unfairly, and makes it so that no one can be denied admission to a private club or cult. It guarantees the right to an abortion and other misconceptions.

Usually, a sentence beginning with "I know my rights!" or "I have rights!" are the standard constitutional fighting words. They form the soapbox we stand on when a wrong needs righted, or when an injustice needs to be justed. And by George (who, by the way, was a British monarch), Americans will whip out the Constitution over most anything that needs fixin'. So, as an American with certain inalienable rights, I assumed this Con Law class would be an exercise in common sense, a walk through the valley of justice because I knew my rights.

Wrong.

Con Law was not called Common Law because there is already something called Common Law and because it is not based on common sense. Instead, this course is a study of the Supreme Court's interpretation of the Constitution. "Is it constitutional?" or "Is it unconstitutional?" The Supreme Court is made up of nine justices, supposedly the smartest lawyers in the land. Half the time they split five to four, or sometimes four to five, meaning five of them saw the issue one way and the other four saw it exactly the opposite. Not particularly reassuring.

The suspense of knowing that at some random moment completely beyond my control, I was going to be called on to give an answer had me terrified. The waiting was killing me. I had to get over this fear, and so I decided to take matters in my own hands, or hand, in this case. I raised my hand and immediately wished I had not, but it was up there. Why, oh why again, *why* did I do this? It wasn't like me to want to be humiliated.

Professor Con asked a simple question of the mute group, most of whom were making eye contact with the concrete floor, or appearing to be absorbed in note taking, or trying to hide drool spots on their notebooks.

He stood there waiting for an answer, looking at the room of non-responders, simply hoping someone would take the bait. His question had to do with the application of one of the twenty-seven amendments to the Constitution. He gave a scenario, or hypothetical, as law school test creators liked to call them.

He asked, "Which amendment applies?"

I had read the Constitution, including its preamble, articles, and amendments. It really wasn't all that long, not like the Bible, only a few pages, but about as cryptic as the Bible. Something in his question reminded me of something I had read in the amendments. I felt as if I knew the answer. This could be my only chance to get something right and get past the godawful waiting.

It didn't occur to me there would be another reason other than fear that no one else raised a hand. And for some reason, I had forgotten that these professors knew all the tricks. They were the house (Vegas) and we were the hayseeds from Dayton.

I thought I knew the answer and desperately needed to get this behind me, so the hand went up, not high, like in the third grade when our hands yell, "Me! Pick me! I'm over here! I know! I know!" My hand was above my head enough so that when he turned to his right to scan the room, he saw it before I could chicken out.

"Yes, sir," he said with obvious pleasure. "What's your name?" he asked. I knew this one too, but it took me a minute. I had to think for a second.

"Fraser, Denny Fraser." I had to stop myself from saying Mr. Hazel.

"Well, Mr. Fraser, what do you think? Which amendment to the Constitution do you think applies to my hypothetical?"

"The fourteenth."

I figured he'd say, "Right, good job," or "No, it's the thirteenth," and move on. But he said, "That's a very good answer, Mr. Fraser, why do you think it fits in this situation?"

I felt pretty good because of the "very good answer" comment, but the follow-up was unexpected. I had to shuffle a little to offer my reasoning.

"That's very good reasoning, Mr. Fraser, and I see exactly how you arrived at that conclusion, but yours is a common misconception regarding that amendment. Let me tell you how the Supreme Court has interpreted that amendment and why it may not apply in my story. Then we'll talk a little about the amendment I had in mind. And again, thank you for offering your opinion, Mr. Fraser."

Okay, he was clearly and unquestionably the nicest man in the universe. He just said I was wrong, but he did it in such a nice way that I actually felt good about myself even though, according to what he then explained to the class, I was completely wrong. I couldn't have been more wrong if I had stood up and recited a Tom Waits album in dialect.

I was happy the ice had been broken and immediately thought I should swing by the USC School of Medicine to have my right arm removed at the shoulder so this would never, never, ever happen again.

Eventually class ended, and just like in sixth grade, pandemonium erupted while nice Professor Con tried to announce an upcoming assignment or interesting lesson. Who cared? We were armed with a syllabus. Hell, we knew what was next. We were nearly lawyers, for Christ's sake.

I distinctly heard Matt say, "How'd that work out for ya?"

Smiling, Matt bludgeoned his book into his nylon bookbag, then spun toward the door without waiting for my smartass comeback. Matt could dish it. I liked this guy.

CHAPTER SEVENTEEN

The Professors

Two classes under my belt, and my second free hour hit me at noon. Nourishment would help me survive the day. The school had a food service area, a small room with sandwiches, fruit cups, yogurt cups, beverages and four tables with plastic chairs. Still afraid caffeine might make me do something stupid, like raise my hand again, I went with a cup of grapes, added a cup of yogurt and a bottle of water. Ever aware of the likelihood that this day, which had gone pretty well so far, could turn tragic at any minute, I figured my food choices had some built-in advantages, depending on which outlet might decide to erupt later.

It was there I met Lunch Lady Judy, a genuinely nice person. Judy was short, round, brown, and she had an incredible smile. She spoke to everyone in line, many by name. She seemed to always have something nice to say to everyone passing through her line.

"What you teachin'?" she asked, right off the bat.

"Nothing. I'm going to school. I'm in the learning biz," I said, trying to sound cool, although I didn't fool anybody.

She stared momentarily, probably to size up my demographic. She did not ask the "W" question, which I appreciated because people were waiting in line and I didn't feel like coming up with another Dale Carnegie answer.

"What's yo name, Honey?"

"Denny," I offered, leaving off the last name.

I have never liked being called Mr. Fraser, or Mr. Hazel, for that matter. I kind of understood the Mr. and Miss thing with the professors—that was the professorial way. I was called Mister because I was older, and I was already sick and tired of the reminder. It was only day one, actually day one point five, and I had heard mister more times than I could count.

"You mind if I call you Denny?"

"Sure, if I can call you Judy."

"Honey, everybody calls me Judy."

"Cool. Nice to meet you, Judy."

We were tight from then on. I really liked her, in spite of not having had a good history with lunch ladies back in the day. It's marvelous when someone is perfectly suited for their job, and Judy, it seemed, never had a bad day. Judy was an extraordinary person.

I had no illusions about the life of a middle-aged black woman with modest educational skills, working at a minimum wage job in downtown Columbia, serving elitist kids who were preparing for a life very different from her own. No doubt she had days that sucked. Bad days for Judy most likely involved every kind of worry that poverty, race, poor health, government budget cuts and mean bosses could pile on a person. Yet, she came to her job joyfully. Each day was a gift, as was she to me. Judy made everyone feel liked and good. She was living proof that people on this earth have something of value to offer, no matter how seemingly insignificant.

Kindness can mean the world to someone. I think of Judy when I encounter someone who seems unhappy with their position in life and wants to make certain everyone around knows it. I think of her when I'm the one having a bad day and want to hold back a kindness.

Judy, in fact, reminded me of the widow in the Bible. Remember the widow who put two pennies in the offering? She was ridiculed for the small amount she gave when compared to the gifts of the wealthy. Although the wealthy gave a greater amount, the widow had, in relative terms, given more. I've put in my time at Catholic school, then as a grown-up, served as a Deacon and was ordained as an Elder in the Presbyterian Church. Plus, I've taught Sunday School—don't get me started.

All that to say I think God has a special place in heaven for those who give generously. I saw Judy give away nearly all she had, and I loved her for it. She made me feel good in a foreign land where very few offered much in the way of friendship. I'm not definite about the special place in heaven, but I truly believe Jesus really, really likes Lunch Lady Judy.

Last class, day one, and back to the old horseshoe classroom. I took my same seat and watched Matt bash his way into the room and maul his bookbag, which looked like he had put out a fire with it. His handicap did not allow him the luxury of delicate page turning. He beat that sucker into submission, found a clean page, and strapped in for some serious note taking. It was time to meet the third new professor of the day.

Middle Eastern looking and short-ish, Professor Civil Procedure could have been a close relative of Danny DeVito considering both his appearance and his accent. And guess what? He gave an opening speech about how much enjoyment we were about to have during his class. All we had to do was come prepared, answer every question correctly, and we'd all get along just fine. I knew the spiel pretty well by now. He seemed like a decent fellow.

I have few words for this course. It was two semesters, as were all of the first year courses, so the schedule of this first day would be the routine for the whole year, which in school years is nine months. This course addressed the rules of civil procedure—confusing as hell. Some might say it was more like being in purgatory, but I'd go with it was more like hell— long, like eternity. Whether Civil Procedure equates to eternal hell, or a giant maze as seen in the wiring of a spacecraft, the damn thing was confusing.

For the benefit of anyone who doesn't actually practice law, civil procedure is the court rules of procedure, both state and federal. Things like who comes under the jurisdiction of the court, what courts have jurisdiction, how you complete service, how information is obtained from adversaries, how to conduct a trial, how a case is ended, and how a judgment is handled, and the list goes on. It is a rulebook, not unlike a giant cookbook filled with ingredients and how-to instructions.

The first semester was all the theoretical case law that supports these rules. To this day, it is confusing as hell. The rule book didn't come out until the second semester. The rule book covers the procedure of how to start and end a law suit, a kind of A to Z, something my mind can deal with. But for one whole semester, I was mostly lost.

The first day was a laydown for the rest of the semester. I was driving flat out in the fog with the lights out. Oh, what the hell. I read the cases, briefed the cases, and went to my classes. I was called on only once and somehow managed to stumble my way past the point. My answer may have been so confusing that our Danny DeVito professor didn't know what

I had said, causing him to move on to another victim without comment.

With terms like subject matter jurisdiction, in personam jurisdiction, in rem jurisdiction, res ipsa loquitur, stare decisis, directed verdict, long arm statute, summary judgment, demurrer, Civ Pro is where the legal rubber meets the mumbo-jumbo road.

Yep, this is how the money is made in any industry. First, create a foreign language of words that are not used anywhere on earth, or even in the Star Trek universe, and if possible, reduce all known words to acronyms. A real FUBAR (noun) for…look it up if you don't know it.

I hated the theoretical semester of Civ Pro. It's like studying volumes of theory behind the shape of Arabic numerals, not what they represent, or how to add and subtract them. Imagine a four-month study of why numbers are shaped the way they are. Transport me to semester two where we get the rulebook and start on page one, and I'm on board.

I'm the guy who gets a 200-pound box from IKEA, finds the instructions, sniffs for meatballs, highlights the directions (in English), groups the fasteners by size, and then, and only then, do I start with STEP ONE. And that, friends, is what Civil Procedure is—one big meatball smelling book that starts with RULE ONE on page one: How to Sue Someone—Civ Pro solves the mystery.

Civil Procedure shouldn't be confused with its country cousin, Criminal Procedure, which is a recipe book of how to put folks in jail, or in the alternative, how to get them out of jail. Of course, "civil lawsuits" is an oxymoron because there is no such thing as a *civil* lawsuit, never has been and never will be. Nobody likes being sued. "You have been served" is the last thing we want to hear. It's right up there with "it's not you, it's me."

Meanwhile, I was mired in first semester Civ Pro, where hours upon hours were dedicated to the horrible theory and rationalization behind the rules. The serenity prayer was said many times during the first four months of Civ Pro.

Finally, the imaginary bell rang, however, there are no bells in law school. It's more like when the barometer falls, the angle of the sun changes, or something shifts in the atmosphere. The change causes movement to begin within the building at exactly ten minutes to the hour. The professor checks his watch on the lectern (an obligatory professorial gesture) and declares that class has ended.

With day one classes over, it was time to tackle the nine hours of study still ahead. For the moment, I was free. I could walk through the cavern of a lobby, past the scowling brown-face bust of Old Strom, down the back stairway that nearly killed me five hours earlier, get in my Volvo, forget all my stuff, including all my newly purchased books, and leave Columbia, never to return. Hell, I'd made it. At forty-eight years old and against all odds, I was accepted to the state university law school, and I'd survived a day of law classes. To my credit, I even said words in class. What more did I need? Check out of the Holiday Inn, get in the car and get the hell out of Dodge.

Here it comes again–*why* didn't I do that? Why didn't I go back to my wonderful life and beautiful wife and kids? Still no answer to the big "W." It was a good thought, but I had a couple of strong reasons to stick it out for at least one more day. First, and foremost, it was past checkout time at the hotel. I was going to pay for another night, so why leave? Second, I had not been to all of my classes. I had two more to go on day two, Contracts and Torts.

The first day resulted in my confidence becoming a little inflated, just a little. I spoke in class on my own terms by raising my hand, which I would never do again, so help me God. The professors were pretty good guys, no sadists or monsters, just really decent, smart guys. So that fear about law school was more urban myth than reality.

I could do this if I wanted to, at least until I failed all my exams. The idea of having to face one final exam with no little tests along the way was weighing heavily on my mental stability. How in the world could there be just one comprehensive test at the end of a course? It was beyond me. I come from the world of pop quizzes, midterms, term papers, and all sorts of stuff that gets averaged into a grade so you can "screw one up" and still get by. One major test means the concept of "screw one up" and still get by is out the window. So I knew if I felt like it, I could hang around law school for four months before taking the walk of shame.

I went straight to my room on the business floor of the Holiday Inn to decompress. The door was standing open about three inches. How could this day get any worse?

Had I been robbed? No housekeeping cart was nearby, so I eased the door quietly open and scanned the part of the room I could see from the doorway. Nothing unusual. No sounds. In stealth mode, I ventured inside, entering as much as necessary to see into the bathroom. Nothing there, except maybe in the shower.

Ghost-like, I eased in far enough to see the whole of the room—bed, desk and all. Still, no predators, well, except maybe in the shower. I slipped silently back down the little hallway to the bathroom door, eased into the shower area, and gently peeked behind the shower curtain. No one there. One last look under the bed, and I was pretty sure that no human was in the room with me. My important possessions, my computer, printer, my thousand-dollar pile of books, my clothes, toiletries, and food, all appeared to be untouched.

Apparently, the housekeepers rely on the automatic door closer to lock up. I checked the door and discovered the automatic door closer didn't close all the way on its own power. This would never do. Time for some one-on-one with the manager.

"Ms. Manager, my most important possessions in the world, well, I mean the ones that aren't human, are kept in that room and I can't have the door being left open like it was. The housekeepers came in because the bed was changed and new towels were hanging in the bathroom. My door doesn't seem to lock when it closes on its own."

She apologized. "We never have a problem with theft and there are security cameras on all floors and at both ends of the halls, but I'm still so sorry your room was left open."

"That's great," I said, "but I just can't put in a day trying to concentrate at law school while thinking all my stuff is exposed to the world. I tell you what, I don't need my sheets changed every day and I don't need new towels every day, so howse 'bout nobody goes in my room until I check out on Friday? It's easier for you and safer for me."

She lit up.

"Great idea, Mr. Fraser. We have the same staff on that floor every day, so I will tell housekeeping to never go into your room. Just leave the Do Not Disturb sign on the knob as a precaution. And howse 'bout I give you a break on your commercial room rate? How would that be?"

This day just got a little better.

After high-level negotiations at the front desk, it was late afternoon before I made it back to my room. I settled into a few hours of reading and briefing cases. The routine would be to study the cases for the next day's classes.

Some say to do it the other way around. They say we should study the ones we just finished and then cover new material. The idea was to spend a whole day on the same subject matter. But I knew I'd do better if I prepared right before the class. I couldn't imagine studying something and then waiting two days to get grilled on it.

I had learned that study theories varied widely. Some relied on study groups. Some were devoted to outlining. Some simply studied all the time. I figured briefing every case and adding class notes to the brief would become my study outline. I had yet to see a passing grade, so I had no definitive answer on whether or not my system was any good.

Only a meager dinner meal interrupted my study. Dinner consisted of a freezer bag of goodness in boiling water, a fruit cup and instant tea. This would have to do until I had a better handle on the food process and could come up with some better engineering.

I gave up on the studying at ten, about the time the trains started rumbling through town, horns blasting. I slept slightly better, in part because some of the horror was demystified by the first day's classes, and in part because I was exhausted to the point of needing hospitalization. Still, the damn train horns blowing five blasts every ten minutes at every street crossing interrupted what little sleep my body would allow.

Five-thirty mercifully came so that I could get out of bed and face day two. Early rising was always my ace in the hole. A shower and coffee, and I had three hours to study before class.

CHAPTER EIGHTEEN

Doctor Bond

First class of the day was Contracts and the non-code-compliant steps didn't get me. Though I spared a second helping of pain and embarrassment, I retained the memory, as did others. As usual, the lobby was abuzz with the now familiar chaotic commotion, but this time around it was not as intimidating. I was somewhat over my shock from day one and even Old Strom's brown-face looked a little less menacing—not welcoming, just less scary.

To get to my Contracts class I had to go past the admissions office, and as if on cue, I heard, "Good Morning, Mr. Hazel. How was your first day?" There she was, and there she would be most every morning.

"First day was great, and by the way, it's Fraser." I tried.

"Have a nice day, Mr. Hazel!"

"Thank you. You too." I gave up.

Arriving early, I had time to study the people in my section. The first day was a bit of a blur, so this viewing served as a refresher course. The girl who sat next to me previously chose a different seat. My feelings were beyond being hurt, so it didn't matter. And then Matt came charging through the door, also a little early. He had time to begin getting his books out of his bookbag using his systemized martial arts style of unpacking.

"What, no grand entrance today?" I quipped.

"Nope, I got a parking place just before some fat chick with a borrowed handi-tag could pull in."

"Awesome! I'm proud of you," I offered.

"It was the last one, too," he said.

"Maybe this law school thing isn't going to be so bad after all," I added, the master of small talk.

Most students were seated. Hushed conversation filled the place as the second hand swept toward the stroke of nine o'clock. When the big hand touched its mark on the big clock, the door opened and in walked the professor. He strolled slowly and deliberately bypassed the lectern and stopped when he got to the center of the room.

Something about his entrance brought with it a chill. He stood motionless, staring at his students. He sported a thick brown beard, General Grant-style, and thick brown hair to match, combed to the side. If one were looking for a hairstyle from 1969, his would have been the photo under Fraternity Brother. Tweed jacket, tie, dress slacks, dress shoes. No one made a sound for an awkwardly creepy long time, including our instructor.

Finally, he spoke. "My name is Doctor Bond."

Another long and frightening pause. I suppose this was designed for us to absorb his DOCTOR status, as opposed to mere Professor status. Nobody missed the point or the dramatic pause.

"I am here to lead you in a study of contract law. The single most important and fundamental nucleus of all human transactions." He stood there, in the middle of the floor, ramrod straight, looking forward, not blinking, not showing any emotion. He appeared to be fond of letting his words digest, as if our ears needed time to chew his ideas to pieces.

"You will follow a few rules." He was in no hurry to rush through this well-practiced monologue. "Yesterday was easy. You had a love fest with your other professors, and by the end of the day you probably thought law school was a warm and loving environment...like they do in California."

He carefully delivered each word and sentence allowing his dramatic influence to be absorbed by everyone in the room. Mesmerized, we realized he was the ONE—the ONE we've been dreading.

"Well, that is not the way it works in here." His eyes were now shifting to scan the room without moving his head. "You will come into this class prepared, or you will not come in. When you take a seat in my class, you have given me a statement that says you have read the assignment. If I should discover that you are in my class without having read the assignment, then you have violated the honor code and I will report you to the honor committee for discipline."

He allowed at least a full minute for this to sink in.

"When I call on you to address the class with whatever wisdom you have assimilated from the case study, you will stand and answer in the same manner you may use in a courtroom one day."

He took another minute to inspect our faces. All of us fixated on his expressionless and fearless presence. I was pretty certain it was during this moment that I smelled urine. I stole a glance down to see if it was me—it wasn't.

"Not long ago, in every law school, men wore ties, women dressed professionally, and every student stood to address the class. That, of course, has gone by the wayside. People shuffle into class as if they' re on their way to the beach. It used to be that law schools, including this one, respected the tradition of holding future lawyers to high standards. Frankly, by lowering the standards, the quality of lawyers entering the profession has affected the current state of public regard for the legal profession. I will not lower the standards. Not in this room. No, sir. You will stand when you speak. You may dress as you see fit and I will afford you the respect you demand. You will study harder for my class and you will become better public speakers because of my class. Ultimately, you will be better attorneys because of my class, and that, ladies and gentlemen, is why I am here. And I do not care if you don't like my rules."

He gazed upon the dazed assembly for what had to be two full minutes. "Understood?" Dead silence. No one made a sound. I couldn't detect any breathing.

"If these rules are not to your liking, there are four doors through which you entered this room. I strongly suggest, no, I insist you pick one to your liking and use it to find somewhere else to spend this hour."

Nobody moved, but not because they wanted to stay. They were glued to their seats because they were paralyzed with fear. I think if the right twig had snapped, it would have sent the herd into a stampede and the room would have cleared in two seconds, leaving Stoneface standing there alone, except for the dirty piece of masking tape stuck on the floor where he stood planted, growing roots. No twig snapped and no one bolted for the door. No one breathed.

"It appears everyone is staying. By your presence, you are making a declaration that the assignment for this class has been studied and we will talk about contracts."

Then he unpacked yet another fun surprise. He announced that we would have the pleasure of completing a midterm exam. He, for some reason, was going to give us an extra bite of the apple.

"As for attendance, I don't take it. If you sit for the final exam, you will sign a statement that you have attended the required minimum number of classes, and if it is discovered that you have lied on that statement, your exam will be thrown out and you will be brought before the honor committee."

Ummm, if he doesn't take attendance, how will he know who hasn't been in class? He then answered our unspoken question.

"First and foremost, *you* will know if you haven't been attending class, which should be enough; but secondly, there are always students who feel the need to take attendance for the perverted pleasure of throwing classmates under the proverbial bus."

As law students, we had heard about these attendance-taking rats, but we thought it was an urban myth. Apparently, the antagonists were not mere legends. They were real. We found out who they were soon enough. We had two of them.

My ears perked up with then mention of a midterm exam. Maybe I was reaching for something human in this guy. But why would he care? Why would he bother? Most professors are not looking for more work to do. Making up a fact pattern for a test would be no big deal because these guys can do that in their sleep. But reading and grading eighty essay exams would be work, that is, assuming he grades them. He could have a research assistant (slave) read and grade them, or he could use the stair step method, another urban law school legend.

The stair step method of grading papers in grad school is where you take all the test books to the top of a stairway and throw them down the stairs. The bottom step is an A, and because each step represents a half letter grade deduction, the next step up is an A-, the next is a B, and so on. This method follows the physics principal wherein heavier tests, having more verbiage, will go the farthest. Pretty sure this is urban legend.

However, I sensed a motive other than meanness at play with this midterm. My theory was that he wanted to offer two bites of the exam apple while diffusing our one-exam anxieties. I tried my theory out on a couple of students; however, they already hated the man enough that objective reasoning was out of the question. They were determined to hold onto the belief that the man was a sadistic goon who took great pleasure in torturing frightened freshmen.

One thing I've learned about college professors, and not just law professors, but those with time under their belts, is that they know their subject inside out and upside down. They know every trick and every trap. When they say something, anything, it should be given weight. Even Bond's opening monologue was planned. Syllable-by-syllable, pause-by-pause, word-by-word, not one utterance, expression or gesture was by chance.

Here is a great piece of advice. When a professor gives you a hint, an admonition, a suggestion, a warning, a clue, a task, an extra mention of a fact in a case, or gives a crap, that's a gift.

These gifts should be accepted and banked somewhere because it may save your rear one day. This little rule works in life, too. If your boss gives a hint, warning, clue, or word of praise, make note of it. Say you come in twenty minutes early to work one day and your boss, who is early every day, says, "Hey, I see you are here early. I like that. Thanks" That's the ball. Run with it.

Okay, so this guy was going to the trouble to give us a midterm exam. I chose to believe I sniffed some human qualities, yet I didn't win any points with my contemporaries by voicing my theory of human life within Bond's granite casing.

Hey, what do I care? I'm a dad, and most of these other people were just big kids. I'm expected to have unpopular ideas, and like the DOCTOR, I didn't give a damn who liked or disliked my ideas. Dear God, I was becoming the guy who says completely rational and unpopular things designed to rain on someone's pity party. Was I becoming my father? Although I don't like the whole turning into your dad concept, it was kind of fun.

Dr. Bond selected his first victim. "Mr. Hazel, please give us the facts and holding of the first case, Mr. Hazel."

My heart skipped a beat. I had to take a breath. For God's sake, I had to remind myself that I was not Mr. Hazel. Happy to be Mr. Fraser, I felt pity for the poor guy—two times in two days. Welcome to law school, Mr. Hazel.

CHAPTER NINETEEN

The Trap

The law of Torts. Torts, what a curious word. It stands for the law of recourse of civil wrongs, as opposed to criminal wrongs. Government takes care of the criminal cases and punishes the bad guys. The victim is just a victim, although the idea of restitution is becoming a part of the scheme.

Even in biblical days you are allowed to get yourself an eye if someone gets yours—same with a tooth. But torts is the law of civil lawsuits, and that is what about ninety percent of the law students are in school for; they want to learn how to sue people and get rich.

In torts we were going to learn when someone could sue someone else for a wrong suffered. The wrongdoer is the "tortfeasor"—what a cool word! I immediately began calling my children "tortfeasors" and they sort of liked it. One of the tortfeasors was five and the other was twelve, so they may have just enjoyed the way it rolled off the tongue. They certainly enjoyed tortfeasing their dad.

The break on Tuesdays and Thursdays was a little longer because the classes were an hour and a half, or eighty minutes, which in school time equates to an hour and a half. I guess the last ten minutes could be used to go puke, if needed.

The little extra time was useful because the first case was the one about the driver who suffered a seizure and while seizing took a shortcut through a bike shop, crunching the bike shop guy. Yep, the same one where the courts held that the driver, who had taken all necessary medical precautions, owed no duty to the bike shop guy; therefore, the crunched bike shop guy could not sue the seizing driver for damages, which were significant.

I still could not come to terms with this one, no matter how many times I read the case and its accompanying notes. Just could not get this one. I was looking forward to seeing how it would be explained in class.

Professor Torts was an average-sized, angular guy, well-dressed and articulate. He certainly appeared to be the master of his game. He didn't give much of an opening speech. He jumped right in.

"Mr. Fraser, are you here"? Jesus, Mary and Joseph!

Surely he meant Mr. Hazel.

"Mr. Fraser?" Crap, I looked like an idiot who didn't know his name, perhaps deaf, or dumb, as in incredibly stupid.

"Here, Professor," came from somewhere inside me.

"Mr. Fraser, please tell us the facts of the case of Crunched Bike Shop Guy v. Seized Driver."

He wanted me to tell the facts of the case I hated. Great, I would state the idiotic facts and he would probably move on to someone else to sort out the backwards holding. I did a fairly respectable job of reciting what happened to the bike shop guy and prepared to relax.

"Now, Mr. Fraser, please tell us the holding and the rule of law in this case."

Okay, I could certainly tell the world what the court held because I had read it in my lap while negotiating I-26 just two days earlier, and I had read the damn thing another dozen times since. So I laid it all out—the seized driver was off the hook.

"Great, Mr. Fraser. Now please tell the class what's behind the court's reasoning in determining that the seized driver owed no duty to the crunched bike shop guy."

I could have, no, I should have parroted the court's belief that sometimes crap just happens and nobody has to make it right, but no, oh no, my mouth was in motion. I felt I should defend the situation as a dad, and with that in mind, I didn't necessarily agree with the court.

Snap. The trap snapped shut on my paw. I forgot what I had learned a few short hours ago. I had done exactly what Mr. Know-it-all had spent his whole summer hoping some ethical hayseed would do.

I made his day, maybe his year, oh hell, maybe his wormy *career*. The SOB picked me because he knew I was older and probably a dad fully saturated with the concept of right and wrong. I wandered right into his trap.

A trapped animal has two choices. A) Chew one's leg off and run like hell, or B) make a stand with three legs and fight the trapper to the death. Since gnawing my leg off seemed out of the question, I stood there like a baby seal.

Oh, he was ready for this and grilled me on the case for the entire eighty-minute class. About two-thirds of the way through the interrogation, I took another look at the leg in the trap and wondered how bad it would really hurt to gnaw it off.

To be perfectly accurate, he called on another victim during the cross-examination, only this guy opted to bolster the court's position. Smart.

Other than this little digression, he had me on the spot for the whole class. I survived, bruised and shaken but alive. I also learned that his MO was to call on one or two students each class for the whole class and never call on them again for the semester. So my trial by fire was over, and although my feet were scorched, I got to sit on the sidelines for the rest of the game, or semester, I should say.

Maybe it was that first stupid case, but I never warmed up to the Law of Torts. Contracts, on the other hand, which I fully expected to hate, turned out to be my favorite class. I liked the coursework. I didn't actually hate the professor like most first year students. I simply feared the stone-faced semi-human. My belief is that there is a distinction between fear and loathing. He was just a scary guy, not deserving of loathing. Perhaps my business background made the law of contracts more interesting.

And then there was Legal Writing. Legal Writing came with a great professor, a young female. She was both challenging and witty. She would probably be a hoot to talk with over an adult beverage, but I still hated the class even though it was only one hour each week. I detest legal writing to this day. Skilled legal writers impress the heck out of me. It's a whole different way of talking, and the ones who are good at it have my admiration.

People excel at the things they like, I guess. This reminds me, I should ask my doctor exactly which courses in med school he hated.

The Dream

All my adult life I've had a reoccurring dream, which is more like a nightmare than an amusing dream. No monsters, or boogeymen, or falling from a cliff, or murderers chasing me through the house, but the damn thing scares the crap out of me every time. It's the college dream, and I'm told many people have had some form of it. I had the dream late in my first week but this time it was different.

It goes something like this.

I'm in college and things are going pretty well. I'm having a good time, possibly even in love, and then I realize I haven't been attending a certain course and it's late in the semester. The realization is shocking because the course is required for graduation, and for some reason, I have not gone to enough classes to pass. When I get this wakeup call, it is well past the drop date and the professor is a jerk.

Technically, cutting the class too many times is an automatic F. If I start going to class, the jerk professor is going to realize I haven't been there all semester. To compound matters, I can't find a textbook and exams are just a few days away. My only chance is to get a book from somewhere, read its entire contents in a couple of days, show up for the final exam and not be noticed by this not-so-nice professor.

If this house of cards comes down, as it surely will, I will not graduate as expected, which will be a great disappointment to my family. I will have to go an extra semester in the spring because this weird course isn't offered in the summer or fall semester.

Yes, I know, it's a dream with many details. The point is I'm facing embarrassment and financial ruin. A whole year of my life will be in limbo. I am in an absolute panic and that's when I wake up and have to run through the checklist. *It's just a dream. I'm in my bed. I'm okay. My family is okay and I'm not flunking out of school.*

Like I stated earlier, this time the dream was different. This time I was in law school, Contracts class, to be exact. I got my final exam packet, and low and behold, it was multiple choice. This should have been a screaming red flag because there are no multiple choice exams in traditional law school. Dr. Bond, mean in life, meaner in my dream, begins to deliver his menacing warnings and threats of honor violations, promises of punishment for cheaters, etc. After a litany of admonitions, he says, "You may begin."

I can't help but notice upon opening my exam packet that my test was thicker than everyone else's. Mine has many more pages. I start working on the first page but can't let go of the idea that mine is bigger than all the others.

I look through the packet to see how many questions are in the whole test. This way I'll have a better idea of how much time I can devote to each question and still finish in the allotted hour. Of course, the hour should have been another red flag because law school exams are a three-hour minimum.

But this was a dream and I should never question the logic of the things my subconscious has dreamt up.

I leaf through the exam. Everything seems in order until the reason for my extra large test packet hits me right between the eyes. There, right in front of me, is the answer key with all the right answers clearly marked.

For a fleeting moment, I think, "What a bonanza!"

But then I realize cheating isn't my gig. I look at the clock and see that half the hour was gone. The first tiny lightening bolt of panic begins to set in. I didn't know what to do in my dream-like dream stupor. *Should I take it to the professor? Would he think I had copied some of it? Should I try to hide it? Hide it where? The tables had no book compartments. Should I let it fall to the floor?*

I wrestle with this stupid dilemma for way too long. Then I notice students handing in their tests and leaving the classroom. The clock says ten minutes to go and I have only answered a few questions. I'm out of time. I can't possibly finish the test. I don't know what to do with the answer sheet. More people leave. Now I'm the last student in the class. It's just me and Dr. Bond. He looks at me. I am going to fail Contracts. My heart races and suddenly I wake up.

I start the process of calming myself down with the usual real life analysis—*I'm okay, the kids are okay, Debbie's okay, and I haven't failed Contracts.* This post nightmare calm down was different because I realized all wasn't completely well in my world, nor would it be for some time to come. My future was undetermined. I had many final exams to pass.

But the point is I survived my first week. I was called on and raised my hand once. Time to pack it up and head home for the weekend. I performed a short yardage sweep of my room and initiated my shut down procedure, neatly repacking all my stuff—clothes (worn, but neatly folded), books, computer, printer and the food prep stuff. This Friday departure, if I could finish this marathon, would be the first of several hundred.

I don't know why I gravitate toward metaphors like marathon races or mountain climbing. Marathons and mountains don't take years. At the most they take hours, days or weeks, definitely not three years. Even when my sailing heroes, like Dodge Morgan, Tristan Jones, Philip Weld, Johnny Bertrand and Dennis Conner do their thing, difficult as it may be, it doesn't take three years, dammit! And if you count the advance prep and the bar exam, then let's call it what it really is, six years.

Yes, I know adventurers get hurt, go crazy, go broke and come close to death, but it doesn't take three freaking years to complete an event. When Tristan Jones ties his bony frame to the mast of a small sailboat and sails alone for six straight years, then we'll talk. Right now, I am two years committed to this process and have three years (plus some) yet to go.

My trip home would have been terrific if the "W" word hadn't tried to haunt me the whole way home. Leaving Columbia on a Friday, on I-26 headed to the confluence with I-95, was somewhat surreal. I didn't care how fast I was driving. I listened to a CD by a band called Everclear, a semi-talented group without the staying power to make it in the 2000s. I must have liked their sound enough to buy their CD, however, as I drove, I noticed most of the songs were about the abused and neglected childhood suffered by the front man, or lead singer, or whatever he's called. So I switched to Van Morrison.

As much as I was looking forward to being home, it seemed as if everyone was passing me. Somewhere on I-95, I started getting really excited about seeing my family. Suddenly nobody was passing me. *Boy Howdy, I need to see those little ladies.* I was going home, the most wonderful place on earth. It was beautiful and bright all the way home. It was August. The sun would be up long after I got home and found my way into my favorite chair. Ah, the back deck. I could hardly wait.

I live on Hilton Head Island, which is not an island like Bermuda, a spot of dry land way out in the ocean. Hilton Head is a coastal island separated from the mainland by only a couple hundred yards of water and flanked by the Atlantic Ocean. When I cross the bridge over the intercoastal waterway, I am presented with an unobstructed view of the Calibogue Sound. At some point, I can see clean to the horizon, well into the Atlantic Ocean, at least thirty, maybe forty miles out, past the shipping channels leading into the Savannah River inlet. This incredible visual dramatically amputates all of North America from my world.

Home is a good and beautiful place. Home is a sanctuary, a place of safety, no matter how humble, no matter how grand. Home is a place for healing and happiness, comfort and rest. And my modest home was built by me. If asked, Debbie will tell you I have an intense emotional attachment to our home. It could be an unhealthy connection to a building that would probably fall over at the thought of a category one hurricane, but I could never leave it.

Finally home, I was at peace. For the first time in days, I did not have a single anxious thought. No thoughts of Monday. No fears or worries.

The bell had rung—RECESS—and I had made it to the playground, although the place looked quiet. There was a car in the driveway but no sign of my people. I knew they were inside, possibly waiting for me with a big "Welcome Home, Dad!" banner on the second floor landing. They knew I was coming home. Debbie has the Mom's sense of perpetual timing. She knows within fifteen minutes, plus or minus, where all her kids are, and here I was, her husband in the driveway.

The week had been cruel. My nerves were shot from driving three hours on two interstates on a Friday afternoon. That alone is worthy of an adult beverage. But then there's the stressful, anxiety-packed week of trying to integrate while at the same time disappear in an environment where I could do neither.

I needed to be inside my house and embrace my family, but I also needed to decompress. I had to let go of the school and just look at my old house and let the tension leach out of my system. As if on cue, Debbie's face peeked out from behind one of the fogged windows. I was busted.

I went around the house to the laundry room entrance. Debbie was waiting for me there, and dear God, did I ever need to see that woman! First, I had to hold onto her for the longest time. It was a monumentally comforting moment.

The only other moment that even came close occurred when I was ten and had the crap beat out of me in the schoolyard. I came in the back door and buried my face in my Mom's apron while she convinced me everything was to be okay. In that moment, in that spot with Debbie, I was safe—safe against any and every foe.

CHAPTER TWENTY-ONE

The Homecoming

Mom was my consigliore, agent and mouthpiece because my dad worked away from home. My bad history with school started the first day of kindergarten. We didn't have Montessori preschool, faux babysitting back then. Moms stayed at home and so did we until real school started. I couldn't wait to go to kindergarten. The kids on my block were five years older, and I wanted to go to school like they did so bad I couldn't stand it.

Day one, Saint Angela's kindergarten—we were running a little late. Mom and I got in the old '53 Ford station wagon and Mom shut her finger in the car door. She must have been in excruciating pain, but like all moms, she got through it.

And like all kids who have been waiting for this special day for forever, I made it all about me. Mom's pain didn't bother me too much. The school was housed in the back of a two-story convent. This is where I would meet the Dominican nuns who had dedicated their life to teaching future world leaders like me.

I thought we had entered a madhouse, nothing like I had imagined. I didn't like it from the start. Kids were running everywhere and I didn't know anybody. Mom took me to the front of the room, up by the blackboard where two black-habited nuns were arbitrating some disturbance. She handed me over to the care of one nun who attempted to say something of reassurance, I guess, to me, maybe to my Mom. I don't know. I was transfixed on the godawful chaos happening everywhere around me. Shocked and in dream-like slow motion, I remember that I forged my way through the unhealthy and foreign environment. *How in God's name did I ever want to be a part of this?* Fear, disappointment and panic replaced the excitement that had been thumping in my veins earlier.

Mom said words of comfort, I'm sure, but I was too stunned to hear them. She probably put her hands on my shoulders, pulled me close, and said something about having fun and something else about loving me. *Was she crazy?*

I saw a large kid named Philip with a tiny chair stuck on his abnormally large head walking around bumping into things like a lost space alien. We would become buddies, but on this day, Phillip was a stranger in every sense of the word.

A hugely obese lady sat against the wall on a chair made for elves. She had an obese infant sucking on one of her massive breasts, right there for us all to see. She did not care.

Dazed, I surveyed the scene and at the front door, to my horror, I saw my mother outside...leaving me! She walked right past the first window and then the second. That's when I decided I'd had enough. School was a bad idea. It was not what I had in mind at all. I had a great life at home with my dog and all my stuff. What on earth was I thinking?

The flight instinct took over and I bolted for the door and safety. A nun, obviously a seasoned veteran of many such rodeos, had a premonition of what was going to happen and tried to block my run.

No old lady wearing a black circus tent could ever catch me. I faked one step right and broke left, leaving her stumbling into the fat nursing mother with the exposed boobie. I cleared the front door at full speed and caught Mom walking up the gravel drive leading to the convent's parking area.

I called out her name. "MOM!" She stopped and turned around, and that's when I ran flat out, hit her midsection and wrapped my arms around her.

"I'm through! I want to go home!"

She held me for a few minutes and let me cry it out. She knelt down on the gravel, took my hands in hers, looked me deep in the eyes and straight into my soul and said in a near whisper, "It's going to be okay. I know you'll like it, if you give it a try. You'll make new friends and this afternoon, I'll pick you up right here and I'll have Skippy in the car. How 'bout that? You can be my big boy and go back in there, can't you? You can do it, I just know it."

I looked down at my shoes. Mom shined them so people would know I was a good boy from a good family. She mopped my face and nose with a tissue. She always carried tissues in her pocketbook. Once my slobber-covered face was as good as it was going to get, she tilted my face up to meet her gaze.

"Okay?" After a moment, I blubbered, "Okay, I'll give it a try."

"You know I believe in you?"

"Yeah."

"You know I love you more than anything in the world. Don't you?"

"Yeah."

I didn't like the first day of kindergarten and I didn't like being the oldest kid in law school. I didn't want to go back but

Debbie, without saying a word, told me the same thing Mom did. "It's going to be okay. I believe in you. I love you more than anything in the world."

After a long embrace and welcome in the comforting reassurance of our laundry room, I unpacked my clothes straight into the washing machine. That is, in fact, why I went around back to the laundry room entrance.

For this law school episode of my life, I became a routine-loving creature all about efficiency of time and motion. After making the laundry deposit, I went straight to my closet and stuffed the empty duffel bag with four tighty whities, four polos, four pairs of pants, and then zipped it shut. This piece of luggage was not to be touched until five a.m. Monday morning, that is, if I decided to go back to school like a big boy.

That took ninety seconds. It was the ideal change over—fast and smooth with no additional time deducted from my weekend. I found the kids in Page's room and did some major catching up, tickling, wrestling and kidding around. We encouraged the dog to get up on the bed, a real no-no, but all was forgiven. Dad was home.

A great day was made even better by a late afternoon UPS delivery. My FoodSaver®, the device made famous by infomercials and TV pitchmen, had arrived. My hucksters sold me the contraption that sucks all the air out of a plastic bag and then vacuum seals it shut. I had to have one, and law school was just my excuse.

And there it was waiting for me—the commercial kind, not the wimpy cheap one. Only the best. In anticipation of my food euphoria, Debbie had stocked up on massive quantities of food from Sam's Club in accordance with my very specific instructions. We were going to shop smarter, seal smarter and save money.

After playing with the kids and the appropriate grown-up hellos, we ended up in the kitchen cooking. It was Friday night at the Frasers, just like always. A couple of adult beverages and then some major pre-cooking for my next few weeks at law school, again, that is if I were to go back.

Grilled chicken breast with lemon, chili, hamburger steaks, and spaghetti—we cooked it, vacuum packed it, and froze it. Clearly, I was going to eat better in law school than my younger contemporaries. We filled the freezer. Three hundred bucks for the vacuum packer and three hundred bucks for the food, it seemed like quitting was out of the question, at least until I had eaten all the food.

I was totally exhausted but stayed up late for fear I'd miss a minute of my weekend. Saturday was a blur of yard work, housework, and kid time. I didn't want the weekend to conclude before it had began, so Saturday and Sunday were days of denial.

We held onto the belief that we had plenty of time and Monday was far, far off. We hung out on the back deck feeding the mosquitoes in the late August twilight until it was pitch black. I lingered well after the family had wandered off to bed and allowed the Saturday Night Live monologue to do what it does best—knock a person into unconsciousness.

Sundays we go to First Presbyterian. We didn't much go to church until kids came along. In fact, during our adult life on Hilton Head, we didn't go to church. Church was a duty observed while visiting Debbie's parents, which seemed to tide us over pretty well until we thought our first little heathen could benefit from an association with faith and the faithful.

We researched several religions, churches, and sects. Our list of criteria was comprehensive. First, we wanted a church that wasn't likely to pass a snake around. Second, we wanted one that would not require one of us to don an explosive vest and run into a crowd of innocents screaming, "All aboard, next stop heaven!" Yep, that was a big one. And third, the church had to be across the street from our neighborhood, so it ended up being the First Presbyterian Church on William Hilton Parkway, which is located down the street from our gated community, Port Royal Plantation.

I've never quite understood calling gated communities "Plantations," with the bad name plantations have picked up along the path of American history. Whatever. Northerners aren't in the least bit deterred. They flock to them in their euphoric state of early retirement.

Yankee refugees from the frozen north didn't always inhabit Port Royal Plantation. During the Civil War, my plantation was home to two Union forts, Fort Walker and Fort Mitchell, also a safe haven for slave refugees fleeing the plantations and carnage of war. Historical records state that as many as sixty thousand freed slaves inhabited the area. To provide perspective, if you have ever visited Hilton Head Island during the fourth of July weekend, it'd be like that—crowded. Knowing my little neighborhood held a city of sixty thousand freed slaves is pretty cool.

First Presbyterian fit the bill. No snakes, no explosive vests and right across the street. Now, I come from more true southern evangelistic preaching style, plus I was educated at a Catholic school, so Presbyterianism was quite a gear-shift backwards.

I soon found out that nobody reads a sermon better than a Presby minister. Imagine someone reading Martin Luther King's "I Have a Dream" speech in monotone—that's Presbyterian preachin' for ye. Retired northerners enjoy cookies and juice in the social hall after the service where one can often hear, "Wasn't that a great sermon?"

One time I heard someone say. "...that part about a burning bush, talking to someone. I saw a burning bush floating down a river in Jersey one time. So God does make these things happen. What time do we tee off?"

Okay, that wasn't very Christian of me. Presbys do have lively preachers but the ministers on Hilton Head must take care not to introduce too much emotion to a congregation that actually likes to be called the "frozen chosen."

On the other hand, when Frasers go, we go all in. Debbie got involved with children's ministries on all levels, even served for years as the Sunday School superintendent. I taught Sunday School to the middle school age gang. They had trouble with me from day one. I brought too much emotion, noise, and passion to the room, but the kids seemed to love both learning about Jesus and having fun.

I was routinely called on the linoleum carpet for allowing my class to become too loud when expressing the joy of Christ. Of course, I believe Christ is worth getting excited over, so I kept up the racket. We rebelled, kept it loud and were tolerated by those within earshot, just barely. I didn't care. As it turns out, I have a passion for teaching young folks about the goodness of Jesus. Fun, I discovered, was the best way to create what smart people call a "teachable moment."

Before class, I'd slip in the back of the church kitchen and steal a platter of freshly made cookies for the grown-ups to munch on after enduring a sermon. With a full tray of sugar stimulation, I led my group of hooligans in a warm-up chant:

"Who was Jesus?"

"Son of God!" screamed the entire class.

"I'm sorry, Jesus can't hear you," said Mr. Fraser, the Sunday School teacher.

"SON OF GOD!!!" they shouted with gusto.

"Do you love Jesus?" I queried. "If you love Jesus, stomp your feet and tell Him you love him so he can hear you in heaven!"

The room came apart at the seams. My classroom was right next to the Senior bible study class, a truly bad idea.

Usually during the stomp session, an emissary from the old folks group would come in and sternly ask us to quiet down so they could do whatever they do in relative peace. An old man approached me at church the Sunday after my first full week of law school. I was ready to apologize for my class being too loud when he said, "I hear you have gone back to law school?"

"Why, yes, I have. Just finished the first week."

"You know, I really admire that. I don't think I could have gone back to grad school after being away for so long. I always wanted to get my law degree and my parents always said I liked to argue so much that I'd be a good lawyer. I had kids and then took care of my parents, and time just got away. But I really admire that you're giving it a try. So, how's it going?"

"Well, I've only been at it a week and I'm still a little shaky, but I think I can handle it. We'll see," I offered.

"Please keep me posted. I'd like to hear how it's going."

He shook my hand and went for the cookies with the other old folks and little kids. I had no idea who this guy was but he was the first, not the last, to seek me out that morning. Two more codgers found me. They mostly wanted to tell me about the dreams they had placed on hold due to commitments of all sorts. Over the next three years, dozens, if not hundreds of people who had heard about the path I decided to follow sought me out, each one with a story of set aside dreams.

I must confess that some Sundays while waiting for the family to finish prepping for church, I'd turn on the TV and browse the channels, noting the televangelists and infomercials that dominate the Sunday morning lineup. I have to admit, I'm attracted to, and even love the passion that seems to be taboo at the Presby.

I might stumble across Joel Osteen selling positive Christianity to an audience of what looks to be maybe ten or fifteen thousand strong, all transfixed on his message, some weeping. The power of his words and their obvious impact amazes me, as does his persona, permanent smile, big hairdo, and gorgeous mesmerized wife. This was clearly the American dream.

I might accidentally come across Ron Popeil selling a little cooking machine that could be simply set up and forgotten. I might unearth old Billy Mays, God rest his soul, selling OxiClean, wherein I become truly inspired by his honest enthusiasm about a powder that turns a tub of blue liquid clear, or removes ink from a lace tablecloth by merely dipping it into the same clear holy water that just turned from blue to clear. I had to fight the urge to buy some of that stuff. I love the power of the words.

Benny Hinn, healing people with a hand on the forehead—that was a good stumble. But on this particular Sunday, I paused my random clicking on an inspirational African-American man who goes by the handle of Bishop Jakes. He was somewhere mid-sermon on the subject of prosperity and success through faith in one's self. The message did not appear to rely on a prayer of supplication but rather on a personal belief that within each of us lives the power, albeit often untapped, to do great things.

I had to think for a moment. *Is this guy talking to me?* Here I was, in way over my head, I needed power. I was on the first step of a massive undertaking that had the potential to destroy my life, financially and otherwise. And yet, here I was, resting the remote on a random channel for more than the obligatory three seconds that permits a channel to prove its worth, and this guy was talking directly to me.

Was I to believe that each of us could fulfill our dreams by following the principals of focus, goal setting, planning and hard work? And most importantly, was I supposed to never allow anyone or anything to steal or destroy my dreams, or dampen my self-belief? That is to say, we can do it—with God's help, of course. And somehow, from a televangelist who many mock as a person preying on the superstitious and weak, I received the essential coaching I needed.

I had witnessed the insecurity of the younger students, and for goodness sake, or perhaps for God's sake, I had been admitted to the school just like the little gifted ones. Maybe I needed to start believing that I could pull this off. I belonged just as much as anyone else. Apparently, according to Bishop Jakes, somewhere within me there was a toolbox containing all the necessary tools I needed to succeed.

Bringing others down seems to be a hobby of some people. I recognized the look of skepticism when folks heard of my journey. I could tell it in their faces. Their words contained little faith that I'd accomplish such a gigantic task. Failure was a prediction shared among my contemporaries, practically an expectation. Most weather forecasters yearn to be right.

Their negativity could have been easily absorbed, and without knowing, I think I may have drunk a little of the Kool-Aid, but only a sip. I had the faith to believe that this law school at fifty thing was doable, but along the way, my confidence was destined to be shaken here and there. I'll admit, I let the professors and little geniuses intimidate me into believing that some alchemy of age and education, but mostly age, made me less of a viable candidate to finish the process. Holy smokes, I needed coaching, something more than a loving and supportive family.

I know it sounds odd and maybe hard to believe, but in my slot there is no coach. I'm a dad. And for most functioning dads, there is no dad coach. Most non-dads would disagree, citing Father's Day and Breakfast with Dad at middle school or some other event when a name is signed at the bottom of a card and presented along with a tie, or whatever. That's all good, but what we need is some steady coaching. Someone to guide, criticize constructively, and challenge. We need someone to say, "You're doing great. Here's what you need to fix." Basically, we dreamers need someone who believes in our ability when we are in doubt of ourselves. That coach is not readily available for dads.

I often marvel at how much coaching is needed by professional athletes. They know their sport better than anyone, but they need the coach's perspective to give them the confidence to succeed. Dads don't have that. At least this dad didn't. I was on my own.

I ran a small business, kept a yard and house. I did the dad thing at home by myself, alone in many respects. I am expected to know my job. I'm expected to know how to be a husband, how to raise kids, and how to run a business, even though I had never done any of those things before or studied at DAD University somewhere. I am supposed to know my job, and it doesn't matter if I make it up on the fly just as long as I get it mostly right.

Finding myself running low on self-esteem was a little spooky. Hearing Bishop Jake's message was good timing. The ladies of my house got through fixing themselves for the fashion show we call church and were yelling for their driver before Bishop Jakes finished his sermon with the obligatory emotional crescendo. I hated to miss the event. However, I did get the gist of his message, and along with it, the lift I needed to get back in the ring. I was ready to take a few more punches, and perhaps land a few of my own.

It was somewhere in the middle of the Sunday chores— yard mowing, mulch raking, driveway edging, shrub pruning and roof blowing that the reality of Monday began to demand my attention. I attempted to suppress it with hard work involving dangerous power tools, which clearly state on the label that they can cause great bodily harm if used improperly and carelessly. But even the tools with their whirling blades threatening to take an eye, hand, foot, or pancreas could not completely stave off the realization that Monday was nearing.

Then, just like it was a dream and never really happened at all, the weekend was over and the alarm was going off at 4:30 a.m. Where did the weekend go?

CHAPTER TWENTY-TWO

The Procedure

I found comfort in establishing a new routine. Everything was packed, leaving me only to get out of bed, shower, and get in the car. The ride to Columbia for Week Two wasn't quite as filled with anxious thoughts. I still had a little nervousness for the class environment, which never entirely went away for the whole tour of duty, but many of the demons had been confronted and diffused in Week One.

The biggest challenge on my return trip was staying awake. Leaving at 5:00 a.m. allowed me time to get into my room at the Holiday Inn and spend about an hour prepping for class, which worked out well. My brain needed a refresher. No doubt, Week Two was to be a little better. Not fun by any stretch of the imagination, just less scary.

I arrived in Columbia and began to forge my routine into something that would not require much thinking. That's the way my brain operates. I am creative like all humans, but re-inventing the wheel at every task is something I take off the plate where possible. My bag, already packed on Friday afternoon with the fours—four drawers, four pants, four shirts—took less than one minute. The toiletries live in my bag. They are always packed. No thinking required.

I hit the parking garage early, at 7:30 a.m., well before 9:00 a.m., before all the spaces are taken. The Holiday Inn fills up with meetings and seminars, so the key is not to miss the hotel parking. If I did, I would be completely out of luck. After 9:00 a.m. on a weekday in Columbia, there is no legal parking available.

Parking attained, I grabbed my rolling trunk, duffel bag of clothes, bookbag, my cooler filled with food, checked in, found my room, and set up shop. Set up was simple, and I did it the same way several hundred times. Open the trunk, set up my computer and printer, open my clothes bag on the corner of the king-size bed, away from sleeping side, put ice in my cooler, sit on couch, and start studying.

Do it exactly that way every time and no brain power required. Having a repetitive system imprinted on my mind and imbedded in muscle memory was essential. I didn't have to think about what to do next. I didn't have to wonder, "What did I forget?" or "Where's my toothbrush?" or "Anybody seen my other shoe?" or any such crap. I needed all my brain power for the other thing, surviving law school.

Another important function was taken care of in my morning set-up routine. I placed a little stuffed dog named Washcloth Puppy on top of the open trunk. WP looked out across the room. He was my conscience and reminder of home.

We named him WP because he was made of brown and white terrycloth and filled with little beans of some kind. His intended purpose was initially a bath toy. Lizzi hid him in my clothes bag as a surprise for me to find when I got to law school on my first day. He watched over me every day, still does to this day. If I thought I might watch some television, there was WP on top of my trunk next to the television looking right at me, never saying a word, reminding me I didn't abandon my family to sit in a Holiday Inn in Columbia and watch television. It worked pretty well.

The other surprise gift was the family portrait drawn by Lizzi featuring me, Debbie, Page, Lizzi, Okie the dog, Precious the cat, the sun and a snail. She threw in the snail because she was good at drawing them. I laminated the family pic and made it the first page of my note binder so that I would see this rendering of my family every day. It made me happy and sad at the same time, but I needed that little emotional dagger jab in the heart to remind me of what I was giving up to have my butt in those cheap plastic law school classroom seats.

My routine had a proper foundation. After the foundation came the structure. Study, class, study, eat, study, eat, study, sleep, and so on. The routine was beginning to influence my law school experience. For example, the professor called on me in Property class and I did fairly well. I think all the professors were somewhat interested in figuring out what was up with these older returning students. Not so interested that they would actually pull one of us aside, engage in a conversation and ask the "why" question. Just curious as to what drove these older folks out of careers and into law school.

Law students are not particularly interesting in and of themselves. Sure, they are all smart, well, all except for me, but being intelligent is about the only and lowest common denominator. Everyone was admitted into the school because a set of numbers lined up and intersected. Test scores verses seats. Try as they might, all the testing and analysis of the paper trail of an applicant's past was not a perfect indicator of which humans would make good lawyers. Some of the dullest knives in the academic drawer make excellent lawyers in the real world.

Similarly, some of the brightest students were abysmally lousy lawyers. Of course, law school was the real world, but only for the folks who worked there, meaning the admin staff, professors, janitors, etc. But for the students, it was the hypothetical world of theory and study. It was the same with the older students. Some were gifted and some truly were not, they just made good enough grades to get in the door. The older students' ages ranged from twenty-five to sixty-five, and the higher the number, the bigger the "WHY?"

For instance, my soon to be friend, Mr. Hazel, was at the top of the age range, at the very apex, actually. He was ten years older than me, fully retired on a lifelong pension, something I would never have.

Q: Why on earth was Mr. Hazel in law school?

    A) For self-fulfillment

    B) To broaden horizons

    C) To expand his mind

    D) Eliminate boredom

    E) All of the above

I should have asked him. Obviously, the younger students were hoping to make a better life for themselves. Mr. Hazel already had the better life, so what was he going to do with a law degree? Well, as it turns out, Mr. Hazel was going to practice law, which he eventually did. This fine gentleman joined a respected Columbia firm and pursued elder law, the legal practice that places an emphasis on issues affecting our aging population. Among the bar association, Mr. Hazel has a reputation of being an excellent and compassionate lawyer.

Week Two went by with little excitement. I was able to tame the flock of seagulls in my gut into a swarm of butterflies. They are still there. I've just gotten used to them.

Week Two gave way to Week Three and the procedure began to solidify into a cadence by the numbers. Lost in the haze of work, my days, weeks, and weekends slithered away like turtles on a mud bank. My existence blended into a single time frame, also called semesters. Anxiety was still in attendance, but now many of unknowns were known, which somewhat eliminated the fear factor. Although many unknowns still existed, they lacked urgency, which I learned was a lawyer's starting gun.

As the weeks crept by, the chilling thought of exams began to demand focused attention. The single test for a whole course remained a dreaded fear of all first year students, and would remain so until the bomb squad arrived and removed the fuse from that ordinance. But for the early part of the first semester there was still plenty of time, and time gave the illusion of safety.

CHAPTER TWENTY-THREE

The Wake-Up Call

A couple of weeks into the semester, Dr. Bond (Contracts) announced a date for the promised midterm and laid out the expected rules. We couldn't figure whether to love Bond or hate Bond for being the only professor to give a midterm. Unlike the three-hour final exams, his midterm would be completed within the eighty-minute class period. It would cover all the material studied to date and consist of two fact patterns with essay questions answered in Blue Books, which are familiar in the world of academia.

A mini version of the real exam, our midterm would be a horse race to see how much regurgitation we could spew into a little Blue Book. It was pretty straightforward. We had a week to prepare, and like the final exam, there was no need for any additional information, the test included everything. Supposedly, it would be graded to count as part of the overall grade using the lesser-known but popular method of grading essays, the stair step method.

Test dread made the week intense. Test day loomed in front of us like a dark cloud. At least no one would be called on, which made for little consolation. Was Bond attempting to relieve some of the pressure of final exam time by cracking a window to his human side, allowing us to experience a real law school exam? Was he? I held onto the belief that he was human, but the crack was not open wide enough to tell for sure, and before it would expose any actual humanity, it would soon slam shut on some unwitting fingers.

The test was a true knock-off of the many we would see over the next three years. The test is a story that academic snobs call a fact pattern, or a hypothetical. That's it, just a story, which may or may not be followed by a couple of questions.

Here's the translation in human English.

Dumbass, write everything you think applies to the course you just studied, and do it fast. And because we were also being taught by lawyers to say something that means something else using language sprinkled with some weird lawyer words, the question would not be that direct and to the point.

Here's a law school question for you.

Identify all issues included in the hypothetical which relate to the formation of a binding and enforceable agreement between the parties, citing cases, holdings, rules of law and statutory law which may apply.

That's right, they couldn't just say, "Tell all you know about my little story." As the professor handed out the tests and cheap Blue Books, I suddenly remembered my reoccurring but different dream about this very class. I sat there frozen, then carefully turned to the last page to see if there was an answer sheet tucked inside. If so, that would confirm I was living in a dream world and that I would wake up in Hilton Head, on my island, and comfort myself, knowing that my family was okay, my world was okay, and this whole law school thing was just an elaborate dream.

But there was no answer sheet, leaving me stuck in the real world. Stoic Dr. Bond stood in the center of the room like an Easter Island statue staring straight ahead at an imaginary point somewhere in the middle of the back wall one hundred feet away. "You may BEGIN!" the granite statue spoke.

The explosive sounds of booklets being torn open and frantic writing on formica tabletops filled the room. At first, I was distracted, but when my adrenal gland sent a shot of some steroid to my left ventricle, an electric volt went straight to my fingertips, which started writing. It was as if my hand had a mind of its own. Good God! I hoped my hand knew what it was writing.

I was reading, thinking and writing as fast as possible, yet I could not help but notice that the little genius SOBs seemed to be filling their Blue Books faster. Damn! No time to hate. I could do that later. Now, it was time to write. Like most things where more is demanded than could possibly be given, time flew by, unfortunately.

"Five minutes," the granite figurine barked. He never moved. "Time's up. Put your pens down. Hand in your tests."

And our first law school test was over.

I was shell-shocked, drained and exhausted but still wired. While I was packing up my stuff (two pens), the statue fired a question in my direction. "Would you remain after class, please?"

My head jerked up. Thankfully, he was speaking to a guy across the horseshoe classroom from me. Several students had heard the request, and as I did, sensed something ominous. I quietly thanked God that he wasn't talking to me.

"Sir, you continued writing after I said time was up. That gave you an unfair advantage, which is cheating. I am going to report this as an honor violation. You will be informed of the consequences."

Ouch.

I had talked briefly to the young man during orientation, so I knew only a very little about him. However, I could tell he was in total shock after hearing he was to be reported to the law school tribunal as a cheater.

He was an older returning student, about twenty-eight years old. He moved his wife and daughter to a small apartment near the army base so he could take his shot at creating a better life as a lawyer. My guess was that he was freshly buried under a massive loan and lived off the income from his wife's job while he devoted himself to their new future. He was all in, that much I knew. He had pushed all his chips to the middle of the table. He gambled everything certain they would one day enjoy the payoff. He wasn't some kid extending a leisurely stay in college to stave off the real world. The chance of becoming a lawyer meant everything to him. I could only imagine what the ice-cold horror that was moving through his veins felt like. How on earth could he tell his wife he was about to be kicked out of law school for cheating?

"I finished a sentence. It couldn't have been more than five seconds," he pleaded. He then waited in silence for something, anything, from the stone cold professor, Dr. Bond.

Now, I'm quite sure this was one of his little stunts he pulls every year to drive home the Supreme Court's push to clean up the legal profession's bad name. He selects his prey then sacrifices them so everyone can see that law school is to be taken very seriously. Zero tolerance.

After a measured pause, the professor said, "Cheating is cheating. It doesn't matter if it was one word or ten pages, one second or one hour. You will be contacted by the Honor Council."

The professor looked straight toward the back of the room, indicating there would be no more debate. My pens packed, my presence too conspicuous to stay any longer, I had to leave the airless vacuum of that room before the poor soul broke down in front of me.

The young man caught me in the hall. I guess there was no further discussion after I slipped out.

"Did you hear that?" he asked, shaken almost to tears. "All I did was finish a sentence. I'm sure I wasn't the only one," he told me looking for some human support.

"I know. I can't believe it."

I had little else at the moment, even though I'm a dad, with a capital 'D.' I could surely have come up with something to make it better, so I told him, "Look, the jerk was probably trying to make a point and scare the crap out of you. Worst case scenario you'll explain the situation to the honor council. Surely they're reasonable and fair. Dr. Bond has a pretty lousy reputation. He probably pulls this stunt every year. Why don't you let this cool down for a while, then go meet with Dr. Bond and have a rational conversation."

My words seemed to have a somewhat calming effect, but it wasn't enough. This blow was too serious and way too threatening. I may have gotten him off the ledge, but panic fluids were coursing and pumping. I truly believed him to be at risk, of what I didn't know, but he was out there, scared, humiliated.

"Why don't you let him know your situation and that you didn't mean to take an unfair advantage? Tell him you respect his position and it will never happen again. At least you will know where you stand. Right now, you are assuming the worst. Just go find out. If it is as bad as you think, then you can deal with it. Chances are it is his perverted idea of a wake-up call and nothing more."

It seemed I was quieting the panic a little so I continued, dad-like. "Offer to take a grade reduction. Show him you mean well. Confront the issue right away, then you'll know what the deal is."

He nodded. "Okay. I'll go talk to him. Thanks."

The next day I saw him, but he didn't show any real interest in talking about what was, for him, embarrassing.

"I think we worked it out."

That's all I got. I never found out whether or not my advice was helpful. He did finish law school and graduated with honors, so he and Dr. Bond apparently came up with some modification.

The legal profession has had a public relations black eye for many years. For twenty years or more, lawyering has been the butt of many a joke, some of which are hilarious. We've all heard lawyers are below used car salesmen.

It wasn't always that way in my life. I remember the profession being generally respected, but not so much anymore. The Supreme Court of South Carolina has taken on the task of fixing the public perception problem by implementing stricter rules, harsher disciplinary actions, and making the bar exam harder. The court is both the gatekeeper and executioner for all licensed lawyers. They beefed up the rules and required more ethic courses to be taken annually. They also became more trigger-happy on disbarments. I suppose witnessing someone thrown out should scare us into better behavior.

Actually, the bar exam can't be made more difficult since the test just mandates that the taker write everything they know. It's twenty-four hours of testing over three days. The court ordered examiners to grade more harshly, bumping the failure rate from fifteen to thirty percent. The theory being that the bad lawyers were the dumb ones and failing more of the bottom percentile would prevent those lawyer wannabes from practicing. The problem was public opinion accepted lawyers as being corrupt, or dishonest, and the bar exam doesn't test for character or honesty.

It's my belief that ethically flawed people are everywhere and can be found within every level of intellect, so failing more people doesn't work. In October, we, the freshmen class, heard the passing rate on the bar exam given in July was below eighty percent. Typically, it was over ninety percent.

Along with the reality that the bar results took three months to come out, this was distressing news. I spent too much of my precious study time pondering the possibility that I could fail the bar exam in July, and then have to retake it in February and wait three months to find out my fate. That translates into one full year post graduation before a law practice could begin.

The flunk more bar exam rule gave me one more thing to worry about, but that was way off in the future. At the moment, I was only obligated to pass a semester of law school. I could devote time to bar prep down the road. Like I said, time gives the illusion of safety.

CHAPTER TWENTY-FOUR

The Friend

Older students are not remotely welcomed into the social world of law school, which may be one of the few good things about getting older. The younger students were nice to me in a "Yes, sir," or "No, sir" kind of way. Polite conversation is common here in the south, but for the most part I was invisible. I was not there to have a social life. I had one of those at home. My mission was to get a legal education. It was my turn to gracefully accept an unhealthy dose of age discrimination.

Of course, I cannot complain about the mistreatment of older folks because there is some likelihood my acceptance was influenced by schools racing to bring in more diversity with regard to race, gender, creed, sexual orientation, and, thank the Lord, age. I accepted my age social banishment. Other than occasionally being singled out as an idiot in class, the world of law school neither knew of, nor cared about my existence, and that worked out just fine.

Still, I missed having short bursts of friendly social interaction. I came from a world where I was surrounded by lots of people who knew me as Dad, friend, husband, coworker, Sunday School teacher, or whatever. Now, I was in a world where no one knew me, or even cared to know me, and that was strange and, to a small degree, lonely. I started to feel like Robinson Crusoe, all alone and shipwrecked on a desert island, except instead of being surrounded by a jungle, I was surrounded by people.

A daily rainstorm drenched Columbia, South Carolina. For most of 1997, it was either hot and rainy, or cold and rainy. The days without rain probably outnumbered the rainy ones but it seemed like it rained most of the time. Wet weather, stress, and confinement in a closed space with lots of other people breathing the same stale air caused half of the students on any given day to be sick.

It was that wet, sick year that turned me into what my kids call a "germaphobe." I became friends with Purell way before anybody knew what it was. Antibacterial lotion, a constant companion, insulated me from the sickos who left their little balled-up Kleenexes all over the place. It wasn't unusual to find the little infected tissues in the study carrels in the library next to those vile communal computers we were forced to use from time to time. I kept sanitizing lotion on me at all times to fight an onslaught of pathogens, which were clearly bent on my personal and physical destruction. And, as a testament to my virus-killing spree, I managed to stay well and healthy in a crucible of sickness.

Washcloth Puppy and a bottle of hand sanitizer as personal friends were my refuge. Those two protected me emotionally and physically. The harmful effect of too little casual human interaction became evident when I found myself regularly discussing my day with WP. Sure, Robinson Crusoe talked to coconuts, and Tom Hanks talked to a soccer ball named Wilson, but they were crazy, and I wasn't quite there yet.

The story starts out the same. It was a dark and stormy day in Columbia. The vast lobby guarded by Ol' Strom was filled with more than its usual humans waiting to catch a break in the rain before heading to the parking lot. And there was Matt, the guy who occupied the space next to me in nearly all my classes.

Matt looked like a puppy waiting for a school bus to drop off his playmate. No one talked to him, which was somewhat standard since handicapped people are even more invisible to the passing throngs of humans than old people. He was alone, sitting in his wheelchair, watching it rain, looking somewhat hypnotized by the dreary rainscape outside.

"Sitting there" is obviously redundant descriptive. As a C-6 quadriplegic, his choices were somewhat limited.

"So, what's up Matt? You waiting on a break in the rain to make a run for your car?" Dammit! *Make a run for your car*, what was I thinking? Clearly, I am incredibly awkward around people with severe handicaps.

Spinal injuries to the sixth cervical vertebra typically mean the whole body below the neck is non-functioning. Matt's injury allowed some use of his arms and hands, albeit limited. He could push the wheels of his chair and get around pretty good. Some quads can't move anything and require a respirator to breathe, so I guess in an embarrassingly odd usage of the word, Matt was lucky. He could at least move himself around.

Matt had thrown a nylon parka haphazardly over his head and shoulders giving him the appearance of a piece of furniture that someone had tossed a garment onto to dry.

He looked at me like I was an idiot. "I can't push my chair uphill when it's wet."

Columbia was not only wet, it was hilly, still is. The parking lot was uphill from the school building. I should mention that the parking lot adjacent to the law school building was off limits to law students, the ones who pay to be there and also pay the salaries of everyone in the building. The school required law students to park several blocks away. However, this parking lot had fourteen handicap parking spaces specifically set aside for the law school. Matt was lucky enough to be parked in one of them.

"I'm pretty good at pushing things. You want me to give you a push to the car?" I offered.

"Sure, if you don't mind," he said without giving it much thought.

The main entrance had an automatic door for handicapped folk, which Matt pointed out. All I had for protection was an umbrella, so I popped it open and was immediately confronted with the dilemma of how to push a chair and hold an umbrella. What's the big deal?

Well, it is a big deal. First of all, Matt is a big guy, probably pushing two hundred pounds. Secondly, the hill was a slight incline, but a hill nonetheless, which meant that the wheelchair had to be pushed with oomph. Lastly, the wheelchair had to be pushed with two hands or it had a tendency to go in circles, and I needed one hand to hold the umbrella to keep from drowning. This was my first lesson in wheelchair 101.

Every time I pushed using two hands, my umbrella tumbled, and every time I grabbed my umbrella, the chair took a hard left. So we serpentined our way up the hill to the parking lot. The scene was probably hilarious to watch.

Matt pointed to a row of cars and to his baby blue van. His parking space was the kind with the extra blue lines, indicating the space would accommodate a wheelchair lift. He had me stop at the rear of the van where he fished out a magnet on a cord from his pack. He stuck the magnet on a spot next to the taillight and the van's double side doors opened.

After the doors were completely spread open, an aluminum ramp appeared and dropped like a drawbridge in slow motion. Once the drawbridge was level, it lowered itself to the ground. Matt had me roll the chair onto the ramp where he pulled a small hand lever on each wheel to lock the wheels into place. He hit a switch and the process started all over again, except this time the ramp rose upward and stopped when it was level with the floor of the van. Matt then rolled in, guided himself into a locking mechanism bolted to the floor where the driver's seat was removed.

Once locked into the driver's position, he began to operate the equipment that allows him to drive using just his hands. The beast of a van had a column shift and a giant lever sticking out of the floor that was both accelerator and brake. Forward for gas, backward for braking. He hit another secret switch and the ramp began its slow transition from horizontal to vertical, at which time the two doors closed automatically. What a process! The whole thing took about five minutes. Not long, unless it's raining.

I knew Matt from several weeks of sitting next to each other in class, which tempted me to claim some knowledge of his difficult life. Having been exposed to the workings of his complicated customized van, I realized I did not comprehend one molecule of the difficulty this young man dealt with on a daily basis.

He locked onto the custom peg handle on the steering wheel, something akin to what we used to call a suicide wheel. Matt then drove the top-heavy baby blue behemoth Ford out of the space and the lot and miraculously hit nothing. Off he went, to carry out the rest of his life, a life I thought about for the first time. It had to be like mine only a thousand times more difficult.

In the world of quadriplegics, each level of mobility loss creates a new level of diminished independence. Paraplegics have the full use of all but the legs. They can get in a car, get in bed, get out of bed, get in and out of the chair, get in a shower and care for their personal hygiene needs. Quads can do none of those things. Quads are dependent upon other humans to do things for them, such as getting in and out of bed, getting in and out of a shower, getting dressed, cooking, shopping, all those things. If there is no human to help with things requiring mobility, then the quad is SOL.

Rolling a wheelchair uphill in the rain was hard, but it was not much easier on a dry day. Matt and I had exactly the same schedule, so I started pushing Matt up to the parking lot every day. It's not like I had to be anywhere.

I found the big blue van to be intriguing, possibly designed by a mad engineer. Magnetic secret spots that opened doors and lowered a drawbridge—how cool was that? Being a gadget guy, a full contact, do-it-yourself dad, I was drawn to this beast like a guy staring at a Shopsmith demo in a shopping mall back in the 80's.

For those who don't know what a Shopsmith is, it is a large multi-purpose woodworking machine and a lifetime partner for guys interested in making stuff out of wood. It replaces five (maybe more) full-sized power tools in one massive unit. Personally, I spent many hours in the mall completely mesmerized by the Shopsmith demo dude who took a block of wood and turned it into a wall sconce right before my very eyes. I tinker, fiddle, and occasionally make things. It took all of my self-control to keep from buying one.

Pushing Matt up the hill to the parking lot turned into, "What's for lunch? Where should we go?"

Matt took the big blue beast and me to some of Columbia's finer grease joints. Columbia is not overloaded with five star dining places, which is fine with me. My palate is geared toward barbecue, fried chicken, burgers and wings, and in that genre, Columbia is king. There are grease joints on every corner, and Matt and I found and frequented most of them within a ten-mile radius.

Matt and I shared the same taste for all things unhealthy, and Columbia, being the state capitol of the number one state in the nation for both coronary disease and obesity, placed us in the epicenter of what is appropriately known as "hog heaven." It's the very nucleus of the universe of clogged arteries and fat people.

On the national level, my beloved state is outstanding in few significant areas. At the time, we were forty-seventh out of fifty states in education and number one in house trailers per capita, obesity, and heart disease. As it turns out, we were good at some things. We also had a few things to be thankful for, most notably, Alabama, Louisiana and Mississippi. Thank God for those wonderful states.

As we ate our way to an early grave, Matt revealed a little more of the complexities of a wheelchair-bound traveler. Nothing much stopped this guy. He could have been paid to test pilot wheelchairs and handi-vans. With the right sponsor, he could have been a cross between Chuck Yeager and Joie Chitwood, the world's most famous test pilot and stunt driver, respectively.

As long as there was enough room for the drawbridge to fold out, access was never denied to Matt. If a small gap existed, he would cram the blue beast into the space. As for the wheelchair, he could take it almost anywhere, frontwards, backwards, sideways, or upside down if need be.

Being handicapped isn't for sissies. It is not. In order for a handicapped person to get out and take part in the world, they had to be tough as nails, emotionally and physically. Everything is hard. I'll say it again and hope it sinks in: *Everything is hard.* Let me flip that around. *Nothing is easy.* Nothing. I don't care how crappy you may think your life is, I assure you, your things are easy. Movement, writing, eating, walking, talking, breathing, sleeping, pooping, scratching, turning pages, holding a fork—easy as pie. But for the severely handicapped, nothing is easy and everything is hard.

For some burdened with a severe handicap, it might be easy to do nothing and wait for the grim reaper to show up, but not Matt, or countless others who maintain a non-cooperative body. Matt kicks the crap out of life. Witnessing Matt's bravery and his forgiving attitude toward a world that makes him struggle for every inch of access changed me. I came to law school to learn the nine elements of civil fraud and the like. I didn't expect to be handed the greater life lesson, but that is exactly what I received.

CHAPTER TWENTY-FIVE

The Friendship

Somewhere along the way, I suggested Matt should join me for dinner on Thursday evenings. A restaurant meal once a week with a friend sounded pretty awesome and would only require giving up an hour or two from my studies. God only knows what Matt normally did for dinner, but Thursday night dinners became a regular thing.

Like I mentioned previously, Columbia has a bumper crop of two and three-star dining establishments, so for a two-star guy like me, this was a plus, as in A+. We had our choice of Outback, Olive Garden, Red Lobster, Piggie Park, Lizard's Thicket, Ruby Tuesdays, and a dozen other mom and pop places specializing in sushi, barbecue, hamburgers, Chinese, Italian, and whatever else thousands of college students and other two-star guys supported. Columbia took good care of us on Thursdays.

I received my first driving lesson in the blue beast at the Outback Steakhouse. We came out after dinner and discovered that some thoughtless jerk had parked on the blue striped handicap space designated for passenger loading and unloading, the side where the six-foot drawbridge folds out.

There was no way to get in, or at least Matt couldn't get in, which was the problem.

"What do we do? Should I go in the restaurant and find the jerk driving the Lexus so he can move his car before we take a Louisville Slugger to it?" I asked.

"No, you can back it out," Matt said, calm and forgiving as usual.

"Do what? I can't drive that thing. Hell, there's no seat."

"It's just like any other car. You start the engine, put it in gear, grab the big lever, and give it some gas." This was his attempt to reassure me.

Not wanting to look like a wuss, I said, "Okay, but don't blame me if this doesn't go well."

Driving a car without a seat is just plain weird. I climbed in the rolling coliseum and tried a few positions in the place where the driver's seat used to be. Sitting was not an option, first because I wouldn't be able to see, and second, because a huge eight-inch vertical steel bolt stuck out of the floor.

The steel bolt was there to grab hold of and lock down the wheelchair, preventing it from rolling all over the van while driving. Getting impaled on that bugger would be difficult to explain at the hospital. So sitting was definitely out. Kneeling was a slightly better option, at least I could see over the dashboard, but just barely. It would have to work. The kneeling position somewhat negated the chance that I'd have an intimate encounter with the standing steel bolt.

I started the beast and grabbed the suicide peg on the steering wheel with one hand. I put the thing in reverse, taking hold of the giant GO FAST and SLOW DOWN lever. Was it back for brakes, forward for gas, or the other way around?

I gently pushed forward and then backwards until the beast rolled away from the jerk's car. One big pull back on the big lever and we stopped rolling. I put it in park and surrendered my driver duties to Matt, the beast's handler. This brave act was my first experience driving the blue beast. It wasn't my last.

As Matt and I fell into a routine, something unexpected happened. I am tempted to say I stopped noticing Matt's handicap but that would be as stupid as my phony liberal friends saying they are colorblind and unable to detect race. Everyone notices race, just like everyone is aware of the burden imposed by a physical handicap. It's always there and will stand for nothing less than full attention. Somewhere along the way I lost the awkwardness and fear that I'd say or do the wrong thing. I was no longer concerned about being offensive or insensitive. Hell, handicapped people have been hurt more than any able-bodied person could possibly imagine, yet we fear we'll offend them when and if we acknowledge their limitations.

It felt good to accept our respective handicaps, his being a quad and mine being old. His sucks worse but mine was less fun with each passing day.

I certainly appreciated Matt treating me like a friend, a peer, and not some old guy who needs "Yes, sir" and "No, sir" and "Mr." I hate those terms of elder respect, especially when I've told a young dope to please call me by my first name, Denny, and the idiot says, "I can't do that, Mr. Fraser. My parents raised me to call old people Mister."

I want to grab the amoeba by the throat and scream, "What kind of piece of firewood raised you to believe it polite to address someone in any manner other than what they requested?" But for obvious reasons, I don't do that. I simply tolerate the stupidity of youth because we were all young and stupid once.

Matt was a supremely regular guy. He had a wicked sense of humor. He indulged in horribly inappropriate jokes. He mercilessly, and quite accurately, rated the female physique on a ten-point scale, which I enjoyed. Matt and I made great sport of ridiculing the dumbasses who obviously suffered a noticeable lack of attention to the extent that they felt the need to speak constantly. Except for the fact that his body didn't work right, he was just like any other young person, and he was kind enough to befriend an old guy like me.

While pushing his chair around the city of Columbia, I got to witness the physical world from the disabled perspective. I've already mentioned that the fourteen handicapped parking spaces in the law school lot were filled every day, and over my three years there, the SOL never had more than one or two physically handicapped individuals at any one time. This became a real pisser for me.

When I saw people, some of whom I knew from my section, hang their borrowed handicapped tags so they could consume those spaces without remorse I wanted to strap them to a wheelchair for a month. I wanted to put them in jail, but only after showing them how their inconsiderate actions hindered the life of someone who actually suffers the burden of great physical difficulty.

Not Matt, though. He had been at this handicapped game longer than me and seemed to have made peace with the way the world works. The more accessibility issues I witnessed, the more I realized that Matt (or any wheelchair bound person) would be one perpetually angry individual if they got upset over every little (or big) thing.

Matt was invited by the SOL to a group meeting established to identify ways in which the school could make the SOL campus more handicap-friendly and accessible to the wheelchair community. This meeting was to be held in the library. Matt asked if I would go in his place.

"Sure, but why aren't you going?" I had to ask.

"Because I can't get in," he said. "The library doesn't have an automatic door opener."

He crumpled the invite and we pretty much laughed our collective asses off. We passed on that fact-finding expedition. Surely, the SOL didn't need the keen eye of the handicapped to point out that the first phase of accessibility was to get the people in the building. The meeting must not have been that successful because no automatic opener ever appeared on the library door during my three-year tenure.

CHAPTER TWENTY-SIX

Ironsides and Me

Diversity was in its hay day at the SOL and everywhere else as far as I could tell. I was on the outskirts of affirmative action due to my age, and Matt was one of the SOL's poster people.

Poster people are hauled out from God knows where so they can appear in photos, the ones used for school advertisements. In this case, they rounded up Matt, a couple of black students, usually one male and one female, and Mr. Hazel. I never made the photo ops—wasn't old or pretty enough, or something. A professional photographer arranged the diverse tribe in several thought provoking poses intended to ensure that the USC SOL brochures would display the right mix of ubiquitous diversity, just like every law school in America.

Schools must make a major amount of money off of the many hundreds of applicants who have no chance of gaining admission but who send in their application anyway, and most importantly, include a check. Why not encourage everyone to apply? It was fun to see the SOL round up a diverse group in their effort to show the world that the old south and this institution welcomed all of God's people with open arms.

Aside from photo ops, life in a wheelchair comes with its own set of dangers. The simplest task becomes difficult, impossible, even life threatening, especially in Columbia. Crossing six lanes of traffic, for example, is a great example of difficult and dangerous. Making such a dash provides both the rider and pusher with a genuine adrenaline rush. Thank God I could still sprint.

Many of Columbia's hills were made for mountain goats. Shoving a wheelchair up a hill is without question difficult; however, going down a steep hill can be equally difficult with an extra added measure of danger, should things get out of control.

The Holiday Inn is situated at the bottom of one of Columbia's steep drop-offs. On one of our Thursday outings, this hill provided an excellent opportunity for our collective lives to pass before our eyes. On this particular night we planned to eat at a restaurant only a couple of blocks away. It made sense to leave Matt's blue beast at my parking garage.

We decided to walk and roll given that we could have ended up killing an hour looking for parking. We were headed to a little wing joint. It had good food and college prices. We successfully took on the dangerous ascent up the hill to the next street a block above. With much pushing, Matt on the wheels and me against the handlebars, we eventually made it to the summit. We found our restaurant and made a stab at wiping them out of food.

After putting a healthy dent in what had to be a small flock of chickens, we headed out to resume the chore of reading cases in preparation for the next day's interrogation. The sidewalk down to the intersection of our street had a gentle incline in our favor, so Matt slowly crept along under his own power. I was a couple of paces behind but close enough for us to continue shooting the bull.

Matt reached the intersection slightly ahead of me and pulled up on his right wheel, which caused his chair to hang a sharp right. This move began Matt's fast-paced dissent to unyielding Assembly Street one block below. As soon as the nose of the wheelchair pointed downward, it took off at an alarming rate. I sprinted after him but realized in three strides that I would never catch him. I could only yell, "Matt! I don't have you!"

He glanced to his left and saw his shadow on a building wall. The silhouette told him the horrible truth: he was on a rocket ship ride toward a street with non-stop traffic. Matt pushed on both brakes but by that time the chair had gained so much momentum he could not slow it down no matter what he did.

By the way, this dude plays wheelchair rugby in his spare time, so he's no stranger to flipping over in that contraption, but the real obstacle was the relentless traffic at the bottom of the hill. No grassy field in sight, Matt was headed for concrete and asphalt, the kind of stuff that leaves a mark.

Halfway down the hill on the left was a gravel parking lot that during the day was usually filled with cars. At night it was empty except for the ominous warnings that unauthorized vehicles would be towed at the owner's expense. It was Matt's only chance. When Matt's rocket-powered wheelchair reached the entrance to the parking lot, he hammered down with all his might on the left wheel brake, causing his chair to take an immediate high-speed left turn right into the gravel parking lot where he did a full 360 and vanished in a cloud of dust.

I could hear him laughing long before enough dust cleared. When the dust finally settled, I saw him sitting upright. I ridiculed his driving, he ridiculed my pushing, and we laughed. That's what guys do when they've done something stupid. We joke inappropriately and take another stab at whatever nearly killed us.

For those who may not know, men, dads in particular, have two modes, unflappable, and the polar opposite, flappable. The two modes are not easily concealed. They are more or less emotional states left over from caveman days, or they could be the guy version of cool. I'm too simple to figure it out, but I do recognize the two conditions tend to serve us well.

"Flappable" works like this. When a man is asked or required by law (or family) to do something he really, really does not want to do, and he really, really doesn't care who knows how little he doesn't want to do it or how miserable he think the chore is, he flaps.

Perhaps he doesn't flap in a big way, like Bill Clinton flapped when he became a conscientious objector and ran off to England at wartime. Or like when George W. Bush used his political might to move up the National Guard waiting list so he could quietly sit stateside and avoid the same nasty little skirmish going on in Southeast Asia. Those guys "flapped." They really, really did not want to go to war, but those are big things.

Just so you know, something small, something comparatively insignificant, something ordinary can spark a full-blown flap. I'm talking about being asked to take out the trash or watch your kid in the Nutcracker for the umpteenth freaking year in a row. Sometimes all it takes is being invited to watch Dancing With The Stars. These little things trigger instant procrastination, our favorite defense mechanism.

Procrastination is the one thing we will not put off until later. No sir-ree. We get right on that one. Then when procrastination fails to save us from that which we really, really don't want to do, we go into "flappable" mode, which includes whining, pouting, and incessant complaining. We often complain loud enough so those passing by will know a guy in that house is doing something he really, really did not want to do. All of this is followed by a great deal of incurable sulking. I'm pretty sure people have died from sulking.

Unflappable, on the other hand, is when a guy, more specifically, a dad, is cast into a terribly difficult situation such as WW II yet acts with unbelievable, uncharacteristic coolness, appearing super calm and having superhuman capacity for superhero-like behavior. At least that is what my dictionary says. All that said, Matt is pretty much unflappable. He's been flapped plenty, so he can take a whole lot of life's crap with coolness and calmness.

One day he called me around four o'clock. "Hey, I'm locked in my car."

I did not see this coming. How does one get locked *in* one's own car?

"My ramp won't work and I can't get out of the car. Can you help me?" he asked, acting like it was nothing at all.

He had probably been there all afternoon trying to MacGyver his way out of the conundrum until finally he had to call for help. And of course, the go-to person in all situations requiring help is a dad, at least when there is no Mom around. Being the closest dad, I got the call.

"What's the deal, Matt, do I need tools?" I asked, wondering how to cut open the blue beast.

"No, the ramp can be lowered manually. If you have a drill, that would help. You wouldn't happen to have one, would you?"

"Nope, no drill at law school." I now keep one in my car.

"No problem," he said. "The ramp can be worked with a screwdriver. It's just a little easier with a drill."

"Cool, I'll be right over," I replied, already in unflappable mode.

Matt lived about six blocks away in housing set aside by the university for students needing assistance. I decided to walk since parking in Columbia is never an option. I got to his old, worn housing unit in about half an hour. I found him in the blue beast, looking a little flapped.

The moment he saw me, he switched to unflappable. I tapped on the passenger side window. "Hey, you livin' in a van now?" It's appropriate to quote Chris Farley anytime someone is stuck in a van, plus dads always use humor when things are lousy. Matt smiled and said something. I couldn't hear through the closed door but I'm pretty sure it began with "F."

I hopped in the passenger seat and asked, "So what's the plan?" He gave me the magnet key and told me to go to the secret spot at the back of the van where the magnet causes the side doors to open, which I did. Then he told me to climb behind the passenger seat where the ramp was in its vertical position, get a screwdriver, find the "let down" device, and manually lower the ramp.

With great calmness and steady stream of dad comedic one-liners, I started to turn the screw that was supposed to begin lowering the ramp. Ten turns of the screwdriver only moved the ramp about half an inch. The ramp was five feet tall—do the math. Plus, I was responsible to move the ramp from vertical to horizontal, like any drawbridge operator. I also had to make and keep the ramp moveable with Matt on it, all the way down to the ground.

Needless to say, it took a couple thousand turns of the screw, first with one hand, then the other until the ramp followed its full arc to the horizontal position. Then, with Matt on the ramp and another thousand more difficult turns, my friend was finally extracted from his van. Only three thousand more turns to get the contraption back into the van. An hour and a half later, my work was done. Dads, we have our moments. This was one of mine.

Matt's life is surrounded by mechanical devices. Breakdowns are an inevitable. Matt told me while in his apartment, the back of his chair broke sending him backwards onto the floor with feet and legs still in the air on the chair seat. No cell phone handy, he remained like that until his evening caregiver came hours later to fix his dinner and get him to bed. So yes, Matt got flapped a lot but he never showed it.

Matt was a great friend in many ways. He was also one of those extremely smart brainiacs who coaxed and coached me into a better understanding of the more difficult theories of the law. Maybe he got me through law school. I'll never know for sure if it was me pushing him, or him pulling me. In the end, we both got diplomas.

I will always be grateful for the kindnesses and life lessons Matt passed on to me during my SOL years. I never had to muster the courage that each day demands of him. Matt is a good person. If life ever presents me with a horrific and unchangeable reality, his example, along with my dad's, will be my guidepost.

CHAPTER TWENTY-SEVEN

Friend in Low Places

The SOL building has a basement of sorts. Not a basement like the one under the house that the Goonies kept the goon in, but another floor under the main entrance. This space houses the South Carolina Educational Television studio. Sets, props, lights, mike booms, cameras, and miles of wires and state employees going everywhere.

And it just so happens I found my friend Andy in the SCET studio that sits below the cavernous SOL lobby. Andy was a producer, not like Martin Scorsese, but more like the guy who pulls together all the stuff necessary to film an educational program and broadcast it around the state to the USC satellite campuses. I'm of the opinion that his was a pretty cool job, one with enough of a technical edge to it to give Andy job security, mainly because he was one of the people who knew where all the wires went.

Andy and I go way back, all the way back to 1973. He had just come back from Vietnam and was working as a carpenter for the company I worked for, Daniel Construction. We became fast (or slow) friends. Our friendship resulted in many adventures, some of which are unsuitable for publication seeing as we both have impressionable children who should not be exposed to the gory details of our misspent youth.

Andy's personality defies a simple description. He is uncomplicated on a complex level. A creature of routine and an avowed pacifist, and I don't mean he was the Gandhi type. He artfully dodges confrontational human interaction at all cost. He goes silent, doesn't run or lay down and play dead. He just goes silent. This little trait helped him stay single for most of fifty years though he had plenty of girls along the way. Most left after they understood that he was never going to modify his routine in their honor, nor was he going to play any relationship mind games. If the leaving took place during the hour in which he drank his black coffee and stared at the newspaper, he might not even look up as the door slammed shut.

Yet, Andy is sociable. He's the guy who walks into a bar, and by the second or third time he shows up, everybody in the place knows him. He is like the tomcat that frequents multiple homes for meals and affection. After a while, each home believes the cat belongs to them.

Andy maintained a counter-culture phase in the early seventies. He moved to Colorado, did masonry by day, and in his spare time, backpacked over the Rocky Mountains, mostly alone. After his stint out west teaching his method of passive indifference during his hippie phase, he came back to South Carolina and got a master's degree in God knows what. For most, college is a brief way station along the path to somewhere, but not for Andy. College became a home.

USC liked his passive bohemian style so much that they gave him a job in the basement of the SOL. As for me, with no actual planning or forethought, and with an entire universe in which to make landfall, I end up thirty feet directly above one of my oldest and dearest friends. How's that for cosmic ordering?

Of my list of friends from the past, I wasn't sure who knew I was at law school. I had made a concerted effort to only tell the "need to know" bunch and the "ought to know" bunch, but I cannot remember if I told Andy that I had enrolled in law school. This was 1997. We weren't texting, emailing, Facebooking, Tweeting, or using any other form of social connectivity that is an obnoxious character flaw in modern society. Except for email, none of that other stuff existed. Mark Zuckerberg was still in diapers.

Back then, as well as now, Andy and I talked on the phone about three times a year, and maybe saw each other once a year around the Fourth. I probably told Andy about the law school thing, I must have at some point, but for the life of me, I can't remember. I do know that if I told him, he would have been the only person to not ask "why." He would have just said okay and then gone silent.

Low-maintenance friends are the best kind. One thing was certain, however. I did not know where Andy worked. Never in an eternity did I imagine he would be working in the basement of the law school, right below where I was being interrogated on a daily basis.

One day, while traversing the cavernous lobby guarded by Ol' Strom, I saw Andy aimlessly or perhaps zombie-like walking through the milling mass of students. I flagged him down, and in our usually efficient *modus operandi*. (Yeah, I use legal terms indiscriminately and incorrectly when I feel like it.) We caught up on each other's lives in about five minutes then drifted back to our separate paths. After our reunion, we had lunch every once in a while but we never went out at night. I know my demons and staggering around the bar scene with Andy was one of them, so that was not an option.

Andy had a revelation to share. He doesn't say much, so when he does, I try to listen. He asked to meet me at a restaurant called the Basil Pot, or as I like to call it, the Pot. Weeks earlier I had an altercation with the Pot's manager over handicap parking for Matt's van, which ended with a vow to never darken their doorstep ever again, but friendship often trumps grudges, so I agreed to meet Andy at the Pot. The food wasn't horrible, in fact, it was pretty okay as far as Columbia cuisine goes.

Andy's news was much better than the food. He told me he heard from a girl he had known from the past. I believe it was in a letter she confided that she had harbored feelings for Andy, and that over the years, those feelings had grown stronger. She told Andy she and her husband were on a marital break that would likely end in divorce. She wanted to visit with him to see if her feelings could lead to a happier future. This was the best break from reading law books ever.

Andy remembered her being a good bit younger, like thirty-two to his fifty-two. He asked me for my opinion, and in the crudest of guy terms, I said, "Sounds like it's got 'sure thing' written all over it. Go ahead. See her, what do you have to lose? Maybe she's really nice, or at least not crazy."

"She's got a kid," he told me. Andy clearly did not know what to do with a kid and was about to venture into the unknown. He was scared.

"Look, Andy, she's coming to Columbia. I'm sure your lifestyle will work its magic, causing her to leave and never come back. But I say keep an open mind. She could be the one."

I was half kidding. It was great fun to see the freest person I have ever known deal with anything that encroached on his secure little world. I shouldn't have taken pleasure in it, but, dammit, Andy was the last of us, no mortgage, no kids, no wife, no car payment, no club dues, no worries, and most importantly, no desire for any of that junk. The rest of us were like Dickens' Marley dragging miles of chains through life. Only Andy was truly free, at least for the moment.

Her name was Lynn and during her visit to Columbia, I got to meet her. She was young, early thirties, attractive and smart. At first she made a commendable effort to like me. I truly appreciated the effort even though it eventually morphed into acceptance, like the way a new girlfriend accepts the boyfriend's dog, assuming, if nothing else, time is on her side and the dog would eventually die one day.

Most of Andy's friends were an unbelievable mix of truly eclectic and cool individuals. My middle-aged, middle class dadness rendered me anything but cool. After a few get-togethers, Lynn's instinct about me was confirmed. I was not to be the dog she would eventually grow to love. She seemed good to Andy and he seemed to like her, so I was pretty happy. Plus, for some strange reason, I kind of respect people who don't like me and aren't dishonest about the fact.

Still, it was great fun witnessing Andy's bewilderment. He's never been good at relationships. Actually, he's horrible at them. For the most part, he has never had a choice in a relationship because his unique and inflexible lifestyle has almost always served him well by chasing women away. Not this time. Lynn clearly had set her sights on this poor man, and even though he did not know it, his days of freedom were coming to an end.

After a brief relationship warm-up session consisting of only a few weeks, Lynn moved to Columbia, and the two shared Andy's home, an epic adjustment for both. Andy rented a small brick home that housed his few physical possessions, consisting mainly of a mattress on the floor, a couch/chair combo, enough kitchen stuff to make a simple meal for one, and his beloved stereo equipment. That was Andy.

Having a human being interfering in his monk-like existence had to be supreme trauma for Andy. He was now on the threshold of life involving something other than himself. Nature and biology would soon reveal another existence and in many ways raised the bar over Andy's head. At fifty something Andy learned he was going to be a dad, then came the mortgage, a wedding, a move to Ohio, and a baby girl, aptly named Andrea.

Andy had become one of us, a dad, with all the trimmings. And how cool is that—married, mortgaged and a dad at fifty?

CHAPTER TWENTY-EIGHT

The Helpers

Debbie needed help. She was running a business and had two kids in two different schools miles apart and on two completely different schedules. The situation was impossible.

It was another one of those things that seemed to be an insignificant line item on the law school plan we had laid out on the kitchen table. We had faith we could do this back to school thing, but we needed divine intervention to come to the rescue. We learned early on that much of this journey was just not doable in our own strength. Divine intervention happened. I have never known a success story in which some completely unanticipated stroke of luck, or hand of fate, or hand of God, did not suddenly appear at the right time to make success possible. Like most of life's miracles, divine assistance comes unexpectedly and from the last place imaginable.

Debbie and I were friends with a wonderful family on Hilton Head, a mom, a dad, and three beautiful kids. Let me sum it up by saying these folks were good people, I mean really good people, sent to earth by God as an example of what people were supposed to be like. That pretty well says it all, but of course, I'll go on.

They were very nearly the perfect family. I know people of faith might take great exception to anyone using "perfect" to describe anyone other than Jesus, God, or maybe Mary. However, I feel so good about the term "perfect" to describe this family that I would be willing to bet that any one of the Holy Trinity would back me up on this.

The mom was the family glue. She had the chemistry that made this family special. She was a devoted vegetarian, didn't eat meat or meat by-products at all, and had such exquisite culinary skills that she could cook up a meal that would please even a meat addict like me. She was also a stay-at-home mom, homeschooling all three girls, all twelve grades.

And if all that wasn't enough, the family was very involved in their church, namely, the Seventh Day Adventist Church. In fact, they gave substantial financial support to the sustenance of their small congregation and they didn't drink alcohol. These folks were the poster family for what God wanted us all to be.

So, here's the question. What on earth were they doing hanging around with the Frasers?

It's a good question, one I have pondered more than once. This good family befriended a couple of families with kids about the same age as theirs. This way their little homeschooled brood would have a social community. The moms started having play dates for the kids.

Eventually we were invited to the vegan household for family dinners, really good family dinners. When it was the Frasers turn to host the kids' outings, we used the occasion to go to the beach. The good family's house was a very safe, spotlessly clean environment with absolutely wonderful vegetarian cuisine. The mom was caring, patient to a fault, and protective of her babies. She kept a skeptical eye on me because she knew my history with meat.

I have eight grills, most every kind there is, including one that is six feet long and has to be towed behind a truck. That big one I took to barbecue contests with my cooking team, Motley Que, where we often took first place for our incredible ribs and pulled pork, not to mention the occasional whole hog.

She kept an eye on me. Smart lady.

This leads to the fateful New Zealand connection. These folks knew a young girl from New Zealand who was working in America at a church camp sponsored by the Seventh Day Adventist Church. Knowing our predicament—me in Columbia, Debbie at home running a business, our two kids in two different private schools ten miles apart—the good mom hooked us up with the camp counselor, Kim, whose stint at the camp was running out.

Kim, the Kiwi, had a little time left on her visa and wanted to continue her stay in the US. This is where the divine hand of God came to the rescue. I was away in school doing a difficult job, but Debbie was home handling an impossible job. Our friend assured Kim that we were not murderers and convinced her to help Debbie as an assistant mommy. At just the right time, Kim came to live with us through the last six months of her visa. She became Mom II, sort of a nanny, or au pair, as the snooty like to say.

Kim was great. The girls loved her and she truly cared for our family. She watched over our brood, even helped our momma dog, Okie, deliver her ten puppies. Kim was a born nurturer and protector. We will always be grateful to our friends for many things, but most particularly for hooking us up with Kim. Her visa was nearing the end of its term, so we only had her for a few months. However, Kim became the catalyst for a stream of other New Zealanders.

It turns out that New Zealanders, at around the age of twenty-three, have a tradition of doing a bit of world traveling at the end of their formal schooling. Graduates use their savings, or borrow money, to go spend a couple of years seeing the world, usually the US, UK, Canada, and Europe, and then they return to home sweet home with the knowledge that New Zealand is the greatest place on earth—by far.

So began the migration from the South Island to South Carolina. Kim hooked us up with Calie. New Zealanders in general, and South Islanders in particular, are fiercely nationalistic. Calie was a piece of work, God love her little soul. She made the average South Islanders look like bloody turncoats. She loved her home and seized every opportunity to point out to us how poorly the rest of the world measured up to the Mother Land.

This vegemite-packing young lady set about teaching us the wonders of her tiny island nation, New Zealand, the remote neighbor of Australia and Tasmania. She shared the unique appreciation of the sludge, vegemite, that all New Zealanders not only love the taste of, but also carry as a form of identification. I've been told that if a Kiwi loses their passport, they need only to march into an embassy, sing the national anthem, and show a jar of vegemite, and a new passport will be issued on the spot.

I tried the thick tar-like goop on bread and quite liked it. This pleased Calie to no end until I pointed out, "Oh, it's made by Kraft!" That's right, the American company Kraft makes vegemite.

Calie snatched the sacred jar from my grip muttering something about "freaking American world domination," or something to that effect. Calie taught us that New Zealand has no snakes, alligators, bears, kangaroos, or house trailers, and further more, New Zealand has beautiful tiny alpine mountains, primordial forests, and endless seashores. In other words, her homeland has all the world's good stuff and none of the bad. Of course, all that is found in the South Island. Our first lesson about the mini-continent was…South Island, GOOD, North Island BAD. Never mind that Auckland, the capital, was in the North Island.

She was a strong independent woman who took no crap without returning a double dose back to the crap giver. It was great fun to witness how little patience she had for the world's lack of knowledge of her beloved homeland.

Often upon an introduction, someone meeting Calie for the first time might say, "Oh, you're from New Zealand? Where they have kangaroos?"

With perfect posture and a brilliant smile, she would reply, "No, you are probably confusing us with Rorotonga, but that's quite understandable now that I have become more familiar with the American educational system."

We really liked Calie but feared her rejection of all things American also meant a rejection of Frasers. She continued to educate us, though. She revealed the New Zealand secret to making a great hamburger. Garnish it with beet root and pineapple. Also, the best adult beverages are mixed with lemon, lime and bitters.

Despite having been handicapped by the American educational deficiency, we were good students. Then something interesting began to happen. Calie became infected with the US. She angrily denied it at first, but gradually she started coming over to the dark side, and by the end of her stay, she was a pretty committed American girl.

Even though Calie was best friends with Kim, the very religious Seventh Day Adventist, Calie was the polar opposite. And by polar opposite, I mean she ate meat, drank all things alcohol, and subscribed to no religious beliefs, at least none that were visible. She could party with the best of them, which was not to say that Kim couldn't party right alongside Calie. She just did it without the assistance of alcohol.

Calie was with us for most of a year, and that year ended all too soon. She has remained a dear friend to this day, and has blown her savings on several occasions visiting us here in the good old USA. At the end of her stay, Calie hooked us up with Karen.

Karen was number three and just as different from number two as number two was from number one. Karen was quiet, polite, and a voracious reader. She read a book a day, start to finish, usually laying facedown on the couch. Her second favorite activity was watching the television series Weird Science 2000 while laughing almost to the point of needing medical attention.

Karen was deathly afraid of moths. Who knew moths could cause a full-blown panic attack? In Karen's case, it could happen wherever, whenever. It was not good to be in a confined space with her when one of the benign creatures came fluttering into the scene. The family broke standard Fraser protocol of torturing someone with their phobias with Karen. Her hyper level of panic at the sight of a moth, albeit hilarious, was dangerous to anyone within a quarter mile.

Karen was injury prone, which was not funny. On her first day in the states she had a mishap that exceeded the boo-boo level. Americans need to know that a plane trip from New Zealand can last anywhere from eighteen to twenty-four hours, so when a Kiwi arrives in the states, a few days set aside for a system adjustment is required if not requested.

After basic greetings and orientation, Karen asked to take our two pretty big Golden Retrievers on a walk on the beach. It was Karen's first afternoon here, so I leashed them up and warned her that they were pullers, especially when they knew a beach trip was imminent. She looked at me with a tilted head, trying to comprehend the stupidity of an American, as she said with incredible composure and politeness, "I'm certain I will do quite well, thank you." That was the moment they launched off the deck.

The leash was somehow wrapped around her pinkie, and when the full velocity and combined weight of two Goldens snapped the leashes taut, the pinkie broke in the most ghastly of fashions. It stuck out at a right angle to her hand. She stared at it in disbelief.

We had two dilemmas now. Dogs were gone, off to God knows where, and Karen appeared to be going into shock. We sat her down before she could be claimed by gravity and ran for the dogs. Actually, Debbie and the girls ran for the dogs while I loaded Karen in the car and headed out to find a doctor who could reset the pinkie.

A doc-in-a-box medical office took us right away.

"I couldn't possibly begin to set a break like this," the horrified doctor informed us. He called it a "green twig" fracture, meaning that it was splintered and would require surgery. He packaged us up and sent us to an orthopedic surgeon, who also took us right away. It was another miracle because just a few short hours later, he had operated on her hand, set the fracture and put her in a hard plaster cast from hand to elbow. The cast did leave her thumb free for whatever a thumb could contribute to the quality of life. So went Karen's welcome to America.

Come to find out her dad, an ex-cop nicknamed Cracker, was making a go of it in the meat pie business. First, I had to know the origin of the name Cracker. That word is often used to describe white southerners, and not in a good way. Naturally, I had to know, what's with the racist handle? She told me that it came from his gift for cracking cases, and perhaps the skulls of the criminal elements he dealt with, but not like a soda cracker, or whip cracker, as is implied in the good old US of A.

Second in lineage of importance was "What is a meat pie?" This particularly intrigued me, a proud carnivore with eight grills. What could this meat delivery system be? Karen said it was a meat concoction wrapped in a pastry, much like an apple turnover without the apple. She told us they were quite popular in New Zealand and that they are sold in gas stations as a pre-packaged microwaveable item. She said her dad had been making them primarily as a side business—that was until his product took off, requiring him to hang up his case-cracking police job and get cracking on becoming the Donald Trump of meat pies. I liked this guy. I never met the guy, but I sure did like his story.

Karen's time with us came to an end all too soon. She was supremely likable and fun. Before she left us, she had a visit from her mother and sister. All of the girls had their families visit while they stayed with us, which we greatly enjoyed.

We learned that most New Zealanders looked down on Americans a little, although they attempted to hide their disdain just enough to escape our limited ability of comprehension. This slight snobbery was typical of all the visiting New Zealanders, so it was no longer a surprise or an issue when Karen's kin were the same. Besides, all of them openly admitted that they consider the French the most loathsome life form, so at least we were not at the bottom of the barrel.

Karen's Mom and sister were nice, but they were more than a little hard on her. She was so excited for their visit, and had talked of nothing else for weeks to show them her new bold life in the US. But they weren't particularly impressed with America or the Frasers, and they seemed to enjoy making Karen the butt of little inside jokes and sarcastic remarks. This banter had a bit of a cruel edge to it and seemed to come quite naturally to the pair. I suspected Karen had already had a lifetime of this, to such an extent the family may have lost awareness of their hurtful behavior.

When a family from the top down tolerates and perpetuates the making of sport of one of the kids, it becomes such an effortless part of the group personality. I would imagine if they were to read this that they would call me a "dirty American liar." Oh, wait, they already called me that, so maybe it would be a "low down, stinking American liar!"

I hurt a little bit for Karen because with her intellect and sensitivity, none of it snuck past her. She lovingly tolerated their role as family elitists with style and understanding.

Karen hooked us up with Geraldine, the last one of the bunch from down under who stayed with us. And like the first three, she won our hearts in her own special way. Geraldine ultimately returned to the South Island, attended medical school, and became a doctor, dedicated to treating the peculiar ailments of people who live in a country where water spins backwards down the drain, winter is summer, cars drive on the left side, salad comes after the meal and the fork is used upside down. I wouldn't presume to know how they use a shovel.

Geraldine was cool, calm, collected and well suited to look after kids while soaking up Americana—unless she was faking it. Her honest easy smile and comfortable nature told us otherwise. She truly enjoyed her stay in the US. Like all the girls, she also took the opportunity to visit the motherland, England. The trek to the US for a New Zee was considered a life experience with an agenda, one that including several must-sees. New York City topped the list with a trip to Disney squeezed in somewhere. Proximity to the UK made Euro trekking too tantalizing to resist.

Fit, like a distance runner sporting a turquoise, floral tattoo armband, and equipped with razor sharp wit, Geraldine was supremely up to the task of outfoxing two hooligans, ages fifteen and nine. Geraldine was last in the line-up. By this time, our kids were nanny-savvy. The girls thought they knew how to get over a newbie. For most twenty-three year olds, having no kid-rearing experience and being the fourth nanny in three years would be a lost cause. Our kids, whom I love most in the whole world, were skilled con artists. They could bamboozle a nervous nanny out of any thing. Not Geraldine. Geraldine ran the show and seemed to have fun doing it. She never raised her voice and always smiled. She was never mean, though we did discover that she had a severe handicap.

Her right foot was apparently of a very high bone density, and therefore, massively heavy, like lead or krypton, causing the accelerator pedal on any car she happened to be driving to be depressed right to the floor. She drove fast. We named her the "G-force." Thank God we had a Honda CRV and a Volvo, not necessarily super fast cars, although she did manage to get our Volvo up to ninety-three mph on I-95, provoking a local cop to ignore her irresistible smile and cool New Zee accent. He gave her a five hundred dollar speeding ticket and me my very first criminal traffic case.

Thankfully, her fast driving didn't cause any harm. We were grateful for the time she spent with us. We bid farewell to Geraldine, the last of the New Zealanders at the end of the summer of 2000. We had a wonderful knowledge of the little island nation and its good people given to us by the four great girls who stayed with us: Kim, Calie, Karen, and Geraldine. We wish them all the best the southern hemisphere has to offer, and hope their memories of the Fraser household are fond ones.

CHAPTER TWENTY-NINE

The Homefront

While I had settled into a somewhat comfortable routine and home was good, Debbie was another story.

Debbie had managed our business office for years. She knew the paperwork inside and out. She was efficient, timely and meticulous in every detail. By nature, a nice person, kind to a fault, small in stature, gigantic in character, easily intimidated, completely trusting, terminally trustworthy, that's Debbie. She possessed the same qualities God listed for his Archangel when he said "Go to earth and find a woman to carry and care for my Son until he can fulfill my prophecy and bring goodness to all mankind. And don't mess this one up!"

However, I'm pretty sure if God needed someone to look after His construction business, the personnel prerequisite would have been somewhat different. "Go down and find me a business manager. Honesty is a plus, sure that's great, but this guy has to be the biggest, meanest SOB in the neighborhood. David killed Goliath, or he'd been a good one. Look around and see if Goliath has any unemployed relatives. And don't mess this up!"

I say this because I have learned that in business, major screwings come when you can least stand them, and they come at the hands of those you've trusted the most. And come they did. In droves. Poor Debbie.

We weren't stupid. We knew Debbie couldn't be thrown to the wolves in my absence. She needed help. I needed help. No one can run a business without some helpful cooperation. Our business was a good place to work. Our employees had had some pretty crappy jobs along the way and seemed to appreciate our happy little world. We had plenty of work, made good money, and let people follow their own path.

The business make-up was nearly all male, nearly all blue-collar. Ten or so field workers, two sales guys, and an office manager lady. We considered most personal friends, especially the sales guys and office manager lady. In fact, we brought them in on the law school decision early on, and they, honest to God, seemed genuinely supportive, even excited about it. I didn't ask why they were excited. I just accepted their backing with joy. It appeared to us they had a surprisingly outright willingness to be a part of the success.

As I said, we weren't stupid, just naïve. I accept that people work to sustain a lifestyle, at least most people. So the idea that anyone owes me, or any other employer, anything more than a job well done is not one I hold near and dear. However, over the years, we operated under the illusion that good people who are treated well would feel obligated to reciprocate in kind.

When we revealed our law school plan, our key personnel gave us a commitment to stay the course while I flew the coop. As I said, they happily jumped on board.

We experienced a few hiccups here and there right off the bat, but for the most part all went, eh, pretty okay. But gradually things began to fray around the edges. The two sales guys decided they hated each other and that one should be the boss over the other, that kind of thing. No big deal if I had been there because I was the boss.

At first, the rivalry wasn't so apparent. In the end, we knew we had flunked business 101 in that I had left behind a power vacuum. Anyone who studies physics knows nature abhors a vacuum, and so does my dog, but that is a different kind of vacuum. Still sucks, though.

The spat between the two sales guys smoldered. I did the old Rodney King thing by saying, "Can't we all get along?" which didn't work for me, either.

Then, for whatever reason, production declined. First, I thought it was a temporary downturn, one that would self-correct. I was wrong. It was a full-blown downward trend. The only thing going up was time on the clock. Meanwhile, payroll was through the roof and our workers didn't respect the sales guys as managers. They knew Debbie's nonexistent field experience would cause her to believe anything they said. Why doubt them? They were our friends.

Our supplies were leaving the warehouse at a rate much higher than the billable work being done. Apparently, we had unearthed a new scientific discovery—our merchandise had the ability to grow legs and run away. Unbelievable!

It became painfully clear that some of our beloved coworkers were stealing from us. Next in the phase of our biz implosion, we noticed our gas charges were double what they had been. Someone was stealing gas. *What's next?*

Well, "what's next" turned out to be two things—contracts vanishing from our files and money missing from our cash drawer. This took place over some time. And for us trusting and disbelieving souls, it took us some time to connect the dots. Once we got enough dots connected, Debbie and I collectively said, "What the heck, how could that be? Is someone actually stealing supplies, gas, money from the cash drawer, and contracts from our file cabinets?"

The answer turned out to be "YES, they were!" With this much going wrong, it could not stay hidden long.

The first tear in the fabric came when one of the trusted sales guys quit without notice. He stomped off in a cloud of bad and uncalled-for treatment aimed at my sweet wife. This left us short-handed, but so be it, people decide to move on.

The second tear we uncovered with the help of the remaining sales guy. This turned out to be the contractor scam, or the stealing of not only contracts, but also the labor, supplies, money, and gas to perform the work.

One of our installers had been coming into the office after hours and taking contracts from our files. Because he worked late and was, well, trusted by us trusting saps, he had possession of a key and the alarm code. After carefully selecting the best contract for his scam, he then contacted the customer, who was always a retail consumer, not the commercial customers who knew our business well. He gave the customer a story, something like we were very busy (which was true), and in order to relieve our backlog, he had permission to do work independently, on the side. He was only trying to help out with the bottlenecked situation.

Then he offered the bait. He said he could do the work right away at a reduced price. And that was all it took to convince a few usually ethical retirees from places like Cincinnati to go for this scam. He had no problem giving a great price break since he was stealing the supplies from our warehouse.

The guy got so brazen that he started doing the jobs during the workweek, on our payroll, using our truck and equipment, and even taking a helper, also on our payroll. To cover his tracks, he'd return to our office late in the day with a story.

Oh, yeah, the truck broke down, or the gutter forming machinery malfunctioned. We understand. Nope. We caught on only after an honest consumer called and told us he suspected we were being robbed. Of course, that was after many thousands of dollars had vanished from our books, but at least we were able to stop the bleeding.

The sad confession I make here is that I did not have the heart to put the guy in jail. I accepted I would never get the money back and I just couldn't live with the thought of putting this bum in prison. I knew his family. They were wonderful people.

The guy had a beautiful wife and two great kids. I'd rather live with the financial loss than with the thought of destroying a family. Something about the concept of Christian kindness and forgiveness rings true, at least it does for us.

Another hurtful aspect of this letdown was that I really liked the guy. I supported him through a number of personal and financial issues that helped him get back on his feet. Debbie and I had a lot on our plate, too much actually, and the prospect of being involved in what would surely be a protracted criminal prosecution as witnesses—not just us, but many of our employees and customers also—that thought was unsettling. Pursuing this would be too costly, and ultimately, the effort and time involved would have taken our eyes off the prize, so we decided to leave it in God's hands. Oddly enough, in an earlier conversation with our thief, back when we trusted and believed in him, he shared his belief that "kindness is perceived as weakness." Guess he was right.

Next, we uncovered the gas scam.

Three brothers worked in a crew together. We learned that when they went to the gas station to fill up the company trucks using the company credit card to pay, their wives would meet at the station in their family cars. The wives lined up right behind the company truck so that when the company truck was full and pulled forward, the family car pulled in its place and receive a tank of gas on the same charge.

This scam wasn't so difficult to discover. Our gas bill doubled. A little research told us we didn't have any pickups with fifty-gallon tanks, so we followed the crews to the station and witnessed the scam.

I cannot describe the range of emotions I felt as I sat in my car across the street from the gas station, slumped down in the seat like a detective, watching this betrayal of trust. We trusted these guys with our business and reputation. Their families, wives and kids, were in the cars, smiling and happy accomplices. One of the guys brought soft drinks and sweet rolls out for everyone to enjoy. I suppose they were on the house, too.

I watched three families turn into thieves before my eyes, trading their character and reputations for some snacks and some gas. I was angry and deeply disappointed. I even began to doubt my ability to judge people. Everything bombarded me all at once. I called the station attendant to verify the charge was placed all on one credit card, then phoned the men and asked them to return to the office. Change of plans. When they rolled back in, all smiles, I collected theirs keys and company Shell card and informed them their employment was concluded.

Many years earlier, working for a large, heartless corporation, I had learned in the loathsome task of terminating someone's employment to never give a reason, just thanks and best wishes for the future. I wanted to break my rule in this case with these three thugs who had just robbed me and involved their families in a criminal enterprise, but I didn't. They were surprised but at the same time kind of knew what this was about. They might not have been exactly sure, but they were definitely too chicken to ask.

One of the brothers said, "Mister Denny," calling me by an archaic form of respect, which I hate, "We got no way home 'til five o'clock. Whad we gonna do?"

"Call your wives. I bet they've got plenty of gas in the car. They can come get you." They wandered out of my office building, crossed the parking lot, and waited by the side of the street until the blue minivan, still loaded with kids and my gas, pulled up and carried the criminals away from my life.

Next, in the succession of Fraser butt-kickings, the other sales guy quit. The only outside sales guy we had walked in one day, said he had a great job offer and was moving on. He collected his kids' pictures and left the building. With that resignation, Debbie was left with no sales force to bring in work, almost no work force to do the work, and no husband to help run things. Emotionally, we were at the bottom of the barrel.

We coped with these disasters the best we could but the stress on Debbie was far too much. We were in a pickle, like when someone swimming the English Channel gets halfway and realizes they don't have strength to make it, that kind of a pickle. So, here we were, halfway across the channel and everything went to hell.

Faith and untapped strength had to come to the rescue, there wasn't much else. The people we were counting on had abandoned us, so it was just Debbie and me. I offered to give up on this stupid law school thing, but Debbie wouldn't hear of it. "We'll find a way to do this together," she said.

And to some extent we did, but the cost of dollars and emotional stress was unbelievably high. What can you do when you're halfway across the English Channel and you don't have the strength to make it to the other side, you don't have the strength to go back, your life jacket is made of bloody meat, and there is a shark convention going on? What can you do when there are no right answers and nothing but wrong answers and no one to turn to? You can ask God to guide you through one more mess, which is what we did, and what God did for us.

Of course, like in any great thriller, there was plenty more darkness before the dawn. Not only was business going to hell, people jumping ship, thieves having a hay day, then the business scammers showed up. The endless stream of hucksters pulling sales scams by phone—the toner people, safety enforcement people, supply people—all of them selling junk marked up above retail, and all of them swearing I had bought stuff from them in the past. Debbie was unprepared for these unethical scammers.

On top of that, in came the business broker con artist who promised he could sell the business for an unbelievable price. All that was needed was a check to cover the cost of an appraisal, which had to happen before they could list the business for sale to their waiting pool of ready cash buyers.

Oh, yeah, the idea of selling our business for enough money to live on until I struck it rich as a lawyer appealed to Debbie. She was heartbroken when I told her that this "too good to be true" deal was, in fact, too good to be true. No legitimate business brokers operated that way. I got hold of the bastard that conned her out of our dwindling resources and made him return the money.

Poor Debbie was beside herself. The fact that she fell for that one confirmed the proverb that "a drowning man will grab the blade of a sword." She must have wondered if there was a single honest person left on earth. I did too, for that matter.

Somehow, we got past all of this. How Debbie survived, I will never know. Her strength was greater than anyone could imagine. Somehow, we made our business work and kept our family and friends from knowing the real truth of the nightmare we were living. I say "we," when in reality it was Debbie. I was in Columbia enjoying an academic vacation while she swam the English Channel during Shark Week.

Over the years, people have sought me out to tell me their dreams of going back to school for one thing or another, but no one has ever professed a dream of working their ass off so their spouse could go off to follow their elusive dream. I'm not sharing this looking for a pity party. I'm simply telling the facts of the matter. To be fair, our business had some good and loyal employees who did not abandon or rob us. I prefer to call them coworkers or friends rather than employees. There was no escaping the fact that we were abandoned by a couple of key people and had lost many thousands of dollars due to thievery. Truthfully, we were lucky a few stayed the course and upon that decent, humble bunch of good people, we slowly rebuilt our business. We will always be grateful for their loyalty and friendship.

I have searched my ragged soul many times trying to determine what it is about human nature that causes otherwise good people to do bad things to those who are at their most vulnerable. I have tried to shoehorn it into the axiom "kindness equals weakness," or "nature abhors a vacuum," or my bad management, or the statement my absence must have made to a group of workers who saw me leave in search of something bigger and better. I don't know "WHY," but I will accept the blame. I'm a dad, and we get blamed for most everything. Life is so damn full of these axiomatic lessons. Why do we have to climb mountains just to see the beauty of the land below? Ask Beck Weathers. His answer will be better than mine.

By October, I was metaphorically out of diapers and about ready to take the training wheels off. This law school thing was just another ten-hour a day job. Much of the jitters had melted away. I had been singled out for humiliation in class a few times and had survived. I chatted with a couple friends about the enigma of the law, which was helpful because I was still trying to make sense of it. I had assumed there must be a rational, common sense basis to all things legal. There wasn't, but I didn't know that yet. I had not yet learned that the legal philosophy is simple. Legal scholars take really simple issues and turn them into really complex issues so that regular people have to hire lawyers. Ain't it grand?

Bottom line, October started out to be a good month. I was noticeably more comfortable in school. The family was good and weekends were great. I turned forty-nine that October. Business sucked, but that was okay. Everything can't be perfect all the time, in life or business.

I developed a business theory, perhaps worthy of the attention of the Wharton School of Business. Business is like a four-legged table. One leg is you, one leg is selling, one leg is servicing or producing, or delivering what you sold. The last leg, and of equal importance, is getting paid. My belief is that all four legs don't have to work well to enjoy success.

Let's assume you are constant in the equation, then it's up to two of the other three legs to stand up. If one leg goes to hell, you can still balance the table with some finesse. Sales can be good, but production and collections can be off but the table stands, albeit a little wobbly. Production can be great while sales and collections are having a hard time but the table stands. Collection can be good, but sales and production are off, and the table stands. However, when sales, production and collections all suck, you better run for the hills, lest ye be squished by a table.

My life had found a rhythm in the first half of the first semester, the business had not disintegrated yet, and school was working out, somewhat. For a while, it looked like we might make it. The only major stress looming like a black cloud on the horizon was the post Thanksgiving feared exams.

October turned out to be the calm before the first big law school tsunami.

CHAPTER THIRTY

The Call

When the phone rings at three in the morning, it's never good. I said "hello" trying to sound awake and knowing deep inside the call was bad. It's three in the morning; nobody's calling to chat.

My mind began the race through all the possible tragedies. Was a kid hurt, or worse? My heart was racing. Debbie was on the other end, fully awake, speaking quietly.

"I got a call from the hospital in Atlanta. Your father has passed away. I'm so sorry. He went in for a test, and during the night, he had a heart attack. They said he went in his sleep."

Sitting on the edge of the bed, holding the cell phone to my ear, I couldn't react. The message seemed so final. I had never had someone close just vanish from my life. There had always been a health decline or sickness, like with my mother. With my mother, there was time to adjust to the reality. We had weeks to be a part of her battle with cancer. We could do things. We could wage war to keep her alive. But with this phone call, I had to absorb the fact that my father, who was alive and fine when I went to bed in my hotel room, was gone from this earth. No chance for a goodbye, no last visit, he was already gone. My overwhelming instinct was to get it in gear and do something to change the course of events, but that urge was completely derailed with the reality of his passing.

I had to talk to Debbie because she was there, on the line. I couldn't sit there in silence. When a person talks to you, you are supposed to say something back, but I honestly didn't know what to say. As vivid as my recollection is of this particular call—the lamp by the bed, the flip phone, Debbie's words—I cannot for the life of me remember what I said.

I'm certain we must have discussed what we needed to do, who would make which arrangements, what I would have to pack, who would need to know what, etc. These are the things talked about when death happens, so we must have spoken of these things. I know we made plans to get to Atlanta. I was in Columbia, Debbie and the kids were in Hilton Head, and Atlanta was in Georgia. My father's body was likely being transported to the funeral home, the very same funeral home that, years earlier, had buried my mother, then my sister. I knew the place all too well.

The sense of urgency was overwhelming but there was no actual emergency. He was gone. Nothing could be accomplished by a middle of the night race to Atlanta. The process could be started in the morning. A call to one of my cousins activated the family grapevine. Debbie placed the call early enough to start the process before the workday, but not so early as to wake people. Of my father's nine siblings and dozens of nieces and nephews, many had been lost to tragedy. An informal and efficient tragedy telegraph-like system had all fifty or sixty of them alerted by noon. My only job was to get my numb self to Hilton Head by three o'clock. Debbie would have the car packed and kids ready for our trip to Atlanta.

The plan was that by seven that night, I would take control of this lonely business of burying family, something most every adult learns to work through. You have to meet with the funeral director, set a time and date for service, answer numerous calls coming in from family members, go through the same sad news over and over.

"He died in his sleep. Yes, he was a great guy. I'm told it was very peaceful. Just slipped away. Yes, we'll all miss him. The service is in Atlanta on Friday. Sure, I understand you're busy. You'll be with us in spirit. I know you'd really like to come. We understand. He loved you and we love you, too. Thanks for calling."

A three o'clock departure time left me with time on my hands. Sleep wasn't an option. Strange as it might sound, I decided to sit through my morning classes before heading back to Hilton Head. For whatever reason, I decided to go by Dr. Bond's office before class, since his was first up. I told him of my father's passing, why I'm not sure, but maybe I was hoping he'd leave me alone for the day.

He, of course, called on me. I truly didn't know what to think of this guy, still don't. Was he a genius, sadist, wise man, or just a jerk? I just didn't know. I stood up to answer his question and he threw me a soft ball, something fairly easy. Having studied the material seemingly years ago, even though it was the night before, I was somewhat prepared and did okay. He let me off without further interrogation, so I guess this was his version of kindness.

Realizing how stupid it was to sit in class, I packed for the drive to Hilton Head. I dreaded the drive, all alone, with time to think about how I was such a lousy kid to my father. Mercifully, my cell phone began to light up with calls from family, saving me from the self-incriminating beating I was certain to give myself.

The trip to Atlanta was quiet. Debbie and I have always kept our emotions in check, away from center stage and never in front of our kids. We don't want the kids to feel insecure. I know there are differing opinions on grown-ups showing emotions, and some would even say that not having a breakdown at every bump in the road is deceptive and gives the wrong impression of pain and grief. We let our kids know when we're experiencing pain and sadness, however, we focus on getting through whatever life throws at us. The kids loved their Papa, as did we, so our trip was quiet, as was our evening in Atlanta. We were bracing for the next morning.

We found the funeral home at nine o'clock. It was just the four of us. We would connect with Dad's wife later in the morning. To begin the process, we needed to speak with the funeral director. Unfortunately, I knew the funeral home all too well. They had taken care of my mother's services nine years earlier, and more recently, had seen to the last affairs for my sister three years earlier.

Funeral directors are a special breed. Our guy was right out of the quiet, somber, and respectful mold. Helpful and caring to a mournful extent, gray suit, white shirt, maroon tie with small blue dots, matching pocket square, rotary lapel pin, onyx tie tack with matching cufflinks, and an Omega watch to enjoy his wealth without over flaunting. A true professional, he guided us, the zombie family, through the process of submitting obituaries, choosing hymns, urns, dates, times, etc. There must be a test for them like law school, but instead of the LSAT, their test would likely be called the LAST.

The system was good for me, a dad. Most non-dads don't understand that the act of doing things is a dad's hiding place. As long as we're doing things, we can't dwell too much on thoughts that might haunt us. It's been our trick since we dropped from the trees, or crawled from the sea, or God made us out of mud. Focusing on decisions is what kept my thoughts at bay. Fond memories and guilt were waiting patiently nearby, like Jack London's wolves outside the circle of campfire light. Quietly, in the dark, my thoughts watched over me, knowing they would eventually have alone time with me.

I asked our thoughtful helper if my dad had made it to the funeral home. Dad had arrived overnight. I asked if we could see him. I was thinking about how I couldn't have been by his side for that lonely trip in the back of a hospital van. Slightly flustered, the funeral director said, "I'll go see. Since it's a cremation, you understand, we have not prepared as we do for a casket viewing." He left us awkwardly alone and silent until he returned. "You can follow me. We brought him to one of our family rooms just down the hall. Right this way."

We followed him down a long corridor. The building was built to Atlanta-scale. It could handle a lot of grieving. The hall was wide like in a grand hotel with floral print burgundy carpet, raised panel white wainscoting, waist-high up the wall, and ornate brass and glass sconces hung on elegant blue floral wallpaper. A grand arched window at the far end of the hall cast shafts of Atlanta sun onto the floor, giving the place a holy brightness, or a light we were all walking toward. The imagery was impossible to ignore. After all, this was a place of transitioning from life to whatever is next after death.

He stopped at a door halfway down the corridor, placed his hand on the doorknob and paused. "Now remember, we haven't fixed…you know, we haven't taken our usual care."

I forgave him with a nod. Now his concern seemed more genuine, not so much for our loss, but for the reputation of his death enterprise that afforded him the slight indulgence of an Omega watch. With that assurance, he opened the door into a nearly empty room save for chairs pushed off to the perimeter walls, waiting for a later arrangement. Across the room was a gurney, and on it was a man with a sheet neatly pulled up and folded over just under his chin. He lay flat on his back, sleeping. My father. We were scared to approach.

"Please feel free to take all the time you need," the director said as he ever so gently closed the door on his way out.

Lying peacefully with a pillow under his head, Dad looked at ease, asleep even, except for the stillness that only comes with death. I had not seen him in three months. He had a small bruise on his forehead and had grown a bit of a beard. He had died alone in a hospital with no one by his side. Newspaper obituaries love to say the deceased died surrounded by family. This man died alone with no one to hold his hand, no one to thank him for being a good man, and no one to say "I love you."

Debbie, Page, Lizzi, and I stood silently by the gurney. We didn't know what to do. I secretly envied people whose emotions flow easily. Mine were kept in a straight jacket, buckled tight, gagged, and locked deep inside the basement of my soul. We stood there until it became awkward. I tried to mumble something though I can't remember what I said. I feel certain it was something shallow and inadequate. The family decided to leave me alone by the side of this man who so truly deserved a better son.

The faint hint of carpet deodorizer hung the air. Floor to ceiling paned windows flanked the outside wall with lace curtains draped off to the jambs, allowing the searing Atlanta sun to shine brilliant rectangles halfway across the floor. And there we were, in this big empty room, which would later hold another gathering of grief, or what is now called a celebration of life.

For the time being, the vast room accommodated a private ceremony for two. Forty years earlier, the two in attendance could have talked endlessly about any subject that may come up between a father and son, but somewhere along the way, they lost that artful conversation, that comfort, that closeness. *God, is there anything nearby that I could work on, that I could fix, preferably something difficult requiring my complete focus?* I didn't want to think. My only job this day was to stand there not knowing what to say to someone who could not hear. The irony.

At twenty-one, this guy Denson takes a wife of sixteen. She actually turned seventeen the very next day, but they loved to joke about his robbing the cradle. Margaret Elizabeth Patterson graduated the eleventh grade in June of 1933, during the Great Depression in the Deep South. She and my father had met only a few months earlier and shared whatever kind of romance could be had in those hard times between great wars.

August after her graduation, my mother piled in a Model T (or was it a Model A, I forget), and ran off to marry Denson Harris Fraser, Sr. They were married before a justice of the peace and only had one picture taken of them looking out the back window of the black Ford that took them off to their futures. My mother was a kind and gentle soul. She was known as "Little Pat" by the locals who decided to name her after her violent and soon-to-be chronic alcoholic Irish father, Clyde Patterson. She escaped a violent household to join up with my father and his clan.

He, at twenty-one, had long since abandoned his plan to go to college and dedicated himself to being the patriarch, breadwinner and surrogate dad of his widowed mother and seven of his brothers and sisters. His older sister, Grace, had married an affluent but much older Texan. She was off living her dream. His older brother, George, graduated the US Naval

Academy at Annapolis and was beginning the career that would later retire him as an Admiral.

My father was not a man who pondered life's choices and missed opportunities. He had a widowed mother in poor health, seven brothers and sisters, ranging in age from two to seventeen. His job was to care for the needs of his family, and he set about doing it without complaint and with pride.

He looked after his mother until her death twenty-five years later. He raised six of the youngest siblings as well as my mother's younger sister as his own. Later, as various family problems multiplied, he took in the children of siblings, my cousins. He also took in my mother's two elderly old maiden aunts. These ladies had given my mother much needed shelter when things were bad in her childhood home. And yes, he even took in the full-blown drunken and dying Pat Patterson himself when his disease would no longer permit him to safely live alone.

Denson and Pat wanted kids of their own but they did not come easily. Three late-term miscarriages nearly ended their hopes of ever having children, but they kept at it. And then, right after WWII came, the long prayed-for pregnancy produced a baby girl, Margaret Lynn, who was born with a spinal defect that claimed her life just two months later.

God only knows why they tried again, but guess I should be glad they did. Two years later I came on the scene, healthy and sort of normal. Five years later came my sister Margaret Lynn (the second) who was born just fine, also healthy, and sort of normal. Finally, Denson and Pat Fraser had their own little family to merge with the rest of the Fraser and Patterson menagerie.

The crowd had thinned a little by my arrival. The household was down to my maternal grandfather, my paternal grandmother, my mother's sister Jo, and my maternal aunt

Alice. We soon lost my grandmother and grandfather, but gained my cousin Debbie whose mother was going through a rough patch. There were many others along the way, too. Denson Fraser took 'em all in, clothed, loved, fed, and even gave allowances to these people.

He never took a thing in return, not a dime, wouldn't hear of it. Once he took in a batch of cousins from Orangeburg whose parents were having difficulty, and not liking the way they came dressed, he threw all their clothes away and bought them all new ones. He was truly devoted to being the guy who took in any family member or friend who needed a safe place to live.

As far as I know, young Denson Fraser was a model child. The Fraser brothers, namely my father's dad and his brothers, were in the timber and sawmill business in west Louisiana and east Texas. They lived on large remote tracks of land, far from anywhere, cutting and milling timber. They were hard working, self-sufficient country people.

Little Denson was an excellent student, only making one "B" in life, and that "B" earned him a whipping. He took great pride in being the youngest Eagle Scout in Louisiana at the time and boasted that he had to travel sixty miles to attend the scout meetings. He earned all twenty-one of the necessary merit badges for his Eagle badge in less than three years. He kept the sash with the seven rows of three merit badges sewn neatly, and the coveted Eagle Scout badge pinned at the top. Imagine how proud he must have been when I quit scouting just short of earning the same honor because of more pressing teenage matters. He never said a word. He just accepted that I was not cut of the same cloth.

After forty years of marriage involving caring for the needs of so many people and accepting the financial burden so willingly of their healthcare and schooling, Pat and Denson

Fraser finally retired on nothing more than social security. For the first time in their lives, they got to live alone in their modest home. In fact, they had a few good years to themselves.

Then Pat's cancer claimed her life. Then Lynn's liver failure claimed hers. And then the man who didn't get to go to college, the one who took care of everyone but himself, slipped quietly from this world. And as he promised so many times, no one had to take care of him.

There we were in the room, just the two of us. With the realization that any chance I had to make things right with him was gone, I looked down at the white sheet and saw my hand had come to rest on his, the very one I had held long ago with such fondness before we grew apart.

I gave him a kiss on the forehead and said, "I love you."

I desperately wished I had not been so stingy with those words for so many years. He deserved much better.

CHAPTER THIRTY-ONE

The Company Man

I left the enormous room with my father laying on the gurney. I couldn't stay there with the memories and guilt. He would be wheeled off to the place where they burn bodies, yet another trip he'd make alone.

Cremation has always seemed such a practical thing. At the time, it didn't feel right, it just didn't. What a lousy feeling. Upon cremation, a person's time on earth, from beginning to end, is gone. It's like they never existed. I used to have all the answers, but not this day. I was fresh out of answers. While they cremated the man who wanted to go to college but didn't, his son, whom he put through college, was writing his eulogy. The irony. I had kind of hoped my father would be proud of me becoming a lawyer. I mean, isn't that what every parent wants? Don't parents dream of their kid becoming a doctor or lawyer? Isn't that the same as an Eagle Scout badge for grown-ups?

It wasn't much of a funeral service. Dad didn't have a church in Atlanta so we held the service in the funeral home's chapel. It was nice of the director to arrange for a minister to do the religious part of the service—that's what everyone expected. The personal part was left up to me.

After my mother died, my father moved to a retirement home in Atlanta to be near Lynn. There, he remarried at eighty-three, so we had to help the new wife, Grace, through the service. A few people who knew him from the retirement home came to the funeral as well as some of Grace's relatives. A few of my cousins, maybe a dozen, also made the trip. Although quite a few siblings had passed on, most of my blood relatives, the ones who had at one time or another lived with us, were in attendance. I was glad they came.

I tried to do a good job of the eulogy. I had no problems being up in front of a group. I had problems when it was all over. No more Mom, sister, or Dad. All three had been buried or cremated by this funeral home.

That evening we went to dinner with the new wife, Grace, and her son. Grace had survived an abusive husband, thankfully lost along the way to divorce or death, I'm not sure which it was. Her daughter, the love of her life, followed her profession, becoming a nurse at Emory only to die at thirty from an infection picked up during a routine appendectomy. Her son lived the difficult life of a chronic alcoholic. He dried out for the umpteenth time at her expense and with her hopes and prayers that this time would be the time he beat the disease, and he was there to support her through the loss of the first man she loved who wasn't mean to her.

At dinner, I ordered a mixed drink even though I knew better. I know alcoholism; I've lived around it all my life. Debbie and I have it on both sides of our families. My sister died of complications related to alcohol abuse. My mother, wonderful as she was, suffered with it off and on, mostly on. Alcoholism robbed her of parts of her life. My drunken violent grandfather, Pat Patterson, brought it into our home in the most frightening of ways.

My dad, God bless him, was certain he could lecture long and loud enough to make anyone stop drinking, but he'd met his match with that mean Irishman, Clyde Patterson. As a little kid, I witnessed dad's lectures, some of which were real doozies.

My grandfather was a stealthy and creative drunk. He had a small pension from Southern Bell and received some social security, which wasn't much. The program was relatively new. His retirement money liquefied quickly, usually carrying him for only half the month. Of course, he only had to buy booze. The rest of his living expenses were on us, or, I should say, on my father.

The last two weeks of the month, he resorted to the survival skills of an addict. My coin collection disappeared first, then my sister's silver dollar, then the piggy bank. Loose change vanished from dressers, wallets raided. Anything of value that would not be immediately missed disappeared. My grandfather was a regular at our town's one and only pawn shop, known on a first name basis, of course.

My father had to work, which afforded Gramps twelve creative hours to plan his next buy. He preferred the pocket-sized half-pint, which could be hidden most anywhere—under sofa cushions, closets, shoeboxes, even behind the toilet.

As a plus, a half-pint could be guzzled in a single swig, so when the infraction had been discovered and the Denson Fraser hundred-decibel lecture descended upon him, gramps was grooving on a buzz that no one could take away.

My father once said "words bounce off him like bullets off Superman." I thought the Superman analogy was both cool and ironic. Superman, the television series was on the air and that same year, the star of the show, George Something-Or-

Other, committed suicide—gun to the temple. To us kids of the fifties, it seemed impossible that Superman could shoot himself.

My father never gave up believing his lecture therapy would eventually triumph. Back then, alcoholism was considered little more than a bad habit any person of character could quit if they wanted to. So the war waged on while grandfather slowly gave in to cirrhosis of the liver, which in a few slow and painful years mercifully ended his battle with the bottle and that part of the lecture series.

All that to say there was no explanation or excuse for ordering a drink at dinner in front of a recovering alcoholic. Insensitivity, selfishness, indifference. Who knows? As soon as I placed the order for a Jack and ginger, the stepbrother I had met for the first time four hours earlier chimed in, "I think I'll have one, too."

Glancing at Grace, I saw pain. I felt so bad. She told me later that this kicked off a binge episode that took him to his next rehab experience.

I never saw Grace's son again. I couldn't imagine feeling worse on that day, but by managing to screw this poor woman's life up a little bit more and delivering a little more pain to such an uncomplicated person who just wanted to love my father for a few good years, I plummeted to a lower state of misery.

Grace had lost a husband and a son that day. I needed to get home to my power tools. I had things to run, things to build, a lawn to mow and law school to figure out.

Leaving the grip of Emory Hospital, the funeral home, and Atlanta, the town that had killed off my mother, my sister, and now my dad, was therapeutic. Finding our way back to I-75 was a relief. Missed opportunities, laziness, and lack of compassion tend to produce guilt in most kids at some point, and I seemed to have more than my fair share.

And because I have a conscience that is aware of all my deep dark secrets, I recognized that I had done a half-assed job of being a good kid. Once I drove away from the I-20 mega-beltway, away from the killing fields that squeezed the evil honeysuckle goo out of Atlanta, a more rational perspective began to incubate within me.

I wasn't the best kid, nobody could argue against that notion, but I was far from the worst. In fact, there were times when, as a teenager, I actually shined. I played a part in handling the crisis that developed in our household whilst my dad worked far, far away from home. I dealt with things that were horrific in nature. Yep, the kid who dropped out of Boy Scouts, the terminally lazy teenager who cut school like a chainsaw and dreamed of naked girls constantly, actually manned up and took control.

I was involved in situations no teenage kid should ever have to handle. Although these stories would make a bestselling author out of me, they are personal and painful, and the only trip they are going to take is with me to the grave.

My father was a good son and a good man—by anyone's standard. He really did sacrifice his dreams to do the right thing, but he wasn't perfect either. Out of self-imposed necessity caused by the brood he chose to take care of, he had to travel the world over to make a living that no small southern town could offer someone not in the fraternity of the landed gentry. While Dad roamed the world seeking money to satisfy his insatiable need to take care of his extended family, the actual taking care part of taking care of the family fell to my mother. During her occasional breakdowns from living a thankless life as a round-the-clock caregiver to the old and infirm who had moved in to die in our home, I was allotted the job along with all its various tasks.

My father was the hardest working man I have ever known. Literally, no joke, no exaggeration, he was the paragon of working men. In fact, in my fifty years of knowing him, I rarely saw him awake and not working. That only changed when he was eighty, blind, and dragging a bottle of oxygen. At that point, he couldn't do much more than sit around the retirement home.

In those other forty-five years I can account for, Dad was working, eating, or sleeping. And he only did the last two so he could do the first. For at least ten years, I was the apple of his eye, but that apple morphed into a prune when my teenage years hit. My sister, Lynn, however, was the love of his life above all else. When Lynn's well-to-do lawyer husband abandoned her, and she succumbed to health issues aggravated by our family's old buddy, booze, my eighty-year old dad, blind and lugging oxygen, stepped in and tried to take care of his daughter. Lynn was the last caretaking job of his eighty plus year career of being the guy who saved the day for everyone.

Outside the family circus tent, Dad loved his many big construction jobs that took him around the globe. First, he built the "bomb plant" in Aiken, South Carolina. The "bomb plant" is what the rest of the world knows as the Savannah River Site. The SRS is an integral part of the American nuclear arsenal. Anyway, the bomb plant really put little ol' Aiken on the map. Unfortunately, the map I am referring to was on the wall of the situation room of the Russian military command.

The SRS job hardly counted because it was not one of his away from home assignments. SRS was followed by Guantanamo Bay, Cuba, and the pre-revolution construction of the vast naval base located on our not so friendly neighbor's soil. He really loved that one. Of course, that one ended with Castro roaring into town, sending the many thousands of American citizens out on the iconic "last plane out."

His real career started after Cuba. He went to work with a industry giant based in Greenville, South Carolina named the Daniel Construction Company, later renamed Daniel International, then Fluor Daniel, and finally the Fluor Corporation.

We called it Daniel, and Daniel became my dad's very mobile home for the next twenty-five years. Daniel sent him all over the world, from one monster job to the next. Daniel was an industrial constructor, and by that I mean Daniel built huge industrial complexes, like the ones seen while driving on an interstate. Picture complex masses of towers, smokestacks, and hundreds of miles of pipes going everywhere, that's what Daniel built. They built them for the southern textile industry, all of which sits idle since our textile industry moved overseas to a third world country and is likely to move to the fourth world if one can be found to make even cheaper stuff to sell at Walmart.

Daniel jumped on the nuclear power plant bandwagon all across America before Three Mile Island shut that industry down. Daniel built chemical plants galore, and then came the petro industry over in the Mideast. Yep, Daniel built them too, alongside the other giants of global construction—Brown and Root of Texas, for example. My father's world of big construction was a real man's dream world if there ever was one.

During my dad's day, Daniel had a simple division of human resources. Management wore white Daniel hardhats. Worker bees wore green Daniel hardhats. The hierarchy was just as simple, crewmen/workers/green hardhat wearers answered to a foreman, the first level of white hardhats. The foreman answered to the craft superintendent, who answered to the general job superintendent, who answered to the project manager, who answered to the division vice president, who in turn answered to Buck Mickel, who answered only to Mr. Charlie Daniel, who answered only to God or, according to legend, some chose to believe that last one flipped the other way around and God checked in with "Mr. Charlie" on big decisions.

The huge jobs became little cities populated only by men, mostly white, mostly Americans, and they were the roughest, toughest, most self-confident, talented, arrogant, protective, proud, nonunion, construction workers on the planet. Each crew was like a little family under the care and nurturing of a foreman. The elite craftsmen were welders, pipe fitters, iron workers, riggers, millwrights, and machinists. These were the superstar crafts. In the big industrial construction culture, trades like carpentry, painting, cement finishing and plastering were crafts held in slightly lesser regard. My dad was a millwright, one of the guys who assembled and precision set the machinery that made whatever these giant plants made. His craft was held in high regard, and he gradually worked his way into a white hardhat. He even made it to millwright superintendent on a couple of small jobs before he retired.

I remember the day he came home with his new white hardhat. Like hat wearing guys from his generation, he wore it cocked slightly to the side. He had taken it to the sign painter's shop on the construction job and had someone paint D.H. FRASER in gold leaf, outlined in black. These were the days before computers. People actually hand painted signs. He didn't boast of his promotion, nor did anyone ask. It wouldn't have mattered, we wouldn't have understood. He made his bones in a real man's world after years in a green hardhat, and the pride he must have felt couldn't be shared, not at home anyway.

This took place on a Friday, as I recall. He traveled home from wherever and placed the new white hardhat on the kitchen counter. After nobody commented, my mother took notice and said, "Would you please move that off the counter so I can get supper on?"

I have that hardhat.

Dad was a true Daniel man. He did whatever the company asked. His transfer orders came on a Friday with instructions to show up in God knows where on Monday morning. He was given no travel expenses or time to get family matters settled before leaving, just an order to report for duty somewhere across the country at 6:30 a.m. on Monday. And he never once hinted dissatisfaction with this system. He loved it, as did every other Daniel man of his generation.

End of story.

CHAPTER THIRTY-TWO

The Blur

Every mile away from Atlanta shed another layer of guilt, allowing some good memories to take center stage for a couple of miles. Then the awakening of another reality—at the end of this road was law school.

Now I'm the guy with one less reason "Why" to be in law school at all, so why was I going back? Stress climbed its way right back in the car and sat squarely on my lap, obscuring my vision and making it nearly impossible to drive safely. Stress does that.

My family made light conversation, even joked a little bit. We were leaving the town that had claimed the life of my whole first family and the mood was better because we were moving on. I wasn't able to listen to the conversations. My mind was readjusting focus back to the giant brick cube in Columbia. I had missed four days of classes, the only days in three years of legal training I missed. For the first time, I was behind.

Thanksgiving was only a couple of weeks away, and the dreaded final semester exams followed Thanksgiving. This haunting realization rode with me the rest of the way home as my new companion. I had missed four full days of school and had not touched a book in all that time, being selfishly preoccupied with my dad's funeral.

Clearly, it would make more sense for me to go home with the family, take the remainder of the weekend to decompress from the deadly Atlanta trip, and return to my old job on Monday. Never returning to Columbia for any reason so long as I should live sounded like the reasonable thing to do. I lived in a hotel for God's sake, so I had all my stuff in my car. I didn't even have to go back to Columbia to get stuff. The reality was sinking in that I could actually stay home where people loved me and go back to the job I was really good at.

Why, oh why, did I mechanically get in the car 5:00 a.m. Monday morning (the first Monday morning I didn't have a dad) and go back to school? What happened to saying, "Screw it!" to annoyances? I used to walk away from them without so much as a look back. I had no good answer for the "W" question, so I went back to the pre-exam hell of year one.

And that was that. Call it the Nike syndrome—JUST DO IT. I just did it. What the hell, I'd paid for the whole semester, might as well.

Reuniting with the Holiday Inn was strange. What could have changed so much in one week? My carefully established routine was committed not just to memory but also to muscle memory so I could go about my business without thought. Everything was designed so that my brain could remain open to nothing but the study of law. How could one week screw with my limited brain capacity so much? I had to think through the process, what goes where, what happens when, what happens next. It was like I'd been gone forever. Though everything was familiar, I had to rebuild my very necessary repetitive routine, which I began doing immediately.

The first climb up the back steps to the giant lobby guarded by Ol' Strom seemed oddly familiar. It was as if I had returned to my childhood home after a long absence. Halfway up the steps, it was déjà vu all over again. My toe caught a step and down I went, but this time I caught my fall with a stiff-armed Heisman. Thank God I was alone. The last thing I wanted was another episode of someone stopping to help the old incompetent up the stairs. I swore to myself that before I left this place I would measure the stair risers. One of them surely had to be slightly taller. Another promise I wouldn't keep, but since I made the promise to myself, it didn't count because I lie to myself all the time, anyway.

As usual, the place was packed with activity. The anxiety level seemed to be slightly amped up with the exam clock ticking much more audibly. By this time, I was able to glide serpentine unnoticed through the throng and was much more comfortable in my invisibility.

The youthful avoidance of older people, which was at first insulting and unnerving, had now become strangely comforting. I could pass through a mob riding a unicycle, juggling chainsaws and kittens, and no one would even chance a glance my way, or at least not until my back was to them.

The physics of fluid dynamics works the same with crowds. When a big body of water constricts into a narrow channel, the pressure and density increases exponentially. So when a mass of people in a lobby all moved in unison toward the hall leading to the classrooms at five minutes to nine, the pressure and density of human flow increases exponentially. This was my world but I wasn't as tightly rigged as before. Maybe because I was an orphan, I just didn't care about all this little crap so much.

"GOOD MORNING, MR. HAZEL!"

There she was with her ever widening and blissful smile, grinning as if her first Valium had just kicked in. "How are you? Getting ready for exams, Mr. Hazel?" She was able to shriek right through the human river as I drifted past her morning sentinel.

"Fine, thanks. It's Denny, Denny Fraser." For some unknown reason, I was willing to give it one more try.

"That's right, Mr. Hazel! I heard Mr. Fraser's father died! Please give him my condolences if you see him!"

Matt was a bit ahead and had most likely heard the exchange, not because he had exceptionally good hearing, which he did, but because the lady's voice could be heard by passing airplanes. This lady could replace the PA system at the Super Bowl.

Getting settled into our standard seats, Matt was having the first fistfight of the day with his bookbag. "She doesn't have a clue who you are," he said, smiling, clearly intending to mock my very existence.

"No. She thinks I'm Bob."

"Welcome back. We missed you. We only had TJ to make fun of while you were gone."

Thankfully, he was giving me no quarter. The guy condemned to a wheelchair knew a little something about grief recovery. Susan, the really nice and smart person who sat next to the real Mr. Hazel across the horseshoe room, crossed no man's land where the professors roam. She was headed in my direction.

Susan was a returning student, about thirty years old, crazy brainy, graduated number two in our class, and kind, to a fault. She had sent a sympathy card to my home, as did Matt. Susan was a member of the small but growing number of students who were brave enough to speak to an older person.

"I'm so sorry about your father." She meant it, and I caught myself fighting back something, I don't know what. I wasn't expecting kindness in the classroom. She handed me a package of typewritten pages.

"I took notes and briefed all the cases covered while you were gone. Hope it helps," she said.

"Thank you, Susan. I don't know what to say."

It was true. I was overwhelmed and speechless. I wanted to get up and hug her, but I sat there like a lump. Then, the professor walked over and quietly said, "So sorry to hear about your father. I lost my father last year."

I was home. The law school was different. It wasn't just me. There was a heightened sense of reality shared among my fellow first year students that the first semester was racing to conclusion. The professors began to give a little lip service to the fact exams were just around the corner, waiting in the shadows with clubs. A general feeling of panic set in across the first year landscape. One test to cover a whole course— how in God's name would I ever pass? All of this was making its way through the slick large intestine of the system, due to dump everything, all at once, right after Thanksgiving. Where on earth did the semester go?

Oddly enough, I was not feeling the same degree of panic as I witnessed among my peers. Don't get me wrong. I was plenty nervous but something had changed inside me. I was able to recognize that I had done the work, that I was as smart as everyone else (almost), and that if I didn't have what it took to make the cut, so be it. The legal ed gene pool was definitely going into freshman exam mode.

My plan was simple. In order to stay the course with the young geniuses, I planted my backside on my couch and devoured cases. I burned the candle at both ends for a couple of days and caught up. Susan's notes and case briefs helped.

An added plus was that the workload kept me from overthinking the recent events. I'd have the rest of my life for that. Preparing for the upcoming monster exams was my only mission at the moment.

Classes were a blur. Three weeks blasted by and Thanksgiving happened. I was not ready or thankful. Quasimodo was banging out the exam clock atop the bell tower in perfect rhythm with my heart, which I could now easily feel in my carotid artery. My pledge to reserve my time at home for family had to be broken, which I'm guessing is good training for a lawyer. Here a lie, there a lie. I was turning into a liar!

First, the big one, *I'll never work away from home.* Yep, that was a big one. I wasn't going to be like my dad, no siree, not this guy. I was going to live, not work, at home. I would never leave my family. Geez, that was a whopper. *What happens at law school stays there, and what happens at home stays there.* Another whopper. I had to study over Thanksgiving, so I had stepped off the slippery slope wearing soap shoes. "Denny, the Liar," kind of has a nice ring to it.

Anyway, Denny, the Liar, shoveled half a turkey sandwich down and went off to study. My rationale, "being in the best interest of the family, and all," worked for me. As Denny, the Liar, I felt a little bit better about my new role. I studied diligently over the anti-holiday, even able to stave off the turkey drug, the strong Class III narcotic we all know induces sleep.

I was never a good student. My dad told people, "Denny can do anything he sets his mind to, he just doesn't apply himself. If he wanted to, he'd make straight A's, but he's happy enough to skim by with the skin of his teeth. Just doesn't have the drive. Not like when I was coming along."

My dad knew better than to bring home anything less than an A. He knew what would be waitin' on him.

"I brought home a B only once. From where I come from, school was a privilege. Lots of kids went to work on the farm soon as they were big enough to stand up. I knew good 'n well that school was an opportunity. Not like kids today." This was the preamble to an hour-long monologue on Denny, the Sloth. Far easier to just say I wasn't a good student.

Not to say I did poorly, which from time to time, I certainly did, but if you balance work effort to results, I got an exceptional return on investment. I had enough brain talent to know I didn't have to kill myself to get by, so I didn't.

For some unknown reason, perhaps a death wish, I attempted to explain to dear Father, with a degree of pride, that my intelligence was likely above average, exploiting the reasoning that my mediocre grades were the proud product of hardly any work at all. This one took him by surprise to the extent he was actually speechless. I knew from experience he was flipping through his mental file of stock lectures, trying to pick the right one to address my absurd remarks. Clearly, he did not have one for this scenario. It was likely he was custom building the lecture of all lectures, which would include the depression, world wars, and walking uphill to school in the snow with no shoes.

"Gotta go study. Nice talk, Dad. Let's do it again sometime."

I made it to the sanctuary of my room, which was rarely violated. I heard the car leave the driveway. I had a little time to kill, so why not flip on The Three Stooges? It was three thirty and Stooges were on back to back for an hour. I had time for one show while Dad was away doing dad stuff, wherever that was, probably messing around in the auto parts store.

Halfway through the first episode, just as Moe was leading Curley by the tangs of a claw hammer hooked in his nostrils, I experienced the primal, instinctive feeling of being watched. Yep, he was in the doorway, quietly gazing upon his brilliant son, immensely proud of busting me with the oldest trick in the book—pulling out of the yard, parking on the street, and creeping back in to capture me in the act. I had to hand it to him. That was a good one.

He unplugged the set and its rabbit ears, essentially killing television, and said, "Thought this would help your studying. I'll put everything back after report cards come out. Good talk. Let's do it again sometime."

I said all that to say I failed to develop good study habits during my formative years, and here I was in a supercharged mental environment with no curve to help dumbasses. I didn't know exactly how to assimilate large volumes of stuff. My undergrad MO was to procrastinate, then cram. Now, and for the first time, I actually did the work along the way. I was playing by the three for one rule—three hours of study for each hour of class, every day, no exceptions.

One final exam for a course with a three-inch thick textbook was mind-boggling, even though the textbook wasn't really a textbook. It was a casebook with a hundred or so cases, each provided a single example of some specific aspect of the law, and each aspect of the law had elements. For instance, a contract has three elements, a tort has four elements, fraud has nine elements, and so on. There are literally hundreds of things to learn spread across multiple cases and classes. Do the math. It hurts my mind to think about it to this day.

Since I didn't know how to prepare to be tested on such a large body of material, my challenge was to invent a darn good wheel. Law students live by the course outline. Armed with that knowledge, I decided to go from big to little. I reviewed all the cases and studied the outline, which was a slimmed down version of the whole book. Then I reduced the outline, which may have been fifty pages, to a single page, albeit a single page packed with microscopic print. I then took the much more digestible single page and endeavored to commit it to memory. Multiply that times five courses, and I'm ready for my first real law school exam.

Ready or not, I was still nervous. My first three-hour exam was Property. I felt somewhat comfortable with the subject matter. Matt wasn't by my side, which was strange. Handicapped students were given extra time and tested somewhere else. Matt had difficulty writing, so that made sense. Another perfectly healthy looking kid also got to test along with Matt because he had been tested and diagnosed with a learning disability, ADHD, or some such thing.

Damn, I wish I had thought of being tested. LD diagnosis testing was a new high-dollar industry and all the rage with young moms who wanted their little ones to make A's instead of B's. The accepted testing of the day cost about eight hundred bucks but pretty much guaranteed a diagnosis. So this young law student paid to have himself tested, and as predictably as Christmas follows Thanksgiving, got himself a bona fide diagnosis of ADHD, with a little dyslexia thrown in to boot. What a genius! Because of the ADA (Americans with Disabilities Act), publicly funded educational institutions, by law, have to accommodate the handicapped. Brilliant strategy, I must admit. This young man was destined to make a great lawyer.

The Professor handed out the test and gave us his instructions, mostly on the honor code. And the gates opened with the words we had dreaded for four months. "YOU MAY BEGIN!"

Eighty adults filled their Blue Books. The task was alarmingly simple. You just write everything you know. You put down what you think is the right answer and you put down what you think is the wrong answer. In a loose context of a response, you write everything to an exam fact pattern. Three hours vanished from my life in what seemed like thirty minutes. And then, "Times up, pens down, pass your test booklets to the front. Ladies and Gentlemen, you have completed your first law school exam." No one clapped but the words felt good.

One down and four to go. I heard one of the students talking about something I completely missed on the first test. With that realization, a little panic set in, so I tried to shut out the other noise around me to keep from going crazy. Mental exhaustion is my only other recollection of those four excruciating days. And then it was all over. The Christmas holiday officially commenced.

I had worked hard, that much I knew. Maybe I would pass, or maybe my legal career was over. I was prepared for either situation. In fact, I had learned one of the more important lessons of lawyering, which is work hard, do your best, and leave it in the hands of the guy in charge, the professor, at this level. Eventually, everything would be left in the hands of a judge or jury. I left the cavernous lobby for the last time in 1997 experiencing the euphoria that comes from mental exhaustion and complete resignation to one's fate.

Down the back steps to the Holiday Inn and into my car, I was going home for a few weeks of rest, or maybe for the rest of my life. Either way I was ready and counting the minutes until I arrived home. And dammit, the faulty step got me again, except this time, I was going down. I was able to grab a handrail with my one free hand and spun a one-eighty before hitting the wall. My save was so smooth it looked like I had just changed my mind and decided to go back upstairs.

Even though the stairs were obviously trying to kill me, the great thing was I just didn't care anymore. I studied the risers and again vowed to return with a measuring tape so I could identify the killer step and paint it safety orange. I reversed course and left the building.

CHAPTER THIRTY-THREE

The Finish Line

I only have one item on my bucket list, which is to one day have a bucket list. I'm not complicated. My only goal is to be a good husband and father. In reality, I'm probably a solid B in the department, maybe a B- or a C++. I can't beat myself up too badly for not being the A+++ dad I thought I'd be when I started out. The grade is made up of many A's and a few F's. Being gone from my family to attend law school was at best a C.

A good career move could be a good thing for the family, but being a part-time dad wasn't a good thing, which is the reason my goal during my years of law school was to at least be an A+ dad during family time. Therefore, the Christmas holiday needed to be A+ dad time, not just R&R for a tired law student. I had to make every moment count.

Christmas, the Holiday, came and went, as all holidays always do. The whole being with family and exchanging gifts was near and dear to my broken heart, which isn't technically broken in the classical sense, it just doesn't work right. I have a heart murmur. The family got caught up in mocking and ridiculing Dad's every error, major or minor. We fried a turkey, or, I should say, *I* fried a turkey. Since the house nearly burnt down, I got full credit. The main point was we hung out, did a lot of nothing, and then it was over.

It came time to find out if my grades would allow me to return to law school—or not. I passed, with mostly B's except for one stinkin' C, so I had to go back.

School was different. Exam hysteria had been debugged, and apparently, I could do it, and do it better than half the little geniuses. Professors were no longer scary. The first years had toddled their way through their fiery trials, meaning we conquered first day, first time called on, first semester, first exams and first grades. I was no longer a virgin law student.

The two things about being a virgin I never much liked were the uncertainty and self-doubt that comes with the territory. I don't know why people say, "I lost my virginity." I tried for years to give mine away. No one wanted it. And just like the day I finally lost it, the mystery of law school was solved. Law school became another thing I could do, and do well.

The next five semesters slipped by, none so ominous as the first semester. No doubt I would make it to the end. I came close to the Dean's List a time or two, and actually made it a time or two. That was momentarily satisfying, like getting drunk in high school and solidly making it to second base with a girl. It was great at the time, but not something that comes to mind often when looking back. I was going to be a lawyer if I could just keep my business from failing, stay awake on the long hours on the interstate at five in the morning, keep Debbie from going crazy, and keep my defective heart from breaking down.

Most of my law school supporters reminded me of NASCAR fans; some were there to see the race, cheering for me to win, and some were there to see the wrecks, expecting me to wrap it around a post. Naturally, my friends and acquaintances had doubts. At the beginning, the odds were against me wearing a cap and gown. After the first semester, the odds gap narrowed.

Academics being off the table, I only had to keep business, family, Debbie, the car and my heart from going in the ditch. That probably brought the odds to something like five to one against. Each successive semester narrowed those long odds until at the end of three years, they were fifty-fifty, only because I checked off all but the perils of driving on interstates and my lousy heart. The only big winner could have been Debbie. She was the only one who bet on me when the odds were hugely against my succeeding, and her bet was enormous.

Law School was far more difficult for Debbie than it was for me. She made it so that all I had to do was go to school with a bunch of geniuses. Somehow, she managed to keep a business running that had gone completely haywire. She kept the family together, kept up a home and still kept part of her sanity. She protected me from any form of bad news until she reached the breaking point and had to spill her guts. With tears, we figured our way through the many bad situations that gnawed on us during those three years. Faith and a positive attitude was the glue that held us together and got us through.

About two hundred twenty—that's how many times I drove one hundred sixty-five miles of interstate to fetch a law degree. About half of them were in the wee hours, fighting off sleep like nobody's business. Wrecks along the vast stretches of highway were commonplace. My unscientific take on the cause of most interstate highway accidents is driver fatigue, an acceptable way to say asleep at the wheel. Crash scenes usually involved skid marks and one car or an eighteen-wheeler plowed into the median, limbs of trees sheared off, and damaged car or truck parts everywhere. I nearly got an invitation to one of these solo crashes.

It was around six in the morning. Headed north on I-95, I saw a minivan catching up to me in the left lane going at least a hundred. The lone occupant blasted past me like I was standing still, only I wasn't standing still. I was doing around seventy-five. It was beginning to get light out enough to see without headlights, but most vehicles still had them on. His taillights were far in the lead, maybe a mile or so before I could tell I was catching up with him.

Gradually, I was in a position to pass him on the right, and as I came alongside, I could tell something just wasn't right. The driver was a distinguished looking middle-aged black man. His was head down, as in this guy had driver fatigue all right. His head was down but he was still going forward on autopilot. Two notions emerged. My first thought was to do something to wake the guy up, and the other was to get away from what would definitely end up a car crash.

I didn't get the chance to make the decision as his car drifted ever so gently to the left onto the emergency paving, then down into the median which, thank God, was open grassland with no trees. As his car bucked over the uneven grassy soil, I saw him wake up. I held my breath helplessly as he awoke to the view through his windshield, hoping and praying he didn't panic and jerk the wheel or slam on the brakes, two things I would have surely done after evacuating my innards.

This guy must have been a F-16 fighter pilot in a previous life. He gently guided his missile back up the dew-covered grassy embankment and onto the interstate, almost at my side. I was down to fifty by then. He looked my way and waved, shaking his head as if to say, "that was a close one." Again leaving me in the dust, he disappeared over the horizon, wide-awake, of that I am certain.

I remember the last time I spoke with Lunch Lady Judy. "So, you gonna graduate?" asked Judy, still smiling. "I'd never put a nickel on it. You, all growed up, goin' to school with kids. They's smart. I bet you'd make a good lawyer. I knew you could do it. You jus' needed to settle down and believe in youssef a bit. Don't forget me, I might need me a real good lawyer one day, and you's the one I's gonna call."

Lord, I liked this woman! She always made me feel good about my awkward, out of place, old self. I told her, "You call and I'll come a-running. You've been kind to me since the first day I got here, and I'll never forget it." That was my stab at expressing my feelings.

Judy patted me on my lily-white hand and looked me in the eyes from down at her five-foot-two perch. "I know honey, I joy'd knowing you, now go on. These hungry little babies is waitin' to get up here to pay Judy so's they can go learn how to get rich."

"Bye Judy. Thanks for everything."

That was our last conversation. I hope life has returned some kindness to her. I love the Negro Spirituals about rewards in heaven and all, but come on, God, this fine person needs a reward right here on earth.

I took my lunch and retreated to the classroom of my very first law school class. The masking tape 'X' was still on the floor, now black from years of foot traffic. The room was empty save for me, and I took great amusement that out of all the empty chairs to pick from, I went to my standard seat, first one on the first row by the big empty space for the handicapped, Matt's place.

We southerners do that in church and classrooms. No one knows why, although some genius on the psych floor of the humanities building might be able to expound on the topic. When I'm forced to sit somewhere else because of some interloper, the room and all the people in it look different. Sticking with tradition, I sat in my regular seat in this empty room and pondered the piece of masking tape on the floor, six feet in front of the lectern. It has been there three years that I know of, and no custodian, engineer, maintenance person, cleaning crew, professor, or student has bothered to peel the now nasty thing up and toss it.

The school had been abuzz with petitions to build a new law school building. Everyone was absolutely certain a new building would both raise the USC SOL to a tier in the pecking order of SOLs around the country and produce smarter lawyers, a veritable "win/win." But why, oh why, would we build a new building thinking it would produce better lawyers? The one we have is a big brick cube in true Columbia style, made to withstand a nuclear holocaust. It will last forever. Why not take care of it, keep it clean, and make it the best it can be? The dad in me felt it necessary to come up with questions designed to rain on someone's parade for a new building.

"What would Ol' Brown Strom say?" I mused aloud.

The bathroom right across the hall from classroom one, the main one visitors use, the one where my zipper derailed four years ago, still had most of the faucets shut off, just spinning with no water coming out. I wondered what visiting students thought of that fixable situation.

As my brief term in this structure was winding down, I became infected with a case of "short timers attitude." I sat in the empty classroom that once filled me with fear and trepidation and realized the place, the people, the emotions, would be slimmed down into little more than a memory. In the coming years, a handful of events would occasionally pop up while the rest will be lost forever.

I'll remember my first day because guys are good at remembering firsts. First day of school, first date, first kiss, first love, first…and that's enough said about firsts. I will always remember Matt battering his way into the classroom and into my life. I will remember Bob Hazel. I will remember Susan, our number two, who was always kind to me. I will remember many others for similar acts of kindness. I will remember Judy.

I was alone with my thoughts until the light went out. Someone had reached through the door and flipped the light switch."Hey, I'm still in here," I squawked.

"Sorry, I didn't know nobody was in here." A man in a green custodian uniform walked in. "You're welcome to stay long as you want, jus' turn the light off when you leaves. And I's sorry for putting you in the dark."

"No problem at all," I replied. "Just eating my lunch, then I'm out of here."

"You teachin' here?" he asked.

"No, I'm a student, at least for a couple more days."

"Oh, den you's 'bout to graduate?"

"Yep, three more days and I'm done."

"Dat's nice, you bein' old and all. Why'd 'cide to go back?"

"No reason, just thought it'd be a good thing to do."

He took a silver razor scraper from his hip pocket, flicked out the retractable razor blade with his thumb, and walked to the middle of the room. "I been meaning to scrape up this 'ere piece of tape. Been here on da flo' a long time. Spoze it fo' some big shot to stand on fo' makin' a video, or something like dat. They do dat a lot cause we sho got plenty a big shots around here."

He bent down onto one knee and scraped away my tape, then made for the opposite door. "Been nice talkin' with ya, mister. God bless ya going back to school, bein' old and all."

I had eaten my last lunch in this building and the time had come to move on. I took one last look back at the empty horseshoe classroom, turned out the light as requested, and closed the door behind me.

"Hi, mister Hazel!"

The greeting came from behind and was louder than usual, causing nesting pigeons to take flight outside the hall window. This time I did not offer a correction. I was contently resigned to be Mr. Hazel for one more day. After all, Mr. Hazel was a good man to be mistaken for.

"Are you ready for graduation?" Maybe the afternoon meds were kicking in because her volume was still turned up to HIGH.

This woman had gone out of her way to make me, Bob Hazel, feel at home, and for both real Bob and me, I thanked her for her kindness. It truly meant a great deal over the three years to know someone cared. I would miss that wildly smiling face. I don't have a clue as to what she did in her job, but what she did to make a bunch of scared students feel cared for was worth whatever the generous state of South Carolina paid her.

Passing the big lobby for the last time as a student wasn't lost on me. I remembered the first time I entered the building for a pre pre-interview sit down with the Dean of Admissions on a fact-finding mission to see if there was a chance in heaven or hell that I could make it in the elite USC SOL. The word elite sounds pretentious now and makes me feel embarrassed saying it, but when you consider that only about fifteen percent of those begging to get in are actually accepted, the 'E' word doesn't seem so inappropriate.

Now that I am on the other side of the fence, I'm having a difficult time understanding why it's such a big deal. I know many lawyers who should never have become lawyers. They loathe the profession like it's a hideous, disfiguring terminal illness. They seem so marginally qualified, or have so little passion for the job. I have to wonder why they put themselves through the ordeal.

I'm assuming the world of moms, dads, grandparents, and wannabe lawyers can't see that the profession is overcrowded, overregulated, underpaid, disrespected, and overworked. Why does the profession still rank as one of the most desired professions by everyone who isn't a lawyer? Every school has a line at the door and new schools are sprouting up across the nation like mushrooms. It seems to me there is a new batch every day, anxious to accept the eighty-five percent who were rejected by the old schools. The for-profit education industry has correctly identified a need and filled it. Now anyone, and I do mean anyone, who wants to get into some law school somewhere can do so.

Even lawyers who hate the profession still love the title. The 'L' word gets dropped in the first couple sentences of any introductory conversation. Parents will add "the Lawyer" behind the words "my son" or "my daughter" in every conversation. The 'L' bomb gets dropped more than the MF bomb in NWA's Straight Outta Compton. So yeah, I was proud of getting into law school when, by stats alone, I should have never received a fat envelope. Like Beck Weathers and Mt. Everest, I kept after it until they let me in.

From the first pre-orientation lecture with my wife at my side listening to a Dean talk about the institution and profession all the way through to the last lunch in a horseshoe shaped classroom, pride wells up so much that it almost dribbles out my eyes.

I was grateful to have survived quite well academically in an environment not cut out for old brains and thrilled to be only a couple of days away from walking on stage and grabbing a diploma. I walked through the lobby for that last time and tried to imprint the snapshot in my mind. How could I ever forget the cavernous room, the stale furniture, and the brown bust of Ol' Strom Thurmond.

I stopped in front of Strom one more time to gaze into the face of the man who lived nearly a hundred years, who was born during reconstruction, who was governor of a segregated state and senator of an integrated state, and, as the world would soon learn, who had fathered a black daughter whom he cared for financially and by some accounts affectionately. Strom was a US senator in 2000, the year of my graduation from his SOL. I bid his effigy farewell though I would see it many more times.

I took great care on the deadly back steps for the last trip as a student, the word "trip" used intentionally for both its meanings. I examined each step, trying to figure out exactly which step kept trying to reject me as a student. Having broken my promise to measure each one to identify the murderer and paint it with safety orange so that others could live, I resigned to accept my failure and get the heck home. I had to prepare to come back for the diploma ceremonies.

The University of South Carolina, like kudzu, is spread all over a huge patch of Columbia. There is no intact campus behind gates like other college campuses. Located in an already packed city, the school has gradually squeezed out most everything not college related, and I imagine in twenty or thirty more years, Carolina will be one mega-campus. But at the dawn of the new millennium, it was still a scattered-out affair.

At the center of the school, there is the Horseshoe, the historic site of the original campus that dates before Christ. The epicenter is guarded by an impressive set of iron gates and outlined by a narrow but huge U-shaped paved lane designed to encompass an immaculately manicured lawn. The graduation ceremony was to take place on this ancient shaded lawn area behind the two massive gates.

CHAPTER THIRTY-FOUR

The Ceremony

My entourage hit town the night before. About a half-dozen of my true friends, the ones who actually supported me making it to the finish line, came to town with us. My family, along with the band of believers, stayed at the Holiday Inn, my home in Columbia. If nothing else, it was entirely appropriate for the occasion and gave them a sense of my law school realities.

Debbie and I sprung for a crazy expensive dinner at the Capitol City Club atop the tallest skyscraper in town. We totaled about twelve including family and friends, including Andy and Lynn, Andy's soon-to-be wife who entertained a deep skepticism about me as a worthwhile human. On top of all the thousands of dollars spent on the SOL, why not spend a couple more on a Last Supper? It was a great evening of good food, good friends and good adult beverages, but not too many. I wanted to be able to remember my graduation without a hangover.

The congregation of students had been given instructions to appear at a particular building near the Horseshoe at an exact time, with the strong implication of "don't be late, dumbass." I was there early, in fact, I was there so early I feared I was at the wrong place. Thankfully, some familiar faces showed up. Minutes later, our three sections packed the room. Two hundred forty or so of us classmates were about to graduate.

To say excitement was in the air would be an understated use of a tired cliché, but here it goes. Excitement was in the air! The room was a lecture hall, or an auditorium of sorts for one of the schools. Don't ask me which one, maybe neurosurgery, or taxidermy? I vaguely remember it was big and worn, and it smelled like every public school auditorium I've ever been in.

A woman in charge began shouting the all-important instructions for our processional and impending seating arrangements. I tried earnestly to listen but the lively mood of the room made it nearly impossible. This clearly wasn't her first rodeo. She was patient to a point, but when it was evident that no one was listening, she rose to the occasion and conquered the pandemonium.

"If you don't do this in the right order, you won't get a diploma with your name on in!" she roared. That seemed to sink in. We were to leave this building in proper order and march single file to the seating area about a block away.

This was May in Columbia, the hottest city on earth, yet the day was a flawless, showing off a cobalt blue sky day that only exists in the deep south. Like kindergarteners, we formed a line wherein we knew exactly who was supposed to be in front of us and who was supposed to be in back of us. Matt got to the staging room late, most certainly caused by a parking problem. His father pushed him in. I broke ranks to tell him where he was supposed to be. He asked if I would push him up on the stage to receive his diploma. Of course! I would gladly give him this final shove. I had pushed that old wheelchair many a mile and would be honored to do it one more time.

Like a line of proud Emperor Penguins, we waddled out into the glaring sun to find our way across the street and through the gates of our ancient campus. The Horseshoe lawn is several hundred yards long, peppered with massive century oaks, and perfectly suited for such an occasion. A stage was set up about halfway down the grassy area. The surrounding audience had already been seated on metal folding chairs though people were still arriving as we followed our leader toward the rows of empty chairs that would soon embrace the rear ends of two hundred forty, not-quite-yet lawyers.

More handlers were on hand at the seating area, willing to take charge of the brain dead penguins. Their only job was to funnel the exact number into each row of seats, one after the next, until all the future lawyers were in their proper seats, facing the stage occupied by school dignitaries. I only wanted to see diplomas, and there they were, stacked on a table next to my old buddy, the Dean of Admission (DOA). Diplomas were the coveted Holy Grail all of us poor fools had spent three years toiling to achieve. At that moment, I knew what Beck Weathers felt when he was a few feet below the summit waiting his turn to stand on Everest's peak.

When we were mostly seated, I stood up and swiveled my head around like a meerkat. I wanted to get a good look at the surrounding audience filled with families, friends and onlookers, all dressed in fine southern style for this special occasion. Sunday best in spring colors, old and young assembled with pride and fixated interest on the one thing—to see fulfillment of a family member or friend's dream. They were dressed to witness the birth of a lawyer, which translated into a title that could now be owned and frequently used by family. Yep, this day was for everyone, and from here forward, the "L' title belonged to everyone cooking in the bright Columbia sun.

The audience was a pretty proud and attentive bunch, except for one little kid in the front row who was more intent on picking something out of his nose than the useless spectacle he was forced to dress for. Except for the kid, everyone had one thing in mind, and that was to witness the object of their affection get anointed, and my little family was no different.

My head stopped swiveling when I found them. They were sitting close to the front row due to, I am certain, Debbie's lifelong compulsion to arrive early. They had caught my meerkat gaze and were looking right at me, proud as punch. Smiling, each one raised a shy one-quarter waive. I smiled back, not wanting to attract any more attention than I already had as what I am sure the audience assumed was a lost senile professor sitting in the midst of a bunch of young students about to be conferred with the power of the law.

Beads of sweat glistened on the back of the neck of the raven-haired beauty seated squarely in front of me. I noticed her hair was pulled back in a severe, no nonsense bun. Maybe this was to show the world she was nearly a lawyer and would be taking no crap. Then this happened. A slight puff of air caused the delicate wisp of hair not trapped in the bun to stick to her wet skin. Columbia was stoking its cauldron to treat us to a little taste of the furnace. I became convinced that there was a plume or subterranean crevasse right below the city that vents straight to hell. Heat came down from the cobalt blue sky and up from Hades. Even our little oasis of late spring lawn and massive oaks offered little protection from Columbia's thermal specialty, which was cooking up a nice stew under heavy black robes.

The podium dignitaries, each dressed in their previously worn old robes, began to amble up to the lectern. One after the other, they attempted to eloquently hold forth impressive inspiration for the soon-to-be-grads and their fans. Dignitaries passing along their own bits of wisdom, "work hard, play hard," "stop and smell the roses," "wake up and smell the coffee," "give to others," "take time for family," "keep an eye on the prize," "don't miss the boat," "don't tip the boat," "rock the boat," "be inspired to inspire," "have integrity," "be honest," "honor the institution," "don't mess up." Three speakers in, we began to zone out and count the seconds until diploma time.

Then it happened. The good old Dean of Admission began to read out names. Holy crap, we collectively snapped out of our zombie hazes. This long-awaited thing was really happening. DOA ceremoniously announced not just the first and last names of every individual, but he also included the middle names and any trailing titles, such as juniors, seniors, seconds, thirds, fourths, and the like. And he did it real slow with extra drama. The first was Aaron Abatman, or something like that, and right on cue, the first of us walked up the ramp to the stage and received a freaking diploma from the SOL. This thing was actually happening!

That's when I notice the ramp wasn't a long, gentle angle per the ADA standard for wheelchair access; it was more like a forty-five degree incline. Maybe not forty-five degrees, but pretty steep nonetheless. I have pushed Matt's chair up many a hill and knew all too well the physics of pushing a couple hundred pounds of person and his contraption up a steep hill. Also, there was a down side, and it involved the "what goes up, must come down" axiom. There was an equally steep ramp leading down from the other side of the stage. Going downhill was just as tricky as going up. One little stumble and you've got a runaway wheelchair plowing into the audience.

I was worried, to put it mildly. I had become quite comfortable in my role as the invisible man, able to walk into a room of young people and be completely ignored, unseen, looked past as if I didn't exist. Now I had to go up on stage, in a place where I clearly did not belong, pushing a wheelchair up a ramp made for mountain goats. Great.

That worry was soon replaced by another more personal concern, a burning pain in my gut. It wasn't nerves, but an actual rebellion of sorts was taking place in my lower GI. It hurt, causing my vision to blur slightly. Praying it would pass, I diagnosed the jabbing dagger as the reincarnation of the lobster from the night before, reassembling its body parts, shell and all, and it was planning an escape from my body.

This wasn't good by any stretch of the imagination because there were no potty breaks listed in the program. I checked. I wasn't going to jump up and run to the nearest bathroom, bush, or trashcan in the middle of this procession, either. That was out of the question for a couple of reasons, not the least of which was that I was uncertain if I could actually stand and run without letting the lobster loose.

I leaned forward like I was checking my shoes and clamped all the muscles in my body, hoping to prevent an explosion. At this point, the ramp seemed even more ominous.

What if I tripped pushing Matt up the hill and fell, only to be run over by his wheelchair rolling backwards down the ramp just as the lobster exploded? That lobster was really getting steamed, no pun intended. It was pissed. Boiled alive and then eaten by some goon, it was mad as hell and going to kick somebody's butt. As the spiny devil trashed my large intestine, which was by no means large enough, things became perfectly clear.

God had planned to humiliate me as payback for the many things I had done wrong over the past fifty years, this according to my mother who told me I was a crappy kid. Those predestinationists were right. An elaborate plan was set in place on the day of my conception. On the day I bounced down the fallopian tube only to be mugged by a bunch of sperm, this actual day was planned.

"Just you watch mister. One day God is going to pay you back, and don't you roll your eyes at me. Just you wait and see."

Thanks Mom for being right. I assumed she meant I would spend eternity in hell, but now it was obvious that my punishment was to be here on earth, in front of all the world to see me get crushed by a wheelchair, pants blown off, grannies killed by flying bits of lobster shell, and my sweet mother looking down from heaven, saying, "I told you so."

Contemplating the situation, including ramps and lobster cramps, I tried to envision an escape route across the grassy lawn. Surely, I was not the first old guy who should never have attempted to go to law school to have a bowel explosion. Come on. A commotion in my row of penguins distracted my attention away from my assured fall from grace. A stirring, a shifting, and a back straightening caused me to look up from my shoes to see what was the matter.

Turned out that the last person in front of me was leaving to get crowned, which meant I was next. The lobster retreated slightly, allowing my vision to somewhat focus. I was able to sit up straight, in the meerkat position. I was beginning to think this might happen without a medical emergency. And then I heard the words booming over the PA that I'd been waiting for, working for, sacrificing for, missing my family for, enduring humiliation for, and now fighting a gut full of lobsters for: "DENSON HARRIS FRASER, JUNIOR."

CHAPTER THIRTY-FIVE

The Cyclops

Hundreds of photos were taken in front of the wrought iron gate posts next to the nearby stately brick pillars, which has officially become the logo for University of South Carolina, or just Carolina, as we say down here in the south.

It was by the logo that we gathered as a student body. Then it was just me and my girls, sparkling like a kid and his family on graduation day. Pods of families radiated out from the epicenter. It didn't take long for the empty chairs facing an empty podium to begin to look a lot like cemetery monuments. Uniformed maintenance workers began to slam fold the chairs so they could carry them away four at a time to a wheeled cart. The rest of us meandered off like those lost souls who wandered away from the Tower of Babel into a future far from certain.

Matt and I had family and friends coming in from out-of-town, so we concocted the idea of reserving a reception room at a local hotel to spend a little time together with food and drink and more photos. It wasn't a bad idea. People traveling in from all over to sit through a one-hour ceremony then to be sent away seemed a little cold. Also, we couldn't let go so easily. We had to mush it up a little more.

The hotel, worn but clean and standard for downtown Columbia, put out a decent spread of food, took our money, and patiently waited for us to get done and get out. We experimented with every possible combination of portrait photography, hugged, ate, and drank until we had to surrender to the future. Then we ditched Columbia.

Of course, graduation was just an illusion fooling us into believing that it was the end of the road. The real hairy cyclops, guarding the gate to our future, was the bar exam. That giant had to be fought, one on one, with just a brain for a weapon. It had to be killed, or the gate to the future would remain locked, barred, and welded shut. There was no way around this one.

Cyclops didn't give a crap if we were male or female, black or white, tall or short, young or old. We had to slay it or not practice law. We thought about this monster many times. Our professors had warned us plenty but it was always way off in the future. A world-class procrastinator like me finds comfort in things in the future; however, procrastinators are given to panic when the day of reckoning arrives and there is no shortcut (short of divine intervention) to pull the whole thing off.

To be honest, I didn't clear the city limits before the first gut-twisting wave of panic kicked in. At first, I thought it might be the lobster, but I had jettisoned that mother back at Wendy's. The place probably had to close for repairs after I left. So it wasn't the lobster, it was panic despite having a surefire plan of attack to kill the monster.

THE BAR EXAM.

Like in every modern academic threshold, there is a prep course, and since most everyone takes the prep course, the ante is upped by that new norm. I paid my thousands to join the lemmings and set my course for taking the bar review. However, before that pre-nightmare nightmare, I had a week off, and what a wonderful week that was. I got to relax and mentally procrastinate.

I have always found such peace in knowing the last minute is just around the corner, and until the last minute officially arrives, I can float in a warm sea of mental avoidance, and float I did. One day, I sat on the couch too lazy to turn the television on, but I watched it anyway.

The next day I putzed around the yard and the garage, trying to attach myself to a project, but none stuck. Some were too big to start and finish in my short reprieve. Some were too nasty and needed to be put off. Some were too mentally challenging. Some seemed just right until I got started and realized the project I had selected sucked.

I thought I'd get our bikes in shape. At the time, I was thinking this would be both noble and easy until I had to find the air gauge, and a three-pronged extension cord, and the thing that adjusts the spokes, and the chain oil, and the channel locks that used to be in my toolbox. In the end, I said "to hell with it," and left the bikes and assorted tools in the middle of the garage floor. I went back inside to my couch, again without grabbing the remote off the top of the television. There I sat, brain dead, watching a television with a black screen.

A little self-diagnosis told me I was not in good mental condition. The couch was the safest place to be until my brain healed, at least a little. I had taken too many blows to the head. I needed a long rest.

The only problem was that the bar exam comes two months after graduation, in my case, July. Two months of cramming my brain full while living away from home...again.

The only advantage to taking the Bar immediately after graduation is that the brain is freshly packed with law school minutia, those thousands of little facts that tend to slither out of the brain with time. The disadvantage is that right after graduation, a person is beat up and beat, not operating at one hundred percent. The monster doesn't care when you take it.

Killing the monster requires three grueling days of super physical and mental functioning. In a perfect world, law school grads should be able to lock up our brains so nothing can escape, and then we should be required to take a six month long mental vacation before having to kill a monster like the bar exam. This world isn't perfect—just watch the news.

Monday came and it was a back to work day for Debbie. We still had a business to run. If law school was my hell, the business was Debbie's hell. When I was home, I shared Debbie's misery. Things were not great. Three years of people taking advantage of Debbie's kindness and a general softening in the construction market had left us struggling.

Our business had stability from the good old days, but the market was becoming saturated with competition. There had been a massive influx of Latin American economic refugees. The demand for cheap housing coupled with 120 percent sub prime financing was on the climb. Banks were giving away money with no strings attached except that it had to be paid back. People like us who were good business managers and a soon-to-be lawyer were great target for lenders. And I had an extra disadvantage in that my best friend was a banker with baskets of money to give away and plenty of big shot high roller advice. Yep, we drank the Kool-Aid.

My week off turned out to be a week back at work in Debbie's hell, which was a good way to use my damaged brain on some project other than law books. Debbie and I work well together, and that week was good for both of us. We had a good plan. I would get through the bar on the first or second try, get a job as a lawyer, make a good living, sell our business to someone with plenty of money, pay off all our debt, and live happily ever after. It was a very logical plan. Let's not forget the monster guarding the gate to our idyllic plan had to be slain.

July exam results aren't released until October, which I think is part of the sadistic artistry of the bar exam and the reason I keep referring to it as a monster. And on the other side of the coin, there is a mid-year exam given in February, the results of which are kept secret until May.

The horror of this system bears repeating; you take the exam in July and don't find out how you did until October, or you take the exam in February and you don't find out how you did until May. This is the way South Carolina does it. I find this mind-boggling for several reasons. If the souls who are formulating a plan to attend law school that culminates in a happily lived life could accurately imagine the cost in terms of money and time spent waiting, law schools would have plenty of empty seats.

My week off, which seemed so long at the beginning, came to an end too soon. Before I knew it, I was headed for Columbia in the predawn hours in my old Volvo, just like I had done several hundred times before. It was time to begin one last assault on the never-ending mountain.

Bar review was different—plenty of new faces, for one. People from other law schools showed up to cram for the bar. Next, the presentation was all lecture, no Socratic method. The presenters didn't care if we had studied or not. They just talked and never asked any questions, and in usual fashion, no questions were asked of them. Without the chance of being called on, this method was relaxed if not deceptive. We all knew that at the end of the process, a giant monster had to be slain. The event could be clean like when little David hurled a smooth stone at a hundred miles per hour right into the forehead of the beast Goliath. Or it could be ugly and sloppy like the Texas Chainsaw Massacre. It didn't matter, the beast had to be killed, and these lecturing professors had to be listened to, and these classes had to be studied for.

The first week was taken up with a review course specifically for the Multistate Bar Exam. The Multistate is a nasty little eight-hour exam given to all aspiring attorneys. It covers all aspects of the law, criminal and civil. The MBE is administered on a single day in 49 states and the District of Columbia, as well as in Guam, the Northern Mariana Islands, the US Virgin Islands, and the Republic of Palau. It is not, however, administered in the state of Louisiana, which follows a civil law system very different from the other states. It truly is the single most important section of the exam because it is the only section that must be passed.

That is not to say other sections of the bar exam should be failed. Of the other five sections, only one section can be failed without destroying the applicant's chance at becoming a baby lawyer. This bad boy, the MBE, a two hundred question multiple choice exam scheduled for day one of the three-day pain marathon, had to be slain. Exam-takers generally receive three hours during the morning to complete the first hundred questions, and another three hours during the afternoon to finish the second hundred questions. Either you are completely right or completely wrong, there are no gray areas like in essay question exams.

Before law school, most of us loved multiple choice tests because if we didn't know an answer, we at least had a one in four chance of picking the right one. Law school taught me that if I don't know an answer, I could spew some bull crap and hope to pick up credit having given it the old college try. The Multistate was badass. It required a daily lecture that lasted from eight until about three in the afternoon. After the lecture, it was back to the Holiday Inn or the library to study the three hundred-page study guide while flipping through the thousand flash cards that came with the deluxe package.

My first week of bar review consisted of listening, followed by cramming. Listen, then cram. My head was getting so damn full. Studying became a singular imperative, even for a procrastinator like me. It was show time. Pressing through weeks with a slightly elevated heart rate became the norm. Wake up scared, go to the review class of the day, go home to the Holiday Inn, study until bedtime. Even on my Friday travels home, I quizzed myself with flashcards. Each day brought with it more anxiety. By the end of my weeks of bar review, I was thoroughly jacked up. Despite having no need for caffeine, I used it copiously.

On the last class of the last day, the last professor bid us good luck and good riddance. Who could possibly be ready for the impending doom of a three-day hell of a test? Not me.

Bar review ended too soon. Urban legend had it that there was this guy who went through law school without buying books or going to any classes. He just took exams, and of course made all A's. Then the guy took the bar exam without preparation of any kind, after several days of drunkenness, of course, and wouldn't you know it, he made the highest grade in the history. In case anyone is wondering, I was not that guy. I studied everything I could get my hands on, and would have eaten a study guide if I thought it would help.

After being expelled from bar review, I went home to study my butt off, back to our walk-in closet where I had studied for the LSAT just four years earlier. In that closet, I organized my brain so that I could puke up the knowledge I had been jamming into my head. Contracts, ConLaw, Secured Transactions, Criminal Law, everything law.

Smart people only have to see (or read or hear) something once to own it forever, but average learners like me need a system. I don't recommend anyone follow my system because it may be dumb and there might be something better out there.

This was my simple systematic approach: I read and outlined all the course material religiously. And I do mean ALL of it, hundreds (and likely thousands) of pages of material. I trusted most of it went up into my brain somewhere where it could all hide among the useless facts that I'd been storing since October 20, 1948, and I held onto the belief that they would remain there until called on to come out and make me look smart.

My problem has always been recall. The stuff is in there. Getting it to come out, that's the problem. I had to develop a means of getting all the law stuff to download out of my brain and onto a piece of paper. My system was to reduce big masses of knowledge down to an outline. Once thoroughly studied, I reduced the outline into a smaller outline, and so on until I had reduced an entire course to just one page of hot topics designed to open the trapdoor of my brain and let stuff out.

By the end of my home study regimen, I had each course boiled down to just one all-important page. Of course, the print was almost microscopic, but I was able to boil each course down to just one page. Next, I studied the hell out of those pages. Simple? Who knows? Who cares? Anyway, that's what I did. If it feels familiar, that's because it is the same system I used three years earlier to condense a one-thousand-page textbook into a mini outline for a three-hour exam. Make big things small. That was my system.

Ultimately, I would face the giant monster alone, well, not all alone. I'd be in a room with eight hundred other people doing the same thing. Even with eight hundred giant fighters taking on eight hundred giants, mortal combat with a giant is a lonely one-on-one battle. I had to go down into the pit and fight this hairy cyclops up close and by myself.

CHAPTER THIRTY-SIX

The Finale

The dreaded day finally arrived, as do all feared and anticipated events. I wasn't ready, but I didn't know what else could make me more ready. For the first time in my educational career, I was completely prepared, nothing left to study. I had studied every hour of every day for weeks and weeks, and had actually not mentally cheated or procrastinated one single time. Being fully prepared was a new experience. Normally, I would be safely cloaked in some excuse—not enough study time, not enough rest, too much partying. This way, if I failed, I'd have something to show the world as the cause of my failure. This time, if I failed, it was because I wasn't good enough to pass. An odd feeling of nakedness began to gain traction.

I was beginning to feel the presence of the bystanders, my loving family, my friends at home and around the world, my business associates, everyone at our huge church, and my future employer, who agreed to take a chance on me. And lastly, I could feel the ever-present onlookers hovering. These were the patient onlookers, the ones waiting for the wreck, the ones I hated because they posed as sincere, interested well-wishers, but believed in their hearts that I really couldn't pull this off.

These were the ones who were convinced that somewhere along the way I would screw up, that sometime during the five years of financial difficulties, isolation from family and friends, endless studying, menacing professors, lonely commutes at zero five hundred, and the weary baggage of age that I'd wash out, come home broken so they could celebrate that they were right. And this fight with the giant, this bar exam, was their last chance at vindication, the last chance to yell from the mountaintops, "We told you so! This joker is too old and too stupid."

So yeah, I felt a little pressure, but I figured if I didn't pass, I'd simply go home, apologize to my family, and go to Montana or Peru, never to be heard from again. At least I had a plan. The combined exhaustion of five years allowed me to sleep. I had lain down on top of the creepy Holiday Inn bedspread to think for a minute, and next thing I knew, it was morning.

The senior vision-sized digital clock on the wall-mounted nightstand said 5:26 a.m. My heart rate jumped up before my beta blocker could bring it down. I had gone to sleep without setting an alarm. Jeez, I could have overslept. On the most important night in my grownup life, I go to bed without setting a clock. What was that about?

How great would that have been? I could have lost a job and put my career on hold for an additional six months all because I slept through the bar exam. My family would have been so proud, and the onlookers would have had their wreck. I even entertained the idea that the doubters really were right. Thankfully, God decided to give me a great night's rest and wake me up in plenty of time to go fight the giant. No matter how hard you try or how much you plan, sometimes it just comes down to fate.

I found my way to a couple of massive buildings at the far edge of the South Carolina State Fairgrounds. These buildings house indoor events during the State Fair, and twice a year, one of the cavernous warehouses hosts the South Carolina Bar exam.

The fairgrounds are located on about a hundred acres in a decaying, light industrial section, south of the heart of the city of Columbia and a half a mile from the capitol building. The area is largely shunned by anything approaching trendy or glitzy, although it has attracted machinery repair shops, fix-it places and other businesses that don't mind the random snarl of train tracks that crisscross the streets every fifty feet or so. The fairgrounds, by the way, double as the parking lot for the Williams-Brice stadium, where eighty thousand Gamecock fans park and tailgate on Saturdays throughout the fall. For some reason, the University elected to build its massive football stadium in the center of this world.

Obviously, there was plenty of room for eight hundred test takers to fight the giant. Actually, it was a pretty bizarre, surreal setting. I had never imagined such a setting, a building suited for prize cattle, butter sculpting, and an academic hall suited for lofty bar exam. Someone picked a big warehouse, possibly on advice from Quentin Tarantino, or J.K. Rowling, or some other imaginer of strange universes. Imagine a few hundred folding tables, the kind you see in church social halls, and plastic stackable chairs, one for every butt.

I got to the scene early but not first by any means. A hundred or so test-takers beat me. They were scattered all around, on the lawn, in the lobby, even in the restrooms, feverishly cramming in last minute studying. Pouring over books and notes just thirty minutes before a three-day exam just didn't make any sense. Three years of intense study had led to this day, so how on earth could a few minutes of last minute studying make any difference?

The air was so thick it was hard to breathe. As hundreds more filed in, the stressful atmosphere intensified. If this emotional moment could be imagined, which it couldn't, law school applications would see a great reduction, perhaps by ninety percent or more. What person in their right mind would elect to go through this torturous experience? Why did I decide to put myself through this? Now I was asking myself the big WHY. Jeez.

I decided to hit the restroom as a means of escape from the chaos and panic. Seemed like a good idea at the time. After selecting a table and parking my few test supplies, I found a hall leading to the restrooms. I still had the creepy ability to pass through a group of young people completely unnoticed like I was invisible. I had three more days in their world and then I could go back to my world, either as a lawyer or a failure. Either way, it didn't matter. I was almost through this godawful odyssey.

The fairgrounds warehouse restrooms were appropriately huge, with lots of sinks along one wall, lots of urinals on another and a row of stalls. The porcelain palace was empty, or at least it looked that way. It seemed like a good idea until I heard the pathetic retching coming from one of the stalls where some poor soul was puking his guts out. Fear, stress, or leftover last minute partying, I had no idea. All I knew was this slob was screaming it out in waves. I finished my business fast and got out before the contagious nature of someone vomiting caused me to be the next retcher. I had to go fight the giant.

A small army of authority figures patrolled the big room of tables and chairs. One look told us wannabes that members of the bar ran the show. These people designed the very test we were about to take. These people had been given their job with one goal in mind: to keep people from becoming lawyers. Their mission was to stop us right there in that warehouse. This was their day of glory, a day with absolute power over others. The emotion they evoked is difficult to describe. I instantly disliked these people.

I learned in the practice of law someone always has absolute power over you. It's different from anything else in the real world, except for maybe the power a parent has over a small child. Some parents are good and some are bad, but the child has no option but to live under the rule of the parent. For grown-up lawyers, the state bar run by the Supreme Court has power. It can do as it wishes. It makes the rules, rewards, punishes and exiles with complete autonomy and impunity. They can do whatever they want, and if you don't like it, they can summon you to appear before them in their court with your treasured license in hand so that they can relieve you of the paper and tear it up before your teary eyes.

Soon I would meet judges, good and bad. When I use the term bad, I mean sadistically bad human beings. In their club, joy comes from torturing young (and old) attorneys, but that's a story for another day. On this particular day, I met lawyers who want to keep us from becoming lawyers, also known as bar examiners.

The first eight-hour day of testing began with orders from a bar examiner. The start signal activated a heart-pounding race to vomit out everything in my brain. And then it ended. I don't remember what was in the middle. I sucked in a breath. It could have been my first real lungful since nine in the morning. Along with the other spent zombies, I walked through the hundred-acre parking lot and to my car in a daze. Day one. Done, or should I say gone?

I went back to the Holiday Inn, and turned on the TV, the first and only time in three years. I did not want to think about how terrible I must have done. I stared at the TV. I have always considered lying on a motel bedspread a subliminal death wish, but this day I did not retain the mental ability to think about the risk. So there I lay until I woke up at five, again without the alarm set.

Surely I was coming apart at the seams. How could I come so close to blowing the bar exam by oversleeping?

Day one, the exhausting Multistate Bar Exam, check. Day two and three, time to conquer South Carolina. There was a morning section and an afternoon section. Day two was another frantic adrenaline race to empty out everything in my head onto paper, legibly and coherently. Same for day three. Comparatively speaking, the four South Carolina sections were simply super-sized law school exams. The examiner in each case had crafted a story, a rambling, semi-witty story chock-full of legal issues.

Some in my world say the key to doing well on a law exam is to be good at issue spotting. They say test-takers who are proficient at spotting as many issues or questions of law that relate to the section will have better results, that is, if after spotting issues, the lawyer in the making can articulate in writing how the law applies to the situation. It's kind of weird, but I am somewhat sad to admit that the process of legal test taking made sense. That doesn't mean that I aspire to become a bar examiner one day.

So day two came and went in another exhausting blur, leaving me with no keen recollection of its facts or circumstances. I liken it to standing on a train station passenger platform while a mile-long freight train blasts through. You know when it starts passing, and you sure as hell know when it's gone, but there is no clear recollection of any of the individual cars that whizzed by.

Fatigue was my new best friend. I stopped at a convenience store in the crummy side of town where the fairgrounds are situated and bought a six-pack. I don't remember the brand, but I do remember that they were cold. I opened one in the car, not caring whatsoever that I was breaking the law and could go to jail, miss the last day of the bar exam and go home in shame. I just didn't care anymore.

By the time I sauntered through the lobby of my hotel clutching my brown bag of sin and courage, I was slugging the second freezing cold beer, and it was good. Not just good but maybe the best thing I've ever drunk. A family of five boarded the elevator with me for the ride up, a mom and dad, two kids and a granny. Most of them looked at the floor in typical elevator protocol, but not granny.

She looked at me disapprovingly as I leaned back against the wall and worked on my beer. I tilted my beer toward her in a gesture of offering, suggesting, "want a swig?" She looked away sharply, as if Satan had extended a gangrene rotten hand with a shiny red apple.

The family flew out the door about the seventh floor, leaving me to ride the last couple of floors alone, contemplating the new me, the new guy who lost all concern for what folks thought. I was officially a criminal, drinking, driving while drinking, a poor example for children. This wasn't me. This was the temporary, brain dead me. I guess this is how a life of crime starts.

In my room, I did two things: number one, I set the clock for o' dark thirty, then stuck my beloved remaining four beers on ice before going to the Outback for a huge steak. Yes, driving under the influence of two beers, but at least I was not actively drinking a third one.

I don't think I had eaten in two days, so the food was good. Actually, the meal wasn't just good, it was good for my condition. It replenished my soul and sent me back to the hotel to sleep peacefully in front of the television, on top of the bedspread, perfectly resigned to my fate until the clock shocked me awake to go fight the giant one last time.

I had decided during my brief life of crime that I would never take another bar exam. I was pretty sure I was failing the thing anyway, but I was absolutely sure I was never going to do this again.

Day three was a blur, just like the others. It was the same crowd of anxious young people showing fear and exhaustion. They still couldn't see me, and this was the last time I would see them. And just like before, it was the wild ride, and then it was over, but this time, the whole thing was over.

I walked out completely wrung out. My fellow zombies were partying just outside the warehouse. Several cars had driven right up to the main entrance and were throwing down a full-blown tailgate bash. I walked through the mob of revelers, unseen as usual. I simply wanted to get to my car at the far end of the giant parking lot.

I spotted the Volvo, alone in its own sparsely populated corner, and saw balloons barely hidden behind the driver's side. At first, I thought the girls sent me a balloon-o-gram until I looked down and saw the feet of people hiding behind my car. The people who cared the most about me in this world were waiting and hiding in that godawful Columbia heat...for me! I was overwhelmed with such joy. My girls jumped out and hugged me like I had just returned from the war. It was one of the greatest moments of my life.

Debbie, Lizzi, and Geraldine from New Zealand had come to Columbia to surprise me. But the surprise celebration wasn't the only surprise. After the hugging, laughing, and congratulations wound down, Debbie led me, the zombie, to her car in another part of the parking lot and took me to the Wild Dunes Resort near Charleston where she'd reserved a room for the next couple of nights. As she drove, I made several lame attempts at conversation. Ultimately, I gave up and sat in silence.

We ordered room service. Steaks, potatoes, salad, and beer. Debbie did the ordering since I was brain dead. It was the best meal I've ever had, that is, until the next night when we ordered the exact same thing. Five brutal years of grueling effort had taken a toll on Debbie and me, the kids, and our business. We sat in bed looking out at the ocean, thinking back on the long and miserably difficult road that had led us to Wild Dunes. There was too much to even talk about, so we just sat with each other.

I don't think we left the room that night or the next. I had suffered serious mental trauma that only time could heal. At fifty-one, I was law school graduate who, against all odds, had just finished the bar exam. I had given the cyclops beast my best, even sent that bad boy to the hospital.

I had a lawyer job offer waiting for me but I refused to start until after the results were posted in October. I went back to my old job at my old desk at the D.H. Fraser Company, the wonderful little business I started in 1976, and the one I probably should never have left to go to law school. The business needed my attention and I needed someplace to hide out while I waited on the bar results.

Those three long months were peppered with questions from everyone. I tried to lay low and avoid people but inevitably, at church, in the grocery store, and everywhere I went people stopped me to ask, "Have you heard from the bar?" "Did ya pass?" "When will you know?" I didn't want to face these questions, especially if I failed, which I kind of thought would be the case.

One night I came out of hiding to go the Home Builders Association annual oyster roast. It was early October, oysters had just come into season, and I needed a night out. The lady taking money spotted me while I was standing in line to pay admission so I could join the shucking. She knew me so she yelled above the crowd, "Have you heard your results? Did you pass?" At least a hundred people stopped talking, and shucking, and chewing so they could turn toward me in unison.

"No news yet, but thanks for asking," I yelled back, wondering what on earth I was going to do if I failed. One thing was for sure, I could not continue living in this community.

The state bar didn't say when results would be posted. Their instructions were to check the bar website daily. So, after the first week of October, I checked the website every day. Then, on about the fifteenth, just before my fifty-second birthday, I received a voicemail on my cell phone from Matt saying the results were posted.

When I got back to my office, Debbie was there. I told her the results were in and I wanted to be alone while I checked. She nodded and I shut my office door. After a couple of screw-up clicks, I finally got to the bar website. South Carolina posts a list of all the eight hundred candidates who passed. I had to scroll through the list for many pages until I finally came to the F's. My name wasn't on the first page of F's. The last name on the page began with FRAN. If I had passed, my name would appear near the top of the next page. I froze with the curser on the word "NEXT" at the bottom of the page. I was stuck.

I was one mouse click away from the end result of a five-year journey, and I was just too afraid to click. *What if I failed? How would I tell Debbie? How would I be able to leave this room that I should never have left in the first place?*

I sat for a few minutes with my heart pounding all the way into my eardrums. I sucked in a deep breath, closed my eyes, and clicked the mouse. I opened my eyes and there it was, the first name at the top of the page, Denson Harris Fraser, Junior.

The first wave of emotion brought with it tears. I sucked up some manly composure, opened my office door, and saw Debbie sitting there, as scared as I had been. I told her the news and then we shared a moment. The ordeal was over.

CHAPTER THIRTY-SEVEN

The Reality Check

If you, or anyone you know is seriously contemplating going back to school as an adult, then you, or that person needs to consider doing a reality check. I am referring to those who have passed the daydream phase and moved on to the actual planning phase.

In the trenches of life, we've all had moments when we wish we had followed another path. We tend to think a different path would have been much more fulfilling than the rut we are currently plowing. Anyone considering a life changing action should weigh the actual cost against the possible return. I will admit I didn't do that, though I thought I did. After investing five years, from the starting block to the moment the Chief Justice of the Supreme Court of South Carolina handed me a license to practice law, I realized I had never imagined the time and cost, both financial and emotional, that going to law school would take.

Cost benefit analysis should be applied to any big undertaking, especially ones that take five years and has a price tag of about $300,000. Had I known the actual cost, I would have never gone to law school at the ripe old age of almost fifty. Let me repeat. I would have NEVER gone to law school at the ripe old age of fifty. Or forty. Or even thirty, for that matter, unless I could have been assured that the benefit to my family and me would be far greater than the cost. Unless we as a family could have been guaranteed to be better off financially, more fulfilled, happier, and healthier, I would not consider going.

Unfortunately, in life, as in the legal profession, there are no guarantees, nor a likelihood that even one of those previously mentioned betterments will come true—this is the truth, the God's honest truth. Trust me when I tell you that if you are planning to become a lawyer expecting betterment on any level, chances are enormously stacked against you. The odds of achieving financial and personal fulfillment are terrible but not impossible. So the question comes down to, what are you willing to gamble?

For the adult returning to school, the gamble is financial, relational, and even physical. The odds of losing on one (or all) of those levels are huge. As a society of gamblers, we gamble everyday and we love good odds. And only one in a zillion zillions will die from falling space junk. The odds for dying while taking a stress test, or getting in a car or airplane crash are in the millions, so we all get in cars, get on planes, take stress tests, and walk outside with whirling satellites overhead without giving a thought to the odds that we may be the one in a zillion who loses the gamble. But if given the chance to bet our money, relationships, family and sanity with odds of hundred-to-one against a win, I'm pretty sure the answer would be no, thanks.

Of course, there are many good reasons to become a lawyer. For one, the world needs good people to be good lawyers. I only wish to stress that a business analysis needs to done before enrolling. I was a successful businessman with the ability to estimate costs and predict market conditions, and I was off on almost every aspect of our estimation. Debbie and I are experienced planners and estimators. We're not just good dreamers. We are grounded in reality and yet we missed the mark on estimating the actual cost. We weren't way off, but we underestimated the cost.

Let's say you walked in on a convention of a hundred small coffee shop franchise owners, each invested their life savings, or borrowed $300,000 to open a coffee shop. If you could ask the group, how many of you did market research before investing, every hand in the room would go up. If you asked, how many calculated how long it would take to get a return on investment, every hand in the room would go up. If you asked, how many did a business plan, again, every hand would go up.

Similarly, if you walked into a first year class of one hundred law students and asked, how many invested in some actual market research pertaining to the area where they intend to practice, not a single hand would go up. Okay, there might be maybe one guy trying to impress the others. If you asked the group how many called the state bar to find out how many licensed attorneys are in the desired area, again, no hands, or just the one liar again. If you asked, how many called the career placement office of the law school to learn how many grads get good paying jobs, again few hands would go up. If you asked how many did a detailed business plan calculating the return on investment, no hands would go up, and you would be looked at like you had just given a presentation of Swiss alpine yodeling.

The point is, before you make an investment, do the research, and know your likely return on investment. More importantly, before borrowing money to invest in education, make absolutely certain to calculate how and when that education will pay back the investment. Also, understand the rules of student loans. Student loans can be a massive burden and most likely will take many years to pay off. They cannot be discharged in bankruptcy and can even force repayment with court ordered wage garnishment.

More lawyers are being spit out of law schools than there are jobs. And for most, the investment will not pass the cost benefit analysis. It is a great profession that currently is burdened by too much supply for too little demand. But that will change, so if you are hoping to be a lawyer for any reason, study the market and invest wisely.

Lastly, if all the economic planning seems to scream, "Heck yeah, I'm goin' to law school!" then the most important ingredients for success are family and faith—faith in a higher power, and faith in yourself. Going back to school for an adult, especially an adult with a family, is an investment made by the whole family. Everyone sacrifices and everyone suffers during the haul. The family needs to be a strong one. Mine was, and is, thank God.

And on the God thing, I can speak only for myself, but the journey with all its aches and pains was much more tolerable and possible to succeed because of my Christian faith. Surely there were those who assumed it was a miracle that I got into law school, let alone graduate and pass the bar. Maybe they are right. Actually, I don't know about the miracle thing, but I do know that maintaining a prayerful focus on a daily basis kept this procrastinating, easily distracted goof aimed in the right direction. In fact, I'll share my little jump starter, which you, the reader, can use in whatever it is you do with your life:

God, I thank you for this day. I thank you for the many blessings in my life. I ask for your strength to stand up to the challenges of life and to resist the temptation to wander from my goal. I ask you to keep me focused and inspire me to give the best I have to every task, great and small. Never let me forget the sacrifice my family is making for me. Please be with them. Amen.

Change my jump starter to suit your situation, but if you do it every morning for ten days, you may see a difference in your day. I promise, adding a grateful prayerful focus to your life will not hurt.

I made it. I am a lawyer and I like what I do.

With the help and sacrifice of my good wife, Debbie, I not only made it through, I also got a good job right out of law school with a good and well-respected solo practitioner right in my hometown. I helped build a good firm. By local standards, it was a big firm, one that employed several very bright, young lawyers.

Nowadays, I'm in my own little rewarding solo practice working alongside Debbie again, just like in the old days. I have been lucky, or blessed, actually. The cost on us Frasers was great, and the financial reward has yet to be determined, so I guess the nagging question remains. WHY, WHY, WHY? And I finally have an answer.

"None of your damn business!"

ABOUT THE AUTHOR

Denny and Debbie Fraser have made Hilton Head Island and the
Lowcountry of South Carolina their home since 1973. After
many successful years working in the construction industry,
Denny enrolled in the University of South Carolina School of
Law in 1997, and earned a degree of Juris Doctor in 2000, the
same year he was admitted as a member of the South Carolina
Bar. Denny enjoys an active private law practice in Beaufort
County, and enjoys speaking to audiences of all ages about the
challenges and rewards of surviving major life changes.